OXFORD BIBLE SERIES

General Editors
P. R. Ackroyd and G. N. Stanton

10634195

OXFORD BIBLE SERIES

General Editors
P. R. Ackroyd and G. N. Stanton

Variety and Unity
in
New Testament Thought

JOHN REUMANN

OXFORD UNIVERSITY PRESS
1991

Oxford University Press, Walton Street Oxford OX2 6DP

Oxford New York Toronto
Delhi Bombay Calcutta Madras Karachi
Petaling Jaya Singapore Hong Kong Tokyo
Nairobi Dar es Salaam Cape Town
Melbourne Auckland

and associated companies in
Berlin Ibadan

Oxford is a trade mark of Oxford University Press

Published in the United States
by Oxford University Press, New York

© John Reumann 1991

All rights reserved. No part of this publication may be reproduced,
stored in a retrieval system, or transmitted, in any form or by any means,
electronic, mechanical, photocopying, recording, or otherwise, without
the prior permission of Oxford University Press

This book is sold subject to the condition that it shall not, by way
of trade or otherwise, be lent, re-sold, hired out or otherwise circulated
without the publisher's prior consent in any form of binding or cover
other than that in which it is published and without a similar condition
including this condition being imposed on the subsequent purchaser

British Library Cataloguing in Publication Data
Reumann, John
Variety and unity in New Testament thought.
1. Bible. N. T. . Criticism
I. Title
220.6
ISBN 0-19-826201-9
ISBN 0-19-826204-3 pbk

Library of Congress Cataloging in Publication Data
Reumann, John Henry Paul.
Variety and unity in New Testament thought/John Reumann.
(Oxford Bible series)
Includes bibliographical references and indexes.
1. Bible. N.T.—Criticism, interpretation, etc.   2. Bible. N.T.—
Theology.   I. Title.   II. Series.
BS2361.2.R48   1991
225.6—dc20
ISBN 0-19-826201-9
ISBN 0-19-826204-3 (pbk.)

Set by Cotswold Typesetting Ltd., Gloucester
Printed in Great Britain by
Biddles Ltd., Guildford & King's Lynn

GENERAL EDITORS' PREFACE

There are many commentaries on individual books of the Bible, but the reader who wishes to take a broader view has less choice. This series is intended to meet this need. Its structure is thematic, with each volume embracing a number of biblical books. It is designed for use with any of the familiar translations of the Bible; quotations are normally from RSV, but the authors of the individual volumes also use other translations or make their own where this helps to bring out the particular meaning of a passage.

To provide general orientation, there are two volumes of a more introductory character: one considers the Old Testament in its cultural and historical context, the other the New Testament, discussing the origins of Christianity. Four volumes deal with different kinds of material in the Old Testament: narrative, prophecy, poetry/psalmody, wisdom and law. Three volumes handle different aspects of the New Testament: the Gospels, Paul and Pauline Christianity, the varieties of New Testament thought. One volume looks at the nature of biblical interpretation, covering both Testaments. This is designed both to draw together some of the many themes touched on in the other volumes, and also to invite the reader to look further at the problems of understanding an ancient literature in the very different cultural context of the present time.

The authors of the individual volumes write for a general readership. Technical terms and Hebrew or Greek words are explained; the latter are used only when essential to the understanding of the text. The general introductory volumes are designed to stand on their own, providing a framework, but also to serve to raise some of the questions which the remaining volumes examine in closer detail. All the volumes other than the two general ones include discussion of selected biblical passages in greater depth, thus providing examples of the ways in which the interpretation of the text makes possible deeper understanding of the wider issues, both historical and theological, with which the Bible is concerned. Select bibliographies in each volume point the way to further discussion of the many issues which remain open to fuller exploration.

P.R.A.
G.N.S.

CONTENTS

PART II: JESUS, THE GOSPELS, AND PAUL: MAJOR VOICES IN EMERGING CHRISTIAN FAITH

PART III: THE MANY OTHER VOICES OF FAITH WITHIN THE CHORUS OF THE NEW TESTAMENT CANON

KEY PASSAGES DISCUSSED

LIST OF ABBREVIATIONS

AV	Authorized Version, the King James Bible, 1611
BEM	*Baptism, Eucharist and Ministry*, 1982
IBD Sup.	*The Interpreter's Dictionary of the Bible, Supplementary Volume* (see Bibliography)
JB	Jerusalem Bible, 1966
JBC	*Jerome Biblical Commentary* (see Bibliography)
LXX	The Septuagint or translation by the Seventy of the Hebrew Scriptures into Greek
NABRNT	New American Bible Revised New Testament, 1986
NEB	New English Bible, 1961, 1970
NIV	New International Version, 1973, 1978
NJBC	*New Jerome Biblical Commentary* (see Bibliography)
NRSV	New Revised Standard Version, 1990
NTMI	*The New Testament and its Modern Interpreters* (see Bibliography)
par(r).	parallel passage(s)
Phillips	J. B. Phillips's New Testament, 1947–57
Q	Material found in Matthew and Luke but not in Mark; a proposed source (sometimes equated with the German for 'source', *Quelle*), made up chiefly of sayings of Jesus
RSV	Revised Standard Version, 1946, 1952, rev. 1971
TEV	Today's English Version, the Good News Bible, 1966–76

Portions of biblical verses are indicated by a, b, c, etc.: e.g.
Col. 2: 19a = 'and not holding fast to the Head'.

NOTE

The Scripture quotations in this publication are normally from the Revised Standard Version of the Bible, copyrighted, 1946, 1952 © 1971, 1973 by the Division of Christian Education of the National Council of the Churches of Christ in the USA, and used by permission. The author has occasionally modified the RSV rendering in order to clarify the meaning of the text.

PART I

Unity and Pluralism in New Testament Studies Today

E Pluribus Unum? Can there be 'one out of many' in the New Testament? One centre, out of 27 books in the canon? Contemporary scholarship both helps and heightens this problem, which is an age-old one, to which a variety of answers have been proposed as to a unifying 'heart of the New Testament'.

I

Is There a Centre to the New Testament?

WHAT holds the New Testament together? 'Two covers, and a lot of church traditions', some wag has said. And nowadays the covers are probably not sturdy leather but flimsy paperback, and church traditions do not carry the weight they once did. Ours is a day when, in spite of many *rapprochements* among the main-line churches (thanks to the ecumenical movement), there also exist an amazing number of newer and growing 'sectarian' goups, resurgent Fundamentalism or Conservative Evangelicalism, and, perhaps as never before, independent individualism about religions and the Bible in a multi-cultural society. Hence the question of New Testament unity is especially pertinent in a period of pluralism.

What provides a centre for the 27 books and pamphlets that make up what we call the New Testament? 'Jesus Christ', many have said over the centuries. That continues to be a responsible reply from some of the scholars in recent decades who have faced up to the problem of a dozen (or more) kinds of early Christian viewpoint in the canon. 'The New Testament is a "Jesus book" '. Loyalty to the Jew, Jesus, whom God has made Lord, is the thread they find running through each and every canonical book. But who was Jesus, and what is meant by 'Christ' or 'lordship'?

What can help us nowadays to make sense of this New Testament library, developed as it was over a century or so (AD 30–130 or thereabouts) and in so many different situations? A sense of its history, some say. An appreciation of its moral tone and ethical judgements, others suggest. The understanding that God was guiding the development of the church, which will provide clear interpretation of the Scriptures, still others have insisted. A literary sensitivity to its structure, a perception of the social setting in which the New Testament witnesses functioned, the endowment of readers with the same divine Spirit that spoke through them—these are among the many answers offered in our times, as people ask what is needed to see the Scriptures as a unified and powerful whole.

Is there a golden thread, a doctrine or experience of literary insight, that can safely guide God's people and interested readers of all sorts through 'the newer testament' in the Bible, indeed perhaps through both testaments? A host of answers echo down the centuries. Grace, justification by faith, reconciliation, being 'in Christ' are four such themes, each especially pertinent to Paul. The covenant (or covenants); the love of God; experiencing the 'new age'; promise; salvation and *shalom* (Hebrew for 'peace and well-being')—these and variants on them each have had their champions and still do.

By this time it is apparent that the very answers given to the question, 'What unifies the New Testament?' form part of the pluralism! It is not that most of the replies noted above are without foundation. Each can, in one way or another, appeal to the New Testament Scriptures and the experience of Christians, indeed to church denominations formed around such answers.

An old issue, sharpened by modern biblical studies

At the very outset it should be made quite clear that the question of 'variety and unity' for the New Testament writings is not one that has been created by 'biblical criticism' or through pressures from modern, historically minded scholars. It has been around, as a problem, for a long time, even before the rise of modern historical scholarship in the eighteenth century. In a sense, it was there already in the canonical writings themselves, as if (so some of the church fathers suggested) God has placed both this book and that passage in the Scriptures to exercise the faith and minds of believers.

The author of 2 Peter, for example, looking back at the letters of 'our beloved brother Paul', confessed that in them 'there are some things hard to understand' (3: 15–16). That author spends a considerable portion of his 'tract for a time when people misunderstand because of false teachers' (1: 12; 2: 1–3; 3: 3), therefore, setting readers straight on something that had in certain epistles been quite precious to Paul: the parousia or 'coming again' of Jesus Christ. Second Peter insists on the certainty but not the immediacy of 'the day of the Lord' (3: 3–14).

James 2: 14–26 sets forth argumentatively the importance of 'works', instead of mere 'faith', in order to be justified. This seems a bid to correct Paul, or at least to correct a misunderstanding of what Galatians and Romans teach.

The disciple and apostle Peter can be variously assessed, and is, in the New Testament. In Matthew's Gospel, quite positively (cf. 16: 17–19); in Mark, more negatively (cf. 8: 29–33). In John's Gospel he is presented as less important and discerning than the 'beloved disciple' (13: 23–5; 20: 3–8), yet at the end a significant figure none the less (21: 15–17). But Paul says he had to rebuke Peter to his face for denying 'the truth of the gospel' (Gal. 2: 11–14). Will the real Peter please stand up, readers are likely to say! The treatments of the 'brothers of the Jesus' and even of Mary likewise vary from gospel to gospel.

The fourth Gospel teaches at times that 'signs' (meaning miracles) produce faith (2: 11, 23; 4: 53–4; 20: 30–1), but elsewhere states there is a better kind of faith *not* based on signs (20: 29; see 4: 48 as a critique by Jesus of faith based on miracles).

Luke–Acts—the author's double work, consisting of the Third Gospel and the Acts of the Apostles—puts heavy emphasis on the Holy Spirit as the vehicle, after Pentecost, for the presence of God in believers' lives. The presence of the Spirit, during the absence of Jesus at God's right hand until the parousia (Luke 24: 49–50; Acts 1: 11; 2: 33), is shown through 'speaking in tongues' (Acts 2: 4; 10: 45–6; 19: 6). Matthew, on the other hand, sees God's bond with believers after Easter in the presence of Christ himself (1: 23; 28: 20; 19: 20) and is wary of those who boast about charismatic gifts of prophesy and exorcism (7: 21–3). Later liturgies have homogenized these positions by petitions at the Eucharist for God to be present 'by Thy Word and Spirit'. This blends what Matthew taught and Luke emphasized. Such examples in the Bible challenge any easy uniformity and non-historical reading of the Scriptures.

The swing of the pendulum over the centuries

The fact is that there has been for years a swing back and forth in the study of the Bible between 'unity' and 'variety'. Certain periods have responded more to the pluralism within 'the Book' and other eras have asserted its unity. In general, the centuries until the time of rationalism and the critical awakening or *Aufklärung* in European intellectualism ('the Enlightenment') put a premium on the Bible as a unified book. It is the last 200 or so years that have revelled in the Scriptures' variety. But there have often been exceptions.

In patristic times, the School of Antioch probably saw biblical variety more faithfully than did the School of Alexandria. But the allegorical method which the Alexandrian divines espoused, and which blossomed in the Middle Ages, was no monolith. As practised by the schoolmen or church philosophers, it sought in almost every passage, besides a literal and an allegorical sense, a moral-ethical meaning and an 'anagogic' aspect, that which somewhat mystically (or 'eschatologically') leads up to heaven. And much of rationalist interpretation of the Bible in the eighteenth century focused single-mindedly on a moralistic meaning for the biblical text, to improve human manners and mores.

It would be unrealistic to think, moreover, that scholars since 1800 have always been dedicated to ferreting out only the varied emphases in Scripture. Quite the contrary: many of them have devoted their efforts to finding some master theme running through the books—thus, for example, Walther Eichrodt with the covenant, or Gerhard von Rad with 'promise and fulfilment'. Albert Schweitzer concentrated on the heroic apocalypticism of

Jesus and the 'mysticism' of the apostle Paul. C. H. Dodd stressed 'realized eschatology' everywhere possible. Although Rudolf Bultmann has seemed to some a threatening figure, finding disparities in the New Testament and exercising ruthless honesty as to what comes genuinely from Jesus, he actually promoted a quite positive programme: namely, to see how the New Testament texts set forth an understanding of human existence in the light of the kerygma (or proclamation about 'Christ crucified') that leads one to dependence on Christ in faith.

From variety to unity to variety in our century

One can perceive three broad shifts since the late nineteenth century: from unity to 'variety', a return to 'unity' again, and then the present varied situation.

The first shift stems from the rise of modern biblical studies—perhaps in 1778, if Reimarus's work on the purpose of Jesus is taken as the start of the 'quest of the historical Jesus'; or during the first quarter of the nineteenth century, as exemplified by Schleiermacher's probing thought in theology, preaching, and Scripture studies, for example, on the pastoral epistles; or in the 1830s, the Tübingen School and its investigation into Jesus and Christian origins; or the period when the 'synoptic problem' came into its own, from the late 1830s to Streeter's work on the four gospels (1924). From this start until at least the First World War, biblical (or New Testament) variety and unity each had supporters.

The development of 'New Testament theologies' in this period is an interesting test case. Some were convinced that Paul, Matthew, John, and James, plus all the other writers of the canonical books, could be combined in a carefully structured, coherent, and cohering presentation. Others railed against all notions of any such 'well-ordered herbarium', culled from the New Testament as if its books were a garden from which to cut flowers for a florilegium or bouquet; these scholars chose to write at most on 'the theology of Paul' or of Jesus in the four gospels. On the whole, the swing was toward pluralism, especially in contrast to previous centuries when the Bible had been viewed as a single book. In the case of New Testament theology, it must be remembered that this emerged as a specialization within 'biblical theology', and that biblical theology had come into vogue only in the eighteenth century, particularly under Pietism, as a reaction against 'systematic theology' or dogmatics.

The variety so frequently found in this period was probably most widely accepted by, and left its imprint more on, Continental and Protestant, rather than Anglo-Saxon and Catholic, Scripture studies. German theology had long learned to live and cope with scientific demonstrations of New Testament pluralism. British scholarship came more slowly to face its implications. America was somewhere in between, basically Anglo-Saxon but with ties to the German universities and scholarly literature through graduate study there and sometimes through the ability of immigrants to use German. Roman Catholics came only slowly to take up 'critical methods'. The ups and downs of the Dominican École Biblique in Jerusalem under Père Lagrange illustrate the difficulties confronting even loyal sons of the church when entering into these areas after the decree of the Holy Office, *Lamentabili*, in 1907 and the Modernist controversy. It was only as the encyclical of 1943 by Pope Pius XII, *Divino Afflante Spiritu*, made its impact that critical studies stressing biblical pluralism began to flourish among Catholics. In all these places and among all these groups, however, the first third of the twentieth century probably brought more awareness of the New Testament's variety than ever before.

In the 1930s, however, although there had been some earlier harbingers, a movement gained strength in many quarters that placed new emphasis on the unity of the New Testament. Emblematic was C. H. Dodd's small book of lectures at King's College, London, *The Apostolic Preaching and its Developments* (1936). The concern was centripetal, instead of the centrifugal movement Dodd sensed in so much previous work. The centre toward which he moved was the kerygma or 'common proclamation' of the early church. This he sought to isolate in the sermons in the Book of Acts, such as those in chapters 2, 10, and 13, and in pre-Pauline phrases to be found in Paul's letters. These, under Dodd's hand, turned out to blend into a common outline, which informed not only Paul's work (he argued) but also the structure of the Gospel of Mark (and, through it, Matthew and Luke). It became fashionable and profitable to reconstruct 'the kerygma of' each New Testament book, and even, for the Old Testament, of the Yahwist, Chronicler, or Priestly writer.

The period after the Second World War was favourable to efforts to produce a thematically unified New Testament theology. For example, that of Ethelbert Stauffer was constructed around the pattern of doxology to God, soteriology, and the contest with the powers of evil. Alan Richardson worked with strong ties to patristic tradition. Floyd V. Filson viewed the resurrection of Jesus as the interpretative theme. An approach particularly common was that of *Heilsgeschichte* or 'salvation history', as developed by Gerhard von Rad or Oscar Cullmann. The latter's views seemed for a time destined to become the pan-Protestant position, yet also one highly influential among Roman Catholics as 'the mystery of salvation' (*mysterium salutis*) at the Second Vatican Council.

While the 'kerygma' and salvation history continued to be important, and numerous New Testament theologies appeared on into the 1970s, the fuller evidence suggests that, since the mid-1960s, the trend toward emphasizing New Testament unity has declined. This has occurred not simply because one decade or generation of scholars turns against or on its predecessors or because 'the pendulum always swings back and forth'. Some of the reaction has come because what a previous generation found to be a hard-won insight in the face of difficult evidence and rival views had become too simplified. Re-examination of the texts showed the conclusion was not so simple as some had made things appear. The very variety in the texts themselves was to a large extent responsible. And so the 'new quest' for the somewhat historical Jesus fragmented. Redaction criticism emphasized the separate theologies of Matthew, Mark, and

Luke, as well as of John. Pauline studies, which had been in the doldrums, awakened to fresh impulses, such as sociological examination of his world or massive claims that he was through and through an apocalypticist. The results of manuscript discoveries at Qumran and Nag Hammadi began to be felt. New or revamped scholarly techniques were developed. There was an explosion of publication and meetings of learned societies. Literary and narrative approaches flourished. Such factors help to account for what must be termed a period, certainly in the 1980s, when the variety of the New Testament is again dominant. Books (such as that by John Charlot) and articles have even flaunted 'New Testament disunity' as the characteristic of the canon. As if to prove that we are in such a period, here and there one finds signs appearing of new interest in the unity of the New Testament and, indeed, of the entire Bible. The pendulum swings.

Aims, answers, ambiguities

Against this background, the major concern of this book is to present a picture of the unity and variety of the New Testament as viewed in current study. Of necessity, the dominant peaks in any map of the New Testament terrain must involve Jesus and the gospels and Paul. These topics are treated in detail in other volumes in the Oxford Bible Series, by Graham N. Stanton and John Ziesler respectively. But if the mapping is truly to deal with the unity and variety of the whole New Testament, then particular attention must be given to those ten or more books that are neither gospels nor part of the traditional Pauline corpus—books like Hebrews, the general epistles, Revelation, and Acts, often overlooked or slighted in surveys, that are, none the less, part of the canonical world. It would be convenient to avoid them, for they seem a disparate lot, the '*et cetera*' after the gospels and Pauline epistles, and they complicate what might otherwise be a more tidy picture. But they are both a part of the richness of the New Testament and complicating factors that militate against too easy a unity.

Thus, it will be necessary to say something about Jesus, the gospels, and Paul (in Part II) as a reminder of variety and unity in their teachings. The particular emphasis of this book will come, however, in Part III, on the 'other' New Testament writings. They make the problem of unity and variety in the New Testament canon as difficult as it has to be, for any discussion to be complete on the New Testament. Our approach also means that this volume can stand by itself as a treatment of pluralism and oneness, while being part of a series where some New Testament books are also treated elsewhere in the depth they deserve.

There is another way in which the present volume stands between two others in this series, linking and drawing on both while possessing its own identity. *The Origins of Christianity* by Schuyler Brown functions as 'a historical introduction to the New Testament', as the subtitle puts it. There, in the light of discussion of what 'history' is and what historians are competent (and not competent) to do, the focus is first on Jesus, his lordship and giving of himself as the Spirit after Easter. Then, inevitably, the account tells of the rise of Christian self-consciousness (in a period where Jewish self-understanding was also being shaped). This self-definition of those who followed Jesus as disciples and who became members in his body is traced out, especially in the cases of Paul and of the Matthean and Johannine communities, as the churches moved toward a sense of 'the church' (especially to be seen in Matthew 16 and Ephesians).

Considerable weight is placed by Brown on 'the second generation', after AD 66. By then the apostles were dying off. The Jewish War against Rome, culminating (though not quite ending) with the fall of Jerusalem and the destruction of the temple in AD 70, brought considerable change, not only to the political but even more to the religious map. Any examination of New Testament variety and unity must be aware of such Christian origins. Much of the literature we shall be concerned with in this volume falls into the 'second generation' (or later), and represents different situations from those which Paul had faced. Few sharper illustrations of the variety in viewpoints can be imagined than the understanding of 'apostle', first as it appears in Paul (cf. 1 Cor. 1: 1; 9: 1) and then in Luke–Acts (Luke 22: 14; Acts 1: 21–6) (Brown, *Origins of Christianity*, 121–4, 134–5), not to mention later appeals to the concept (ibid. 139–41, 143–6). Brown's concluding emphasis, from his historical survey of origins, is on all the diversity within the New Testament canon, and yet on the continuing appeal of 'one saving gospel' and of 'the one true church'.

Brown's volume on beginnings poses initially the unity/variety question. That by John Barton and Robert Morgan, *Biblical Interpretation*, shows how varied have been the subsequent understandings of the New Testament by later readers. Something of the variety in their answers as to what holds the canonical writings together has already been indicated in the opening paragraphs of this chapter. The pages which follow must be cognizant of both Christian origins and later biblical interpretation while exploring the question of unity and variety for the total New Testament.

More will be said in Chapter 3 about the aims and priorities of this volume with regard to the challenge that diversity presents to New Testament unity. It is already apparent, though, that these aims must include a brief overview on Jesus, Paul, and the gospels; more detailed treatment of the rest of the New Testament literature not covered, or only touched on briefly, in the volumes by Stanton and Ziesler; above all, it must probe for unity amid the patent variety in all this literature. One must weigh the answers and ambiguities of early Christian documents in the canon, along with the ambiguities and answers of subsequent and contemporary scholarship.

Some might wish to speak simply of 'biblical answers', holding modern criticism responsible for introducing the problems and ambiguities. But it has been suggested above that some of the problems lie already within the New Testament texts. Scholarly disciplines can help provide answers. Others might wish to see professorial answers from today's experts as straightening out the ambiguities and problems of the text; but it has been suggested above that modern scholarship itself is quite often pluralist. Besides, the ancient texts may well give answers that are still helpful, when read in their historical situations. We should be slow to judge something wrong before we ascertain the circumstances under which the words were originally spoken. Answers and ambiguities thus occur in both the biblical texts and in modern scholarship. Why not look at the canonical writings and the means of investigation at our disposal as challenge and opportunity, rather than merely as 'problems'?

The New Testament Canon and the Techniques of Modern Scholarship

REPEATEDLY, above, reference has been made to the 27 books comprising the canonical writings of the New Testament. These did not come together between two covers any more automatically or 'perpendicularly from above' (as Karl Barth put it) than the various writings individually came into existence in the first place. So, just as 'historical introduction' exists as a field of study for the rise of early Christian literature or Christian beginnings, thus there is also historical study of the development of the New Testament canon.

There existed earlier, of course, for the Hebrew Scriptures (which we might term 'the older Testament') a canon which was fairly well developed by the time of Jesus and Paul. The Greek term *kanon*—probably derived from a Semitic root *kane* for a reed, used as a tool to measure; literally, therefore, a 'measuring rod'—came to mean a norm or list, even a rule (cf. Gal. 6: 16; Christian writers of the second century spoke of 'the rule of faith', *ho kanōn tēs pisteōs*, Latin *regula fidei*, for kerygmatic, confessional summaries of what is to be preached and believed). Some, like D. N. Freedman (*IDB Sup.*), today see the components of the Hebrew canon as having taken shape earlier than often supposed, chiefly in the period of the exile, the return, and afterwards.

In any case, by the end of the Second Temple period, when Jerusalem fell in AD 70, the Torah or Pentateuch had been in place as supreme authority for at least four centuries, the prophetic corpus (Former and Latter Prophets, in the Jewish system including historical books like Samuel and Kings, but not Daniel) for 200 years or more, and the 'sacred writings' as the third part of the Tanak (*torah* plus *nebiim*, 'prophets', and *ketubim*, 'writings') were settled except for debates over items like the Song of Songs. This involved a process of discussion, especially among the rabbis in the academy or synod at Jamnia, until about AD 90, although we ought not to think of a 'council' there in the sense of Chalcedon or Trent.

Establishment of the New Testament canon had its own long, slow evolution. It was at points interrelated with questions of what books to take over from ancient Israel. Happily, today, virtually all Christian groups agree on the same 27 items for their New Testament list. Here there is more agreement among Christians than with the Old Testament, since Roman Catholics accept books Protestants and others place in the Old Testament Apocrypha, and the Orthodox include a Psalm 151. For the New Testament the Syrian church in its fifth-century translation, the Peshitta, recognized a collection of just 22 books, admitting only James, 1 Peter, and 1 John out of the catholic epistles, and those three belatedly, and omitting Revelation.

The story of the canonization process which stretched over three or four centuries after the final book was written which eventually was accepted into the Christian collection we call the New Testament—probably 2 Peter, as late as AD 130 or 140—has been clarified considerably by recent historical studies, by using some of the same methods of investigation that have been directed to the New Testament writings themselves. To help understand the views on the unity of the New Testament prevalent in the second and ensuing centuries (although these positions also show at times considerable notions of diversity), we need to look at the factors that produced the 27-book collection. Then, to aid us in comprehending recent scholarly methods of interrogating the resulting canon, we shall survey briefly a series of these methods, including one that has emerged as very important for the variety/unity question, that of 'canonical criticism'. But, as one might suspect, the devotees of canonical exegesis and canonical hermeneutics, concepts that have been articulated only in the past two decades, are themselves by no means united in outlook.

The canonization process in the ancient Church

The way was neither easy nor direct from the time when the final document that gained admittance into the eventual canon was written to the time the first listing of those 27 books no more and no less occurred—in a letter in 367 by Athanasius, sometime bishop of Alexandria, during a stormy career on behalf of the orthodox faith.

This road to the canon intersected at points with decisions about the use of the Old Testament writings in the Church's life, including matters of which text and version or language. There had been, as Qumran evidence and other texts from the Judaean desert show, a fluidity to the Old Testament text in the period at least down to AD 70, and a certain pluralism that the church inherited, best seen in the Septuagint (LXX) text and canon. (The term originally designated a translation of the Pentateuch by a legendary group of 70 scholars). Produced over several centuries, the LXX sometimes rests on a different, perhaps at points better, Hebrew text than that chosen by the massoretes or Jewish scholars who shaped the 'official' Hebrew text, although at other times the LXX reveals an expansive, less than accurate rendering of the original Hebrew.

The rise of the New Testament canon was also interrelated with a variety of types of Christianity that were emerging in the patristic period, in Syria, Asia Minor and Greece, Italy (especially Rome), and North Africa, where Egypt was to prove especially important, just as it had been in Jewish development. The battles between what were to become 'orthodox' and 'heterodox' sorts of church left their marks on the canon. There were, for example, Jewish Christians who wanted nothing to do with Paul and produced anti-Pauline writings, like the *Clementine Homilies* and *Recognitions*. There were gnosticizing Christians who readily embraced the Fourth Gospel, writing commentaries on it before more orthodox Christians took it up, and who gladly made Paul one of their own, but who did not welcome books like Matthew, and who treasured dubiously Christian treatises like those found at Nag Hammadi.

Marcion, a wealthy Christian and a vigorous teacher in Rome in the 140s, helped force the canon issue on other Christians by his decision to discard the Old Testament as the work of an inferior 'creator god' and to edit a canon that consisted of 'gospel' and 'apostle'. Such a canon, he held, was true to the position that Jesus and Paul had articulated as authoritative, namely, the new way to salvation in Christ alone. Marcion's single gospel was a version of Luke—probably beginning with how 'in the fifteenth year of the reign of Tiberius Caesar . . . the word of God came down to Capernaum' (3: 1–2; 4: 31), with all the 'Jewish-sounding' infancy material of Luke 1–2 expurgated—and a collection of some ten of Paul's letters, with Galatians in first place, each shorn of Old Testament material.

How pluralistic views on the emerging New Testament collection were in these centuries can be seen from firm evidence we have in early manuscripts. Here, books that eventually turn up in the canon and books that do not are copied cheek by jowl often with no indication that some were revered and others not. The Sinaiticus manuscript (designated *aleph*, fourth century) includes Barnabas and The Shepherd of Hermas; Alexandrinus (A, fifth century) contains 1 and 2 Clement. The Greek and Latin manuscript of Claromontanus (D, written in the sixth century, but with an enumeration of books several centuries earlier) has our four gospels, Acts, ten Pauline letters (omitting Philippians and 1–2 Thessalonians, probably by accident), seven catholic epistles (with Hebrews, perhaps also accidentally, left out), and Revelation, but also Barnabas, The Shepherd of Hermas, Acts of Paul, and the Apocalypse of Peter (these four with a mark indicating someone's hesitancy about them).

When lists appear, as in the Muratorian Canon (variously dated from the late second to the fourth century), some writings are specifically designated as 'not accepted', like 'a new book of psalms for Marcion'; others are to be read, but not in church as assigned lectionary, like Hermas' The Shepherd (because it is known to be after the time of the apostles and not among the prophets); yet the apocalypses of both John and of Peter are accepted (the latter with a note that 'some of us do not want it to be read in the church'). The Christian bishop Eusebius, of Caesarea on the Palestinian coast, presented, in about 325, a triple classification: 'books acknowledged' (*homologoumenoi*)— the four gospels, Paul's letters (with Hebrews), 1 John, and 1 Peter, plus Revelation 'if it seems desirable'; 'books spoken against' (*antilegomenoi*) or 'spurious' (*nothoi*, 'bastards'), including James, Jude, 2 Peter, 2 and 3 John, Revelation 'if this view prevail', plus five others that do not eventually make it into the canon; and downright heretical books, like the Gospel of Peter and Acts of John. For about four centuries of the life of the Christian Church, therefore, the New Testament canon was anything but secure.

Since this story is told in detail in many places (e.g. Gamble, *New Testament Canon*), we need note here only in a general way how the subcollections came together into one collection, and then point out some of the factors that led eventually to a feeling that they formed one single whole. While probably each of our four gospels were originally *the* book about Jesus in a given church or area (cf. Luke 1: 1–4), a collection of four gospels began to have wide acceptance, and to circulate, together, by the late second century. The order varies. A sequence of Matthew, John, Luke, and Mark is found especially in the Latin tradition, where the first two are regarded as the work of apostles, the latter two are not. The attempt to substitute a single harmonized version of the gospels, as in Tatian's *Diatessaron*, had only limited success (his somewhat ascetic recasting enjoyed a vogue, especially in Syrian Christianity). This fourfold gospel collection meant that Acts circulated by itself, not with Luke, and became *sui generis* in category and transmission.

Paul's authentic letters were probably transmitted by a 'Pauline School', which edited (fragments of) some of them (as in the case of 2 Corinthians and Philippians) and added others to address new needs (Ephesians, probably Colossians; the pastoral epistles) and combined them into a corpus of a maximum

13 letters. These were arranged, we may with some probability guess, by length (from Romans to 1, 2 Thessalonians and Philemon), but they could have been structured also by place, so that seven churches were addressed (Corinth, Rome, Ephesus, Thessalonica, Galatia, Philippi, Colossae). In the latter case, the letters to the seven churches of Revelation 2–3 might have been an influence or a parallel.

With the 'general' or 'catholic' epistles the picture is far less certain. Only 1 Peter and 1 John attained prominence and widespread acceptance in the second century. Others that eventually made the canon were debated for some time, and the manuscripts containing them might also include other books up for consideration. When the catholic letters do come together in the fourth century, in the order familiar to us—James, 1–2 Peter, 1–3 John, and Jude—it is as a collection of seven documents. The order may be determined by the reference in Gal. 2: 9 to 'James, Cephas [Peter] and John' as 'pillar' apostles. The agreement of these three, plus Paul and others, as assumed in Acts 15: 6–35, attested an apostolic oneness to the ancient Church. This was seen also in the canon. Hebrews, not numbered with these general epistles, came to circulate with the Pauline corpus. Revelation, a kind of neglected orphan, had its own textual history. The process of putting together the eventual canon has been likened to assembling a freight-train in a marshalling yard; as, for example, in North America, cars from the Atchison, Topeka, and Santa Fe, Baltimore and Ohio, Canadian Pacific, and New York Central lines get strung together in one train, with a new corporate identity and a common destination on the same main-line (church) track.

What factors helped these writings to coalesce into a canon? We have already mentioned the influence of menacing movements like the Marcionite church and gnosticism. More debatable is whether the prophetic revelations claimed by Montanus in the second half of the second century pushed the Church toward a fixed 'revelational book' in opposition to his new claims. Lest it seem that the church's debt for the canon is chiefly to heretics, let it be said that many theologians and bishops (both offices combined sometimes in the same person) who were firmly catholic and orthodox in their outlook were positive influences, as was reading of the Bible in local parish services. The canon became, along with confessional position (*regula fidei*) and church structure (orthodox bishops and churches in fellowship with each other), a means to Christian unity.

The old answer that regarded 'apostolicity' as a criterion is not wrong. But it could take various forms in this period. One might claim apostolic authorship for a document; for example, that Paul wrote Hebrews; or apostolic association, that Mark's Gospel rested on Peter as a source, or that Luke's work is to be explained as apostolic through contacts he had with Paul and on the basis of the supposition that Luke was one of the 70 sent out to preach at Luke 10: 1—the epistle reading for St Luke's Day came to be a passage including 2 Cor. 8: 18 on the grounds that 'the brother whose praise is in the gospel' (as the AV phrased it) referred to Luke and his authorship of a gospel book; or apostolic in the sense of conforming with the kerygma of the apostles.

Nor should the figure of Jesus be disregarded as an influence for what was to be canonical. Directly or indirectly, the Christ, as Christians had come to understand him, was a factor without which nothing became part of the canon. Orthodoxy meant, above all, 'right thinking' and belief about the Lord. Oddly enough, claims of 'inspiration' played little role in shaping the New Testament canon, partly because they could not—other documents which were not included in the final 27 also sometimes claimed elaborate influence from the Holy Spirit—and partly because the Christian community in the process of reception of these writings was deemed the arena of the Spirit, not just the pen of the earlier writer.

Recent trends in methodologies

For our concern with variety and unity in the canonical New Testament it is not merely the well-known sub-disciples of form, source, and redaction criticism that are important. These

methods try to trace the history of the composition of a passage
or book. We must also be alert, however, to the often-ignored
further segments of traditional history—about how, for example, what Paul wrote was edited into the documents we have
in the canon, or how letters positively assigned to Paul himself
came to circulate with writings labelled 'deutero-Pauline' by
many critics. Here, too, redaction is involved, both in the sense
of piecing together sources (in these instances a letter or part of
one by Paul, e.g. 2 Cor. 1–9 with 10–13) and in the way that a
further theology is involved in bringing together 'genuine' and
'deutero' letters, so that the apostle is made to speak not merely
to the 50s (when he lived and worked), or the 60s, 70s, or 80s (or
later) when Paulinists wrote in his name, or to around the 90s,
when (we may guess) his letters and those of the Pauline school
were brought together in a collection, but to further centuries.

There is, in addition, a powerful influence at work when all the
Pauline letters are placed in the shadow of Acts, which did occur
in the canonization process, or when Hebrews was added after
the Pauline corpus, so that 'Paul' is now between two 'book-
ends' that may affect how one views his letters. It is, of course,
true that Paul wrote (or has attributed to him) 13 of the 27 New
Testament books. But that impressive Pauline presence is
modified by the Lucanized picture of the apostle in Acts (where,
with the exception of 14: 4 and 14, he is *not* one of the twelve
apostles or really an apostle at all) and the 'catholic' theologies of
Hebrews and the general epistles. No doubt canon has here a
unifying effect, but it also mutes the distinctive voices of the
original Christian writers. The real Paul has thus often been lost
sight of, in favour of a more domesticated version.

Something of the same effect has occurred in homogenizing
the synoptic tradition and John into a 'Jesus of the four gospels'.
This too was made possible through the canonical arrangement.
It is no accident that critical scholarship approached the
'historical Jesus' question, from the eighteenth century on, not
merely by setting aside the Christology of Chalcedon but also by,
first, separating John and the synoptics, second, by seeking the
first gospel to be written (Mark, as most scholars, conservative

and liberal, came to agree in the nineteenth century), and then by searching after the oldest pre-Marcan tradition in and behind 'Q'. For the unity question in the New Testament, as we shall see, an important step toward a 'Petrine block' of thought was taken when 2 Peter was grouped with the 'Pauline' document we call 1 Peter (a move which perhaps the author of 2 Peter presumed), but when 2 Peter is removed from proximity with Jude (by the location of the Johannine epistles in between), that may obscure a link between Jude and 2 Peter (which the author of the letter may or may not have intended). Such questions are part of the interplay between unity and variety brought about by canon.

Certain trends in scholarship over the last four decades have had a mixed effect on the matter of unity and diversity in New Testament thought. The 'new quest' for the historical Jesus (1953–c.1970) had the effect of levelling the canon in many cases (the gospels became quarries in which to dig for data about the person behind the evangelist's portrait) in the effort to get back to Jesus, if not 'as he really was', at least to the Jesus behind (though in some continuity with) the kerygma. If successful, this quest would elevate the one Jesus in comparison with the four gospel pictures and later Christologies. The 'new hermeneutic' of the 1960s, while a successor to the quest, probably had for some a unifying effect on the way the New Testament was viewed, at least as regards parts of the gospels (especially the parables) and Paul; it is harder to see how it did justice to the rest of the New Testament, the general epistles, Hebrews, and Revelation.

Religionsgeschichte, or the application of texts, insights, and phenomenology from world religions to the New (or Old) Testament and to the place of Christianity (or Israel) in the spectrum of all other religions, can have either a unifying or divisive effect. Overall, it has often served to relativize biblical religion and the canon. The concern here becomes 'Christian origins', not 'New Testament introduction'; the interest lies in 'comparative religion' and not 'theology'. The canonical writings are treated as simply one collection of 'sources', not even the most important one at that, and the four gospels hold no privileged place, for they are to be fitted into 'trajectories' or 'lines of development', where each is but one step along the way; the Gospel of Peter may be more important in such an approach than the Gospel of Mark (cf. Koester, *Introduction*, 2: 162–71).

To some extent, attention to social setting may also operate either to make more vivid the New Testament books in their world and to link them to each other and to us, or to minimize them as 'theology' in favour of 'community dynamics'. With 1 Peter, we shall see, an exciting case can be made for the view that a group of Gentile converts are here being addressed who suffer alienation from the society of which they were once a part. Or, to take a view of longer standing, many of the New Testament writings, including 1 Peter, may have grown out of a situation where Christians faced persecution. But if documents become simply a reflection of the situation in which they were produced, the unity that many have seen in Christology or eschatological hope in God may be reduced to social axioms ('those who are disenfranchised project their expectations of supernatural help into the future').

Structuralism and, to take a trend easier to apply to gospels and Acts than to epistles, narrative theology may yield insights toward unity by seeing deep commonalities among documents that differ on the surface—while at the same time losing historical specificity. All these comments simply call attention to how new ways of doing biblical studies may or may not yield results on diversity and/or unity.

What of the emergence of a 'canonical approach'? The concept means, for one thing, emphasis on the existing canonical form of the text, as we have it, and the author's intention, not putative earlier sources or forms and their supposed meanings, or the concepts of the opponents of the biblical writer, or putting your money on a reconstruction of 'the historical situation' (which may vary from commentator to commentator). To illustrate, this approach could point to a distinction between Paul's thought and the thought of the Pauline epistles. For ascertaining how Paul's ideas developed, and what they meant in the struggles of the day, it would be important to locate, say, Letters A, B, and C in our canonical Philippians and 2 Corinthians 10–13 and 1–9 (or, to accept a more complex subdivision of the document we have: 1: 1–2: 13 + 7: 5–16; 2: 14–7: 4 (minus 6: 14–7: 1), then ch. 8, then ch. 9) in a sequence between an imprisonment at Ephesus and the departure from Macedonia to Corinth noted at Acts 20: 1–2. But in order to get at the canonical sense of the Pauline letters, one would take up Philippians as a whole and 2 Corinthians intact, both as they stand. A further move, canonically, would be to interpret any idea in one Pauline letter in concert with what the entire corpus of Pauline writings in the canon says, and, beyond that, together with what other authors like Luke, James, or Matthew have to say.

To illustrate: Paul's autobiographical testimony on justification in Philippians 3: 4–14 would, on this approach, have to be blended with what Galatians and Romans also have to say on God's justifying righteousness. To get a total New Testament picture, however, one would need to bring in other references as disparate as those scattered throughout Matthew's Gospel and in James 2, not to mention Jesus' parable in Luke 18: 9–14 about the publican who 'went down to his house justified' and Paul's remark, using the same Greek verb, in a sermon at Acts 13: 39 concerning how 'every one that believes is freed from everything from which you could not be freed by the law of Moses'. In some ways this kind of canonical approach is akin to earlier types of study which did not take historical specificity and diversity so seriously. It denies that a sharper historical focus makes for better interpretation, because the canonical approach has a vision of the entire New Testament as sacred Scripture speaking with a unity to us in the church. Canonical criticism takes quite seriously the believing community, whether of the time when a book was written or of today.

Most advocates of a canonical-criticism approach do employ, to one degree or another, all the biblical criticisms, but so as to 're-present' what the text of a God of grace once said or did in that situation for the pulpit and life of today. In so speaking, the canon exhibits both a stability (it is said), since the text is fixed, and also an adaptability, in that it can adapt to new situations and still prove meaningful. Tradition history in this case opens up the past meanings of text but also provides clues as to how Israel or early Christianity adapted material; these clues can be pointers for how a passage speaks to us today. A text can become 'resignified' for us, the biblical 'signs' speaking afresh, when reread in the light of this hermeneutic.

But one may become hesitant about this canonical approach when a tremendous list of achievements is envisioned as a result, such as 'learning from current international wisdom' or challenging anti-Semitism or underscoring the need to pursue social ethics, together with emphasis on a 'divine bias for the weak and dispossessed' and the claim that Luke 9: 51–18: 14 is resignifying Deuteronomy 1–16 (all in Sanders, *Canon and Community*). Then one realizes that as much has probably been brought to and into the canon as is being derived from it. At work is a thematic unifying of quite different biblical passages (e.g. the 'Jubilee theme' of Lev. 25: 8–17 in Luke 4: 19, to be seen together with the 'Holy War' theme of Deuteronomy 20, in the banquet scenes of Luke 14: 7–24: Jesus is present, and it's Jubilee time!). For preachers at least, such insights are a great boon. Hard-nosed exegetes may be more dubious: did Luke see it thus? Or is this an insight that comes with great unifying effect when *we* 'think canonically'? For some in canonical criticism, to address merely unity and diversity in the New Testament is too little; one must think of the Bible as Scripture, not two testaments!

3

Ways Proposed toward New Testament Unity

BY now it is apparent that some of the factors that led the ancient church to canonize 27 New Testament books and the opinions of some segments of modern scholarship come close, or even coincide, especially in canonical criticism or hermeneutics. The fence around the collection is taken seriously, the books gathered within stand in an interrelation that gives each a further meaning. It will help our examination of New Testament variety and unity to look at some ways in which people have sought to grasp an overall oneness in these writings.

Before looking at these unifying themes, we may note some surface similarities among our 27 documents. One is chronology. While Jesus died about AD 30, the gospels which tell of him all date for their composition from around 70 to 95. The letters from Paul are therefore our earliest writings. They fall mostly in the 50s. A great many of the other documents on which we shall concentrate are located between the 60s and the 90s. (There are one or two for which an earlier date can be argued, like James, and several for which a date going on into the second century can be posited, notably 2 Peter.) An extraordinary number of the books in the New Testament, therefore, stem from the two decades or so around and immediately after the fall of Jerusalem in AD 70. This fact, in turn, explains some common concerns in a number of biblical books appearing in this generation, such as persecution or questions of church structure. What kind of ministerial leadership, for example, was needed for such times of crisis or for the lengthening future? That is a different question from the issues faced by Paul, with his expectations of an imminent parousia.

There is thus a certain commonality in dates and interests within what has been termed the 'second generation' of Christianity, counting AD 30–60 or 70 as the first such period, then 60–70 to 90–100 as the second—or the third generation in terms of the sequence suggested by Luke 1: 1–4 (first, eyewitnesses; then, the 'many' who undertook to compile a narrative about Jesus; third generation, Luke and his addressee, Theophilus). But location in the same decade does not necessarily mean similarity among all documents; two other factors are involved. One is geography. What was the place of writing or of the audience addressed? Our writings from the 70s and 80s, while heavily concentrated in Asia Minor (e.g. 1 Peter, Revelation), may also reflect conditions in Palestine, Italy (Rome), Greece, or Egypt. For Christians, conditions varied from place to place as well as from time to time. A second element is the literary genre or type of writing. Just as a gospel is different from a letter, so also an apocalypse, historical writing, homily, and the more formal treatise (Hebrews? James?) fit into different literary and rhetorical categories and must be viewed accordingly.

Given such likenesses and differences, how may the totality of New Testament books be thought of so as to sense a unity? Over the years the following motifs, among others, have been proposed. In one form or another, each still finds support.

Jesus Christ

In the New Testament itself, as well as in the judgements of the ancient Church and statements of certain modern scholars, the unifying factor is Jesus, the prophet from Nazareth, revealed as Christ and Lord. Every writing in the New Testament collection is a 'Jesus book'. But distinctions must be made. From the fourth to the nineteenth century it was the God–man figure, the Second Person of the Trinity, who was thought of here. With the quest for the historical Jesus, the human personage came to the fore, often viewed as prophet or great teacher. So during Protestant Liberalism, especially given this sort of distinction, the Cross could still be regarded as the goal of his life or as a tragic mistake.

Easter might be the supreme interpretative clue or, as read by others, a subjective hallucination claimed by a few of his followers, a notion the disciples spread, but not 'historical fact'.

If one talks of 'Christology', that brings in a most variable factor. Each book of the New Testament has a view of Jesus of one sort or another, but some are minimal (as in James), others unbelievably high (as in John), and most somewhere in between. New Testament books employ so many different titles for Jesus that it has been argued that Christology is the variable in the New Testament, compared with anthropology or the understanding of the human being and the human situation, where the view is more constant! (This position turns out to be not quite true, though, for there is relatively little about anthropology outside Paul, and the emphasis on sin varies in intensity from situation to situation.) At the least, it will be necessary in our investigation to ask how Jesus the Christ is depicted in each document, if we wish to assess unity and variety on this most central topic.

The gospel

In the 'good news' others have found a unifying theme, indeed for the whole Bible. There are 'good tidings' in the Old Testament about the Exodus or the return from exile (see Isa. 40: 9; 52: 7 for the use of such language). Jesus' preaching concerning the kingdom is so described by Mark 1: 14–15. Paul's life centred around what he termed 'my gospel' (Rom. 1: 1, 9, 16; 2: 16). The word as a noun or verb, 'to preach good news', can be traced through most New Testament books, though strangely not in John.

There are innumerable ways in which this gospel of Christ can be spelled out: as righteousness/justification (Old Testament, Paul, and books like Matthew and James); reconciliation (really only in Romans 5 and 2 Corinthians 5, plus Colossians–Ephesians, but not an Old Testament concept); grace; or 'in Christ' (a phrase widely used by Paul, but not a term in the Synoptics or Old Testament). One may well ask of each New Testament book, what is the 'good news' here?

The kingdom of God; love

Of all the topics taught by Jesus, the one that has the widest use throughout the New Testament writings is his chief theme, 'the kingdom of heaven' (Matthew) or the reign of God. While the synoptics present the concept far more than does John, almost every book in the canon uses it in one way or another. That holds for a good deal of the Old Testament too, if one looks to its verbal form, '(Your) God reigns' or 'The Lord is king' (Psalms especially, the prophets). God's kingdom has often, as today, had its supporters, who see it as a shifting symbol, if not the constant theme, running through Bible and church. It suggested to Calvin (and others) the sovereignty of God. For still others, the kingdom has led into ecclesiology, and a church understood in terms of a place where God's rule is realized in human life, or a place where there is divine authority and structured, ministerial leadership.

To many another reader, however, to the 'person in the street', love, in the full biblical sense of *agapē*, seems a more obvious and more endearing candidate for what the Bible is all about. John's words, 'God is love' (1 John 4: 8, 16; cf. John 3: 16), echo in everyone's ears, although we may not realize how many variations on this theme are rung in the New Testament. Jesus in the synoptics, for example, speaks of love primarily as a demand (e.g. Matt. 5: 43–4, love even enemies!). Paul talks of God's love for us (1 Thess. 1: 4; Gal. 2: 20), our loving one another (Rom. 13: 8), but almost never of our loving God (Rom. 8: 28 is an exceptional case; usually in Paul the response to God is faith). We ought to look for 'kingdom' references or how 'love' is used in each biblical book, but can expect differences among writers and situations.

Kerygma, proclamation of the word

Another way investigators have found unity among the books of the New Testament is by asking about the proclamation in them. C. H. Dodd's book on the apostolic preaching gave impetus to further studies of the kerygma. Since this proclamation focused on what God has done in Christ, there is likely to be more continuity here from book to book than if we ask about ethics, where the point of emphasis is often more situationally determined. A host of terms for preaching may be used—kerygma, 'the word' in the sense of message, 'preach', 'announce' or 'herald', even 'tell' or 'speak' are all terms that may crop up, as well, of course, as 'proclaim good news' (discussed above). For some, the lively nature of the word, which does what it says it will, by the power of God, is the important part of the picture. For others it is the content of the word that matters most. Such emphases on proclaiming or speaking are also prominent in the Old Testament, especially the prophets. In a 'theology of the word' therefore biblical unity has also been sought (cf. Ebeling, *Word and Faith*), and this theme can be looked for in each book.

God's (plan of) salvation

This heading can cover a number of ways in which people have looked for unity in the New Testament. There are places where a plan of God is spoken of directly, as 'the mystery' or divine wisdom which has been made known (1 Cor. 2: 7–8; 4: 1; Col. 1: 26–8; Eph. 1: 9–10; 3: 3–9). At times, God's programme in history is spelled out in a series of seminal figures from Adam through Abraham and Moses to Christ and the Last Adam or Christ-to-come, as in Paul (cf. C. K. Barrett, *From First Adam to Last*), or is conveyed through narrative (Luke's Gospel; cf. Acts 2: 23). More often, the talk is of 'salvation', with both present and future connotations. 'What must I do to be saved?' (Acts 16: 30). 'Salvation is of the Jews' (John 4: 22). 'There is no other name under heaven given [besides that of Jesus Christ] by which one must be saved' (Acts 4: 12). Patristic theology spoke of God's plan of salvation as 'the divine economy' (*oikonomia*), God's arrangement and demonstration of salvation culminating in the incarnation (which is another, later sense of the word *oikonomia*) and the various parts of the incarnate life that led to the Cross and resurrection. All the fulness of *shalom*—peace, well-being, wholeness with God—can be packed into the concept of salvation.

The new age (eschatology)

Still others see the New Testament centred in the time of salvation, the 'age to come', announced as imminent or actually brought into history by Jesus Christ. Paul provides a good test case. It has been argued that his message had at its heart apocalyptic categories which set forth the dawning of the total triumph of God through Christ. Such apocalyptic thinking appears in 1–2 Thessalonians, and is never absent from the genuine letters. But others have held Paul changed from this sort of futuristic apocalypticism to a 'realized eschatology', where the promised day in Jewish thought, the 'coming age' (in contrast to 'this present evil age'), was regarded as already here. 'The new being' (creature or creation), as at 2 Corinthians 5: 17, and the church as the locus for the corporate 'new person' whom God intends to come into being, a reconciled humanity (Eph. 2: 14–16), exemplify this view. At times the church emphasis, as spearhead of the new humanity, has led to a stress on its structure, authority, and ministry. A great deal in the debate about eschatology depends on which letters are assigned to Paul and which represent Paulinist developments. John's Gospel is another great example of 'the life of the age to come' being present here and now as 'eternal life' (5: 24). In the documents at which we shall especially look in Chapters 7–16, whether the 'last things' are regarded as future, as 'just around the corner', or already here, will vary; 2 Peter 3: 8–13, 1 Peter 5: 8–10, and 1 John 1: 2–3 each illustrate one of these three possible stances. But eschatology of one type or another can be expected in each of the 27 New Testament books as an interest all share, but again with considerable variations in views.

Faith

A final category, already hinted at, involves belief and all that goes along with it. In terms of classical theology, one may distinguish between 'faith by which one believes' (*fides qua creditur*) and 'the faith which one believes' (*fides quae creditur*); the first is subjective, the second a matter of objective content.

The former entails 'my faith' as a personal response, the latter 'the faith of the church' or of the Bible, often as in a series of propositions to be accepted. Both aspects appear in the New Testament. Another approach to faith is to ask whether the term in a given author suggests 'trust' or 'obedience' or both. Still another is to ask what the object of faith is: whom or what is believed? Some suggest the New Testament is an account of how Jesus' teaching about faith in God, presented in the gospel tradition, became faith in Jesus Christ after Easter.

It has been argued in other circles that the future for any view of the historical Jesus must centre in how he trusted God. Some have in recent years revived the position that the Pauline phrase 'the faith of Jesus Christ', to give the Greek (as at Gal. 2: 16 or Phil. 3: 9) its literal rendering, means the way Jesus believed in God and trusted the Lord, or the faithfulness of Christ into which believers are in turn caught up, so that we are saved literally by 'Christ's faith'. The usual rendering, however, as an objective genitive, where Christ is the object of believing, 'faith in Jesus Christ' (RSV), need not be abandoned, for Christ becomes the focal point of Paul's faith in God. Still others point to a tendency for the belief of those who respond to Jesus (Gal. 2: 16) to be replaced in later documents by 'the faith' as 'a bundle of church doctrines', delivered to the saints to be kept inviolate (cf. 1 Tim. 4: 1; 6: 20–1).

One way or another, faith as a theme in Scripture is an avenue unifying its varied books that is sometimes overlooked. Because of a great deal of recent work on the theme, some of which has just been noted, and the great and flexible variety of senses the concept can include (examine the many meanings it has had in this chapter), we propose to pay special attention to 'faith' as part of the New Testament unity and variety in the pages that follow.

The priorities of this book

It is now possible to arrange in sequence the aims already outlined and to expand them more precisely. They are listed below in order of importance:

1. to explore variety and unity in the entire New Testament (Chs. 4–17), including Jesus, the gospels, and Paul (Chs. 4–6);

2. to examine in greater detail the 9–16 books not among the four gospels and Paul's acknowledged letters: the (seven) general epistles (attributed to James, Peter, John, and Jude), Hebrews, Revelation, and to some extent Acts, and the later Pauline or, if not by Paul himself, deutero-Pauline letters (Chs. 7–16);

3. to look for the outstanding features—e.g. of doctrine, experience, situation—that characterize each book, thereby raising concerns that any discussion of unity must look to as part of the variety (catholicity) of the New Testament (Chs. 4–17);

4. to check each book for certain master themes that appear frequently or that have been proposed as unifying the New Testament, such as Christology, gospel, eschatology, community ('church' concept, including, where pertinent, ministerial leadership) (Chs. 4–17);

5. while not overlooking such topics as the kingdom, love, salvation, or ethics, to analyse how 'faith' is presented in each book (Chs. 4–17);

6. to present, in the light of the fuller study in Chs. 4–16, a further discussion of variety and unity, how and where the 27 books cohere, the limits of New Testament unity and of variety, and implications for today (Ch. 17).

PART II

Jesus, the Gospels, and Paul: Major Voices in Emerging Christian Faith

The gospels, four in number, like the four winds, 'four pillars breathing out immortality everywhere and rekindling humanity' (Irenaeus, *Against Heresies*, 3. 11. 8), and 'the divine Apostle', Paul, became norms in early Christianity because of their proximity to Jesus and use in Church life. They continue as New Testament standards to this day.

Jesus of Nazareth as Starting-Point

To choose a starting-point amid the pluralism of the New Testament canon is no easy task, whether the approach is 'historical' or 'theological' or both. In terms of sheer number of literary references, of course, Jesus is the chief figure in or behind all New Testament writings, along with God.

If historical development is the concern, there are problems, however, even when we wish to start at the obvious point, with Jesus. For, modern criticism asks, how much can we know about the prophet from Nazareth? Even given the more optimistic assessment that we can discover a good deal about this figure (a position strenthened in recent years by appeal to Jewish data and argued in part by Israeli scholars), there is the matter of precisely which background to invoke to account for his message and person and therefore what sort of Jesus to project. Was Palestine so infiltrated by Graeco-Roman cultural currents, especially in Galilee, that Jesus could have been something like the wandering Cynic preachers of the Hellenistic world? If we locate him more firmly in Judaism, is he to be likened to a charismatic rabbi/teacher or to an apocalyptic prophet? Was he a reformer within Judaism or something more radical, a voice of doom like John the Baptist or a political revolutionist like Theudas or Judas the Galilean (Acts 5: 36–7)?

If the approach is theological, does Jesus himself deserve to rank among the theologians of the New Testament or was he *sui generis*, a 'law (or gospel) unto himself'? Some would mark him off from all the later theological witnesses to the revelation that came through his proclamation and person. This they do either because, traditionally, he was the God-man and Second Person of the Trinity, or because Jesus was the one who uniquely spoke for and revealed God, and therefore all theologizing is the response of the community (Jeremias). Debate over the role of Jesus is particularly acute if one thinks at all in terms of an overall 'New Testament theology'.

The place of Jesus in New Testament theology

It once was common, in unfolding any theme in the New Testament, to begin with what Jesus taught or by reference to what he did. He was the Lord presented in the gospels, from whom was derived what Paul and John said. But as the pendulum swung and critical scholars questioned how much, even in the synoptics, really was from Jesus, a position at the opposite pole emerged: to allow very little to the message of Jesus (as recoverable today) and to stress the thought of the post-Easter church which is accessible to us in its letters and other writings. So argued Bultmann's *Theology of the New Testament* (1948–53). While Jesus Christ will be the content of the kerygma after the resurrection, the message of Jesus was but one of the presuppositions for the theology of the New Testament. Indeed, Bultmann allowed the term 'theology' only in speaking of Paul and John. Much of the New Testament material he dealt with under the heading of the kerygma first of 'the earliest [Palestinian] church' and secondly of 'the Hellenistic church aside from Paul', and finally in a section entitled 'Development toward the Ancient Church'. Conzelmann provided a variant on this in *An Outline of the Theology of the New Testament* (1967) by treating Jesus under 'the Synoptic kerygma', after 'the kerygma of the Primitive Community and the Hellenistic Community' but before Paul. In this way, Conzelmann sought both to reconstruct the proclamation of Jesus and to present the theology of each gospel, not just that of Paul and John.

Subsequent efforts have varied. Leonhard Goppelt's uncompleted, posthumously published *Theology of the New Testament* (1975–6) focused massively in the first of its two volumes on Jesus' earthly activities; as the English translation puts it, *The Ministry of*

Jesus in its Theological Significance. From Jesus stem both kerygma and Jesus-tradition. The one volume on *The Proclamation of Jesus* (1971) that appeared in Joachim Jeremias's planned *New Testament Theology* shows a similar emphasis. For these scholars, New Testament theology begins with, indeed is the achievement of, the earthly Jesus. Somewhat similar was the volume by W. G. Kümmel (1969). His *Theology of the New Testament According to Its Major Witnesses* takes up three figures: Jesus, Paul, and John.

On the other hand, the descriptive textbooks on New Testament theology by George Eldon Ladd (1974) and Leon Morris (1986) approach the topic by canonical and chronological groupings, respectively. In neither case is 'the historical Jesus' treated separately. (There is, in part, however, a presumption that the gospels, especially the synoptics, provide reliable information about Jesus.) The approach here is by books and authors in the canon, without seeking prior 'development' or stages from the earthly Jesus to what the New Testament witnesses say.

To include Jesus himself, therefore, among the voices in the New Testament, in the light of but prior to our gospels, involves both historical-critical and theological decisions. Over fifty years ago, Hoskyns and Davey, in discussing 'the theologies' of the New Testament (an accolade they granted to Paul, John, and Hebrews) in relation to Jesus, spoke (*The Riddle of the New Testament*, 208, 246–64, 14) of 'a riddle in the New Testament', a 'theological riddle', namely, 'the relation between Jesus of Nazareth and the Primitive Christian Church'. That riddle still baffles, even though for many nowadays there seem good grounds for attempting to state something about Jesus himself, historically, as we shall do, at the outset of any picture of New Testament variety and unity. In his career can indeed be seen some roots for later common themes, and also for the rich diversity that was to blossom among Christians in their faith.

A general picture of the earthly Jesus

The following points can be made with the agreement of considerable portions of current New Testament scholarship, in the light of our knowledge of the Palestinian world. For fuller discussion of many of the details, see the volumes in this series by Graham Stanton, *The Gospels and Jesus* (pt. ii), and Schuyler Brown, *The Origins of Christianity* (45–71); further, Reumann, *Jesus in the Church's Gospels*; and Conzelmann, Schillebeeckx, Harvey, and Vermes, listed in the Bibliography.

Jesus, a Jew of Galilee, lived in a land under Roman rule. It is clear that he was put to death by crucifixion at Jerusalem, on political charges of sedition (Luke 23: 2) by the Roman overlords, probably in AD 30 (and, if in that year, then on 7 April). His ministry, of twelve months or so, had centred on the preaching of 'the kingdom of heaven' (i.e. of God). This was a teaching marked by ethical demands to turn to God and live in accordance with God's will, a proclamation accompanied by wondrous deeds of healing which signalled that the kingdom was upon the very threshold of his hearers' lives (Matt. 12: 28 par. Luke 11: 20).

Jesus' heritage was that of Israel. This meant, among other things, that his thoughts were rooted in the Scriptures, especially in Genesis, Isaiah, and the Psalms, but also in Daniel and other apocalyptic writings. Jesus took over Israel's revealed understanding of Yahweh as Lord God and Father. Yet he could be critical of legalism, Sabbath laws, and purification rituals (see the testimony in the later accounts in Mark 3: 1–6; 7: 1–23). While he attended synagogue, Jesus had little to do with the Jerusalem temple and its cult and probably saw it as doomed (Mark 13: 2 parr.). He did not 'cleanse' the temple, but acted so as to make its cultic procedures impossible by driving out the sacrificial animals, a key part of the ritual–economic system.

For all the influences in his day from the Graeco-Roman world, Jesus seems none the less to have avoided 'pagan' cities like Sepphoris and Tiberias in Galilee. Perhaps he knew some Latin or Greek, but his preaching was to 'the lost sheep of the house of Israel' (Matt. 15:24) in Aramaic. Any 'universal' hopes he had, for the Gentiles to come into the kingdom, were akin to the vision of certain Old Testament prophets: that at the last day God would lead the nations to a banquet table set atop Israel's holy mountain (Matt. 8: 11–12 par. Luke 13: 28–9; Isa. 2: 2–3, 25: 6–9).

Contemporaries, depending on what segments of Jesus' teaching they heard, most frequently viewed him as a rabbi (though not formally ordained), close in many ways to the Pharisees and specifically to the more liberal or Hillelite wing. He was not at all similar to the Sadducees and Zealots. Yet there were clashes with the Pharisees, especially on the part of Jesus' followers. While his parables and some sayings gave the impression of a teacher figure, other statements by Jesus made him appear a prophet, even an apocalyptist. But he seldom spoke along nationalistic lines, or of cosmic disasters or timetables for 'the End'. Jesus was at points indebted to Israel's wisdom tradition or heritage from the sages (Blenkinsopp, *Wisdom*, 158) and talked about God's providence (Matt. 6: 25–34 par. Luke 12: 22–32).

If among Jesus' followers was numbered a Zealot (Luke 6: 15), he also enrolled pro-Roman tax collectors in his ranks (Mark 2: 14–15). If he spoke a great deal to the poor, he also had time for the rich. If some reconstructions of his life put forth in the last 200 years attempt to make of him an insurrectionist, others try to portray him as a pacifist. He may have discerned the signs of the day and pointers to Jerusalem's impending fall, but there is almost nothing to commend the view that Jesus was a Zealot activist. His outreach to women and children was particularly remarkable for his day. A table-fellowship with the outcasts from society, tax-collectors, and harlots exhibited his gregarious freedom, in contrast to the style of John the Baptist (Matt. 11: 18–19 par. Luke 7: 33–4).

Much of what Jesus said and did was stamped by a deep sense of God's goodness (Matt. 5: 45; 7: 7, 11), even though he did not speak of God's love or grace. For God is a father (*Abba*) who rejoices over sinners who repent (Luke 15: 7, 10) and is like a mother hen gathering her brood (Matt. 23: 37 par. Luke 13: 34). Yet we must be careful not to make his manifestations of God's loving kindness into sentimentality, for there was a bite in what he said. His message was of such a nature as to rouse opposition among certain Jewish groups and powerful forces in Jerusalem that condemned him and handed him over to the Romans to die. That message had to do with God (for Jesus spoke little about himself) and about what God was doing.

He would have been, at best, however, a minor figure in rabbinic annals if it had not been for the claim, experienced by some of his followers, that 'God raised Jesus from the dead'. Certain women found the tomb empty, and disciples, women and men, then saw him alive and eventually exalted at a place of honour alongside God. That led to the kerygma of Jesus as risen Lord.

Themes in Jesus' ministry

As indicated, Jesus announced the kingdom of God. That emphasis immediately related him to the major Old Testament theme that 'Yahweh is king, the Lord reigns' (Exod. 15: 18; Pss. 95: 3; 97: 1; 98: 6; 99: 1). But Yahweh's kingship had receded for Israel in the face of the vicissitudes from the fall first of the northern, then of the southern kingdom, and then from the exile. Often in the intervening centuries, and now under Roman occupation, the hope was that God would one day restore this divine rule and dominion, preferably soon. Hence Jesus' announcement that the reign of God was at hand roused great hopes that God was finally about to do something about it all. At times, Jesus spoke of the divine kingdom as future but imminent (Mark 1: 15; 9: 1), other times as already 'in your midst' (Luke 17: 21) or growing like a plant or an actual harvest among us (see the 'seed' parables in Mark 4 and Matthew 13). Both the 'already realized' and 'future/to-come' aspects belonged to Jesus' presentation.

In speaking so emphatically about what God was doing and would do in the future, how did Jesus picture himself? The topic of Christology with regard to the historical Jesus hovers between the principle that 'Jesus preached God and not himself' and the fact that our finished gospels are studded with christological titles and claims. Those most startling and significant, in John's

Gospel, are especially the result, as we shall see, of a process of post-Easter escalation. Even in the more reserved synoptic accounts, we must remember that the experience of the resurrection helped prompt the accumulation of titles that exalted Jesus, and that these were then applied to the Galilean teacher in depicting his lifetime with greater clarity than actual events and the disciples' discernment during the ministry warranted.

To oversimplify some much-debated areas, we may suggest that Jesus, who lived a life of service to others and spoke as a prophet of God, did not himself use the title of '(suffering) servant' or welcome that of 'messiah' (Christ)—in part, because, although 'messiah' had some Old Testament background (usually for an anointed ruling king), it could in Jesus' day be misunderstood along political-revolutionist lines. Yet Jesus' understanding of God as *Abba* suggests he had a sense of unique filial calling as 'son'. The practice of addressing Jesus as 'sir' or 'master' (used of a teacher) would lead to a deeper understanding of him as lord. Most enigmatic and debated is the term 'son of man'. Jesus' personal use of it suggested both his being a prophet (as in the use of the phrase by Ezekiel) and an apocalyptic sense of destiny for himself and those who heeded his message about God (as in Dan. 7: 13–14).

Jesus' gospel was thus about God's own reign. (He seems at most to have used the verbal form, 'to preach good news', Matt. 11: 5 par. Luke 7: 22; cf. Luke 4: 18, 43, since passages where the noun is found, like Mark 1: 15 are today widely regarded as summaries from the early church, using a term popular with Paul.) Jesus' eschatology was both present and future. The kingdom theme will echo through every segment of the New Testament, though not always as the chief theme. The twin aspects of eschatology will crop up, now one, now the other, sometimes both, in every subsequent early Christian writer.

What of 'ecclesiology'? The term 'church' occurs only twice in the gospels, both in Matthew. (The references are 16: 18, for the universal *ekklēsia*, and 18: 17, on discipline in the local assembly.) Both examples are under suspicion as reflections of post-Easter usage. Because of this paucity of records and the fact that his eschatology scarcely permitted much 'long-range planning', most modern scholars do not talk of Jesus 'founding' a church. But recent gospels study does emphasize the movement that grew up around Jesus during his lifetime and continued after his death and resurrection. This 'Jesus movement' emphasized discipleship (following as 'learners'). It is a forced conclusion, however, to claim, as Paul Hanson does (*The People Called*, 423–6), that under Jesus was affirmed a 'classic triadic communal pattern tracing back to early Yahwism', namely, worship, righteousness, and compassion. Even if such a triad appeared in the Yahwist (J) writer centuries before and had a continuing history in Israel, 'righteousness' appears in the synoptic gospels primarily as redaction in Matthew (cf. 6: 33 with Luke 12: 31), and 'worship' is not prominent. It might be better to stress how Jesus gathered a new eschatological family of God (Mark 3: 33–5; 10: 29–30). His circle of followers included a group of twelve, symbolic of an awakened Israel, but there was a repudiation of hierarchical or even rabbinic-style leadership among them (Mark 10: 42–4 parr.; Matt. 23: 8–12). Jesus had a vision of this egalitarian band of humble servants as 'light' and 'salt' for the world, 'a city set on a hill' (Matt. 5: 13–16 parr.). From them and their efforts to spread the story of Jesus, a church community would grow.

Jesus carried over into his own teachings the biblical concept of faith as confidence and trust in God. Once (Mark 11: 22) he is recorded as commanding, 'Have faith in God' (*pistin theou*, objective genitive; to interpret as 'Have faith the way God does' would be grotesque). More characteristic is the way Jesus spoke of 'faith that moves mountains' (Mark 11: 23 parr., including 1 Cor. 13: 2) and of 'prayer faith' (Mark 11: 24 par., 'whatever you ask in prayer, believe that you have received it, and you will'), which in turn is connected with forgiving when you pray (11:25). Compare Matt. 17: 20 par. Luke 17: 6, about faith like the grain of mustard seed: small though it is, it promises great results. Nothing will be impossible for the believer (Mark 9: 23). A specific area where the power of faith operates is healing, as in the formula, 'Your faith has made you well' (Mark 5: 34 par.; 10: 52). Even Jesus' disciples, however, sometimes lacked such faith (9: 19, 23, 28–9). One must profess, 'I believe; help my unbelief' (9: 24).

An implication may be that Jesus himself had faith, supremely. Some have therefore claimed that, after Easter, to believe in Jesus 'came to mean "to believe *like* Jesus that God grants prayer" '. But never is it said in the synoptics: 'Jesus believed . . .'. The closest any text comes to saying this may be in a dialogue found only in Mark. The father of a mute son possessed by a spirit comes to Jesus with the petition, 'If you can [do] anything, have pity on us and help us' (9: 22). Jesus responds, 'What's this "if you can"? All things are possible to a person who belives' (9: 23). That could mean that Jesus is the person who believes and can do something. But the father takes it to mean himself, as the reply shows: 'I do believe; help my unbelief' (9: 24). Overall, what the synoptics teach is faith in God, not a call by Jesus for faith in himself (Matt. 18: 6 par.; Mark 9: 42 represents a later expansion into belief in Jesus). All this was consonant with ancient Israel's trust in God and petition in times of need (Pss. 107: 6, 8; 145: 8–9).

The Witness of the Four Gospels

JESUS worked in Palestine, using a dialect of Aramaic, among Jews, rarely with even Samaritan contacts (Luke 17: 15; John 4). Our gospels come to us in Greek, written decades later, according to most views (both traditional and current) from outside Palestine. In all four cases, the story of what Jesus said and did and who he was is told with a particular audience and its situation in mind, the situation including a community of people who believe in Jesus as Lord amid a world that is hostile to them or ignorant of Christ.

In the years between the death of Jesus and the gospel-writing period, sayings from Jesus, stories about him, collections of parables or miracle stories, glimpses of the Passion, and resurrection experiences had been told, heard, and eagerly retold. In some cases the material may have been put into written form, perhaps for teaching purposes or for use at worship. Almost midway in the period between Jesus and the composition of our gospels, Paul had dictated letters to his congregation to set forth, defend, or clarify 'the gospel of God concerning Christ' (Rom. 1: 1, 3; 15: 19). There had been time enough for distortions, proclamation of alternative gospels, and downright heretical teaching (Gal. 1: 6–7; Phil. 3: 18). Now evangelists, either individuals or a school of Bible students who had pored over the Scriptures together, who theologized about the coming of Jesus and were concerned to address their communities with the word for a changing time, were moved to put together gospel books.

It has been widely held, especially in German scholarship, that the gospel-book form or genre arose uniquely out of the kerygma or apostolic preaching (compare Mark as an expansion of Acts 2: 22–4). Others would see Old Testament precedents in the 'lives of the prophets', such as Elijah or Elisha, for there one finds a teaching ministry, miracles, and even, in the case of Elijah, an 'ascension' into heaven (2 Kings 2, as the climax of stories beginning at 1 Kings 17). Still others, especially in America, have seen analogies in Greek 'biographies', particularly those of Socrates or Philostratus' *Life of Apollonius of Tyana*, the account of an itinerant teacher and wonder-worker of the first century AD, written in the third. In favour of the last-named theory is the claim that the gospels would then have appeal to pagan readers in a genre with which they were familiar. Some stress also the argument that the gospels thus showed biographical interest. But each gospel obviously has kerygmatic interests also, and is more or less reflective of the Hebrew Scriptures (usually in their LXX form). Each gospel should be examined in its own right for its blending of such features.

For centuries Christianity assumed (*a*) the priority of Matthew as the first gospel book to be written and (*b*) the historical eyewitness value of John. After all, both were held to be by 'apostles'. Critical analysis persuaded many in the nineteenth century, however, of the priority of Mark, and by 1950 much of Roman Catholic scholarship felt free to adopt that view and also the supposition of a Q or Sayings Source as part of the 'Two-Source Hypothesis'. Today some Catholics continue to claim, and some American Protestants have vigorously reasserted, the sequence Matthew–Luke–Mark (without necessarily claiming full historical veracity for Matthew or John). In Israel, a few Conservative Evangelical and Jewish scholars opt for Luke's priority. But careful, pericope-by-pericope analysis continues to suggest Mark's priority; compare with Matt. 8: 16 and Luke 4: 40 the chronological detail at Mark 1: 32, where the double phrase, 'That evening at sunset', fits perfectly the setting at the close of Sabbath. It is hard to make the rough-hewn Gospel of Mark the end-product of a process where gospels with Matthew's careful structure and Luke's polished Greek preceded a writer who could then only be called inept.

For a more detailed chapter on each gospel, see pt. i of Stanton, *The Gospel and Jesus*, in this series.

The Gospel of Mark

Whoever the author was (unmentioned in the book itself, unless at 14: 51–2), he (or she) has put great emphasis on the term 'gospel' (1: 14; 8: 35; 10: 29; 13: 10; 14: 9), indeed as a title or with reference to the whole writing as 'The Gospel of Jesus Christ' (1: 1, RSV). This gospel begins at least with Jesus' announcement of the nearness of God's kingdom (1: 14–15), although Mark may envisage it commencing with John the Baptist (1: 4; cf. NEB) or even with Old Testament prophecies fulfilled (1: 2–3; Phillips trans., TEV). It deliberately includes the story ('in memory of her') about the woman who anointed Jesus for his burial (14: 3–9). A particularly bold move is made in identifying Jesus himself with the gospel in the twice-repeated phrase on his lips 'for my sake and the gospel's' (8: 35; 10: 29); no other gospel, as comparison of the parallels shows, equates the gospel with Jesus so directly.

The author and the group addressed are experienced with 'sowing the word' in the world and meeting sometimes with failure, sometimes with short-term success, or sometimes with enduring response (4: 14–20). They seek to preach the good news in the whole world (14: 9) to all nations as their task before the End comes (13: 10). Little is said about Israel and prior history. The newness of Jesus bursting on the scene is stressed, not least by the frequent use of the adverb 'immediately' (1: 18, 20, 21, 23, 28, etc.) and the glad response of the people in Galilee (1: 28, 33, 37, 45). When the Old Testament is reflected, it is chiefly to point to the Passion (14: 18, 21, 34, 49, 62; 15: 24, 34).

There is no question but that, from 1: 14–15 on, the gospel of Jesus in Mark centres on God's kingdom. While it is openly announced, the reign of God is difficult for the rich to enter (10: 23–5), for one must receive it 'like a child' (10: 14–15), i.e. helpless, with complete trust; without personal achievements but calling on God as *Abba* (Jesus' own term, 14: 36; 11: 25).

Eschatologically, some verses speak of the kingdom as a present or very immediate reign (9: 1), a growing one (4: 26–32), but Jesus also speaks of it as future, though imminent (14: 25). It is God-given, but only to those chosen (4: 10–12, 'To you is given the mystery of the kingdom of God, but to those outside all things are in parables' or enigmas). The predestinarian manner in which Mark speaks of the way of Jesus (14: 21) and of 'the elect' (13: 20, 22, 27) will appear also in Paul and John. Jesus' coming and words bring a division among those whom he addresses (10: 17–22; 3: 20–35).

Mark highlights positively the picture of Jesus and in surprisingly negative ways that of the disciples. The Christology in Mark, while presenting a very human figure (1: 41, 43; 3: 5; 6: 3; 8: 12; 10: 14)—there is no miraculous birth, he simply appears on the scene and receives the Spirit at John's baptism (1: 10)— is powerful. There is frequent reference to the impression that his teaching makes (1: 22; 2: 1–2; 11: 19), though very little content is given (chiefly chs. 4 and 13). He is usually able to perform great miracles (1: 23–6, 30–1, 32–4, 40–5; exception, 6: 1–6). The title 'Son of God' is especially stressed (1: 11; 3: 11; 5: 7; 9: 7; 15: 39; 1: 1 in many manuscripts) and at significant points 'the Son' (13: 32; 14: 61–2). 'Son of man' is Jesus' self-designation, during his ministry (2: 10, 28), concerning the Passion (8: 31; 9; 31; 10: 33–4), and with regard to the parousia (8: 38; 13: 26; 14: 62). The complicated history of this phrase is indicated by the way it can be equated with 'man' or 'humankind' (2: 27–8) and by the distinction to be seen between Jesus and the Son of man in 8: 38. In Mark's day the title was clearly one for Jesus. 'Christ' is a title which Jesus (according to Mark) is cautious about at Caesarea Philippi (8: 29–33) but allows at his trial (14: 61–2), although in each instance Jesus goes on to talk of the Son of man.

The disciples, especially the twelve and even Peter, are treated so negatively at times that some have thought Mark has a vendetta against them. They constantly fail to understand (6: 51–2; 8: 16–21). They bicker among themselves (10: 35–44) and are impotent to heal (9: 18). One of them betrays Jesus (14:

10–11, 43–5). Peter denies him thrice (14: 29–31, 66–72). All the rest desert Jesus in Gethsemane (14: 50), and there is no account reporting that they were reinstated later. Even the women, though accompanying Jesus' corpse to the tomb (15: 40–1, 47; 16: 1–8), can be said to fare little better, for the abrupt ending of Mark at 16: 8 leaves open whether they ever told Peter and the others! But such judgements are too harsh. The very fact that there is a Gospel of Mark and a Marcan community presumes they *did* spread the good news to the disciples and Peter about Jesus' resurrection (16: 6–7).

More controverted, however, is the so-called 'Messianic secret'. While Jesus clearly is the Christ in Mark, he sometimes tells those healed not to reveal his identity (1: 24–5, 34; 3: 12; 5: 43). But the device is not used consistently (1: 44–5; 9: 14–29); 5: 19 demands telling 'what the Lord [presumably God, through Jesus] has done'. The practice could be traced back to the historical Jesus on the supposition that he sought anonymity in order to avoid premature or mistaken understandings of who he really was. But the messianic secrecy material can also be, and more probably is to be, explained as the hermeneutical presupposition for writing a gospel: to present Jesus as now the messiah must be balanced by due reflection of the ambiguities of his own time, in a tension between openness and secrecy. Otherwise, Jesus would appear in the narrative as the object of a series of historically verifiable epiphanies, as if 'a great green jay bird' (Kierkegaard) had taken up residence in an otherwise pedestrian landscape; the result would be to overawe, not bring to faith in a God who works in a hidden way, as leaven in dough (Matt. 13: 33 par. Luke 13: 20–1), a seed growing secretly (Mark 4: 26–9), or a Jesus in the midst of Israel.

The community associated with Mark's Gospel is only hinted at. It continues the Jesus movement through wandering disciples who have broken family ties (1: 20–1; 10: 28–30; 3: 31–5) and follow Jesus, proclaiming him, healing in his name, and suffering for him. These volunteers urge others to join their group and await God's vindication of Jesus as the triumphant Son of man. Forgiveness (2: 5; 11: 25), love for God and neighbour (12: 33), and probably equal rights for women (cf. 10: 10–11 on divorce) marked their life together. The Marcan 'church' can be seen as intensely apocalyptic if the book is dated just before AD 70 and ch. 13 is stressed. Or less apocalyptically, as a call to reconstituting Christian life by going back to roots in Galilee, if chs. 1–9 are stressed and a date after 70 and the fall of Jerusalem.

Jesus' own use of faith as a theme is preserved by Mark, a concept deeply fraught with Old Testament overtones of trust in God (11: 22). In the miracle stories, the term *pistis* stands out as trust in and with a power to deliver (5: 34; 10: 52). The references in the story of the epileptic child at 9: 19, 23, and 24 provide almost a catechetical illustration of the movement from disbelief to effective faith. Cf. also 11: 23–4 on faith, instead of doubt. Mark 5: 36 has the significant enjoinder to a synagogue ruler, 'Just believe' (i.e. faith alone). Mark's initial reference to faith, however, is to believing in the gospel of the kerygma Jesus preached (1: 15). This reflects later Christian use concerning faith as wholehearted acceptance of the apostolic kerygma about Jesus the crucified and risen Lord. The gospel is here the object of faith. It is the 'little ones' who believe in Jesus in the Marcan community (9: 42). Faith can be corporate (2: 5; 6: 5–6), as well as personal. If the added Long Ending to Mark (16: 9–20) is considered, faith becomes even more prominent (16: 11, 13, 14, 16, 17).

The achievement of Mark was to bring together so many disparate traditions about Jesus, as teacher, wonder-worker, or apocalyptic figure, and combine them, under the overarching theme of the Cross. Narratives (3: 6) and Jesus' own statements (8: 31; 9: 31; 10: 33–4; 10: 45) increasingly point readers to the Passion in chs. 14–15. Mark's theology of the Cross is set off, however, by the apocalyptic vision of ch. 13, assuring us that God will triumph in the end, and by the empty tomb narrative of 16: 1–8 that caps the series of 'secret epiphanies' throughout the book (like 9: 2–8) by proclaiming, 'He is risen, he goes before you to Galilee' (16: 7; cf. 14: 28). This geographical reference to Galilee not only points to 'roots', to the halcyon days of the early

Galilean ministry (1: 9, 14, 28, 39; 3: 7; 7: 31; 9: 30) but also summons to mission until God's plan is fulfilled (13: 10).

Matthew's book about Christ and Church

The Gospel according to Matthew (in addition to Stanton, *The Gospels and Jesus*, ch. 4; see also the proposals in Brown, *The Origins of Christianity*, 108–14) is traditionally ascribed to the tax-collector named at 9: 9 (where Mark 2: 14 had 'Levi') and Matt. 10: 3. Otherwise anonymous, it may in reality be the work of a 'school' of Christian scribes, prophets, and sages (13: 52; 23: 34). It describes itself in its opening words as a *biblos geneseōs* (1: 1), which means a 'book of the genealogy of Jesus' (1: 1–17) but also of his birth (1: 18, same word), beginning, and history. The overall thrust is christological and more ecclesiological than any other of the four gospels.

In many ways, Matthew closely parallels and builds on Mark. But this book fills in much more teaching content, chiefly through five great discourses on the lips of Jesus. Each discourse is concluded with a similar formula at 7: 28; 11: 1; 13: 53; 19: 1; and 26: 1. Chs. 5–7 present the Sermon on the Mount; 10, instructions to the twelve on mission; 13, parables about the kingdom (the three parables of Mark 4 are expanded into seven); 18, on communal discipline; and 24–5, eschatology. Ch. 23 is a fierce tirade of some seven 'woes' against the scribes and Pharisees. Mark's abrupt opening and ending are expanded by materials about Jesus' birth and childhood (chs. 1–2) and two resurrection appearances and the Great Commission (ch. 28).

Both the structure of Jesus' ministry and the scope of God's plan for salvation through Jesus are sculptured more precisely than in Mark. The ministry in Galilee and Jerusalem is pegged to parallel sentences at 4: 17 and 16: 21 (cf. also 26: 16) as turning-points—'From that time Jesus began to preach' about the kingdom to the crowds; and later, 'From that time Jesus began to show his disciples that he must go to Jerusalem and suffer. . . .' The content is from Mark (1: 14–15 and 8: 31 respectively), but Matthew has packaged it differently, so as to suggest pre-ministry, public ministry, and private ministry and Passion sections. The work of Jesus is preceded by Israel's history in numerous references (1: 1–17; 11: 13; 21: 33–9; 22: 2–7). Other verses tell of what would follow Jesus' death and resurrection: mission (28: 16–20; 26: 13), a church, Jerusalem burned (24: 2; 22: 7), the parousia, and judgement (25: 31–46; 22: 9–14). Matthew paints on a grand scale.

Throughout this account Matthew lays strong emphasis on continuity. The message preached by John the Baptist (3: 2), Jesus (4: 17), and the disciples (10: 7) is the same, about the kingdom at hand. Jesus and John stand in a sequence with Old Testament predecessors (23: 29–36), and the disciples are to make converts who will further teach and do what Jesus commanded. Continuity with the past of God's revelation is brought out especially by use of quotations from the Hebrew Scriptures (9: 13; 12: 7), often in their Greek Septuagint form (1: 23), introduced by the formula, 'This happened in order that it might be fulfilled which was spoken by the prophet . . . saying . . .'. The quotations occur especially in the opening chapters (1: 23; 2: 6, 15, 18, 23) and often cite Isaiah (4: 15–16; 8: 17; 12: 18–21).

The gospel of Jesus in Matthew, as in Mark, concerns the kingdom. True to Semitic reverence for the divine name, Matthew usually (but not always) speaks of 'the kingdom of [the] heaven[s]'. In the Lord's Prayer, disciples are taught to pray for God's present and future rule (6: 10). The kingdom belongs to the 'poor in spirit' (5: 3), those persecuted for righteousness' sake (5: 10). But the kingdom of God shares the spotlight with Christology in Matthew. There is great emphasis on the parousia, when Christ will come again (24: 3, 27, 37, 39), and hence on a parable vision where Christ is the final judge, as Son of man, of those who are not disciples ('the nations' or pagans, 25: 31–46). Hence also Matthew makes an unusual distinction between 'the kingdom of the Son of man' (13: 41, which seems to denote the church) and 'the kingdom of the Father' (13: 43) which will one day supersede it.

The Christology of Matthew's Gospel calls for special

attention. The titles in Mark are all carried over and sometimes enhanced—'Son of God' (see 2: 15; 14: 33; 16: 16; 26: 63); 'Son of man' (8: 20; 11: 19); 'the Son' (11: 27); and 'Christ' (1: 1, 16–18; 11: 2). There is particular emphasis on 'Son of David' (9: 27; 15: 22; 20: 30–1), linking Jesus to Old Testament messiahship. A new feature is the presentation of Jesus as 'wisdom', a theme from the Old Testament (Blenkinsopp, *Wisdom*) found also in Paul and Q (11: 19; cf. 23: 34 with Luke 11: 49). Most startling is the application of the name 'Emmanuel' to Jesus (1: 23). The evangelist explains that it means 'God with us', and one can argue that a great deal of the authority of Jesus in Matthew stems precisely from the fact that he speaks for, if not also as, God. Within the framework of 'Father, Son, and Spirit', the closing words of the risen 'God-with-us' are the promise, 'Lo, *I* am with you always' (28: 20).

It is in the light of this majestic picture of Christ that Matthew's view of the church is to be understood. Jesus says, '*I* will build *my* church' (*ekklēsia* in the world-wide sense) on the rock of Peter as confessor of Christ (16: 18; cf. 16–17 and the contrast in 22–3). Jesus also refers to the local *ekklēsia* in connection with the disciplining of sinners (18: 17). Peter is accorded a significant place (14: 28–31; 17: 24–7) among the disciples, all of whom have previously confessed Jesus as Son of God (14: 33). At the resurrection, however, Peter does not receive the prominence that Mark gave him (Mark 16: 7; cf. Matt. 28: 7). The disciples are more favourably portrayed than in Mark; they become persons of 'little faith', as at 16:8, not people with hardened hearts (Mark 8: 17). There is even greater emphasis on the missionary task (28: 19) in the world, which is their field (13: 38). But the community that results is a mixed body of both bad and good persons, and will itself be judged at the end (13: 24–30, 36–43, 47–9). In the Church, no one is to aspire to titles like 'rabbi' or 'father'; humble service is to mark life under Christ (23: 8–12).

One will not grasp Matthew's total message without attention to the ethical demands. While great promises undergird the disciples' existence (5: 3–11, the Beatitudes; 5: 13, 14; 28: 20), the commands are rigorous (5: 16, 48), e.g. on almsgiving, prayer, and fasting (6: 1–18; 7: 1–12). A more perfect righteousness is to mark their lives than even in Israel of old (5: 20–48). If righteousness is at times depicted as a gift (5: 6; 6: 33) in the course of salvation history (3: 15; 21: 32), it is also the moral response expected of disciples (5: 10, 20; 6; 1).

With regard to faith, Matthew keeps Marcan usages (e.g. Matt. 18: 6) and contrasts (17: 14–18) or expands (21: 21) the theme, especially in connection with miracle stories (9: 22, 29). For he further employs the formula 'to you according to your faith' at 8: 10 and 13 and 15: 28. It means persistent trust in Jesus, and opens the way for Gentiles to come to him (8: 5–13; 15: 21–8). Another application is to link faith with understanding or knowledge (*syniēmi*; 13: 13–15, 19, 23, 51). One must not only hear but also comprehend; this is the presupposition for believing. Those of 'little faith' understand but doubt, or do not yet really believe (14: 31; 16: 8, 12; 17: 19–21). Matthew is thus didactic and hortatory in presenting faith (cf. 21: 18–21), connecting it also, as in Mark, with prayer (21: 22).

The achievement of Matthew's Gospel was to take up the Jesus story, as presented by Mark and supplemented from sayings out of teaching material, and anchor it more firmly in Scripture, God's broad plan, and the church's mission, with a call for ethical rigour before God. The good news is that Christ continues to be present after Easter, not through the Holy Spirit or sacramentally, but quite personally, as an 'I', with believers (18: 20; 28: 20) in community life and disciplizing (making disciples and being a disciple of Jesus).

Luke's narrative

The themes of Luke's Gospel can be fully appreciated only when the Book of Acts is also considered. (Even if one no longer concludes that these are both the work of Luke, a Gentile physician and companion of Paul (Philemon 24; Col. 4: 14; 2 Tim. 4: 11), the two volumes are the product of the same hand.) Some New Testament theologies treat Luke with the synoptic gospels and then take Acts as grist for describing the early church (Conzelmann, Ladd). Others treat the double work, Luke–Acts, together, as a single theology, rating as much coverage as Paul or John (so Morris, *New Testament Theology*). If the view currently advocated by some is adopted—that, after writing a gospel and the Acts of the Apostles, Luke then was responsible for the pastoral epistles—this author's contribution to the New Testament would be even more impressive, almost a third of its pages. But the similarities of 1 and 2 Timothy and Titus to Acts are less convincing than their differences. We shall treat the pastorals separately in Chapter 9, and take a further, though brief, look at Lucan thought from the standpoint of Acts in Chapter 16. Here the focus is on Luke's first volume.

The Gospel of Luke calls itself a 'narrative' (*diēgēsis*, 1:1). It is conscious of predecessors who told the story of Jesus, indeed of being in a succession to 'eyewitnesses and ministers of the word' and the 'many' who have undertaken to compile accounts (at least two or more, including Mark and other sources, perhaps even an earlier edition of this gospel). The famous preface (1: 1–4; cf. Acts 1: 1–2), written in the style of a Hellenistic historian, rightly suggests that the author wishes (*a*) to set his story in the political and cultural currents of the day but also (*b*) to speak theologically, so as to strengthen in the truth the person addressed ('Theophilus', possibly a patron or a Roman official or, symbolically, any 'God-lover'). Luke takes pains to locate his 'life of Jesus' in a world-history setting (e.g. the sevenfold chronological fixing at 3: 1). But he also knows he is treating 'the word' (1: 2; 2: 29; 4: 32; 5: 1; 8: 11, etc., *logos*; 3: 2, *rhēma*). Hence the long debate over whether Luke should be accounted primarily historian or theologian. Both aspects are present.

The result of the author's diligent quest for sources and his distinctive theology of history and salvation is a book characterized by great beauty, excellent Koiné literary Greek, and a different framework for the Jesus material than in any other New Testament writer. No one can deny that Luke focuses on Jesus in volume 1 and on the churches of Jesus after Easter in volume 2. He is thus able to spread out over some 10 metres of papyrus scroll in each case (a luxurious amount for an early Christian group!) a Christology of Jesus and an ecclesiology of the Spirit from the risen Lord.

Luke differs from Matthew, who had to weave his references to the church into a book on Jesus' ministry (and from Mark and John, who had less of an ecclesiological bent). Luke shows a certain interest in the times prior to Jesus, in Israel (1: 54, 68, 80; 2: 25, 32, 34; 4: 25, 27). But it is not the interest Matthew exhibited in the centuries of Israelite and Judaean history, as exemplified in the genealogy at Matthew 1. Rather, Luke talks of Israel as an entity, though ancient (1: 54–5, 68), which existed in Jesus' day (7: 9; 24: 21; Acts 10: 36), and which in Acts the Christian missionaries hope to win to Christ (Acts 2: 36; 4: 10; 28: 20).

On the tripartite structure of Luke's salvation history, as proposed by Conzelmann and modified by others, there is considerable agreement. The centre-piece in this triptych is 'the time of Jesus', when he was here on earth. Preceding it was 'the age of Israel'. Following Jesus' earthly ministry and the uniquely Lucan depiction of a period of 40 days of resurrection appearances (Acts 1) and the coming of the Spirit at Pentecost (Acts 2)—which might be depicted as slivers of divine action from above, between periods 2 and 3—comes the 'time of the Church' (Acts 2–28). It is fair to see a 'plan of God' spelled out in this way, for Luke refers several times to a 'definite plan and foreknowledge of God', where steps are predestined (e.g. Acts 2: 23; 4: 28; 5: 38; Luke 7: 30), and where a divine necessity stands over what is done (Luke 4: 43; 13: 33; 17: 25).

There is a certain likeness between the time of Jesus and the age of the church in that each has three subdivisions. The Marcan structure of 'Galilee/Jerusalem' was the pattern for Jesus' ministry (with a journey to Jerusalem in between) becomes in Luke 'Galilean, Travel or Samaritan, and Jerusalem' sections (4: 1–9: 50; 9: 51–19: 27; 19: 28 ff., respectively). This is matched in Acts by witnessing (1: 8) in Jerusalem (1: 12–8: 3), Judaea and Samaria (8: 4–12: 24), and to 'the end of the earth' (12: 25–28: 31), here Rome. This arrangement minimizes

Galilee somewhat, and makes Jerusalem the goal of the gospel account (9: 51, 53; 13: 22; 17: 11; 18: 31; 19: 28) and the starting-point for the word's advance in Acts (Luke 24: 47). To give such prominence to Jerusalem (19: 41–4) requires different phrasings at times from what the other synoptics have; compare Luke 24: 6–7 with Mark 16: 7.

More disputed are some proposals about the periods of Israel and Jesus. It is suggested that John the Baptist belongs with the law and the prophets in the age of Israel, not with Jesus (compare Luke 16: 16 with Matt. 11: 12–13). Almost all the references to John are concentrated in Luke 3: 1–20, so that he is off-stage, in prison, when Jesus appears for baptism (by God; 3: 21–2). When Jesus preaches and ministers, we sense a unique period in all human history: the 'today', when scriptural promises are being fulfilled (4: 17–21), is 'the time of Jesus'. Some would see the Isaiah 61 passage he quotes as a reflection of the year of jubilee set forth in Leviticus 25: 8–55. It has even been claimed that Satan departs from the story between Jesus' besting of the tempter in the desert (4: 13) and the betrayal of Jesus by Judas at the Passion (22: 3). Jesus' ministry is marked by expressions of God's mercy and forgiveness such as the world of the day had not known. The tender mercy of God (1: 78) is at hand in a 'gospel of great pardonings' (7: 36–50; 19: 1–10; 23: 34, 39–43). All these details serve to underscore the uniqueness of the time of Jesus as unparalleled, indeed the 'mid-point' for all history.

Luke is able to link the ages of Israel, Jesus, and the church through the way certain themes are handled. An example is the temple in Jerusalem. Missing in the Third Gospel is the charge of Mark 14: 58 par. Matt. 26: 61 that Jesus said he would destroy the temple. Instead, there is a quite positive picture of it given for the period prior to Jesus' ministry, in his childhood (2: 27, 37, 46). While the city of Jerusalem knew not the time of its visitation (19: 41–4), Jesus is specifically said to have entered the temple, a house of prayer (19: 45–6). There he repeatedly taught (19: 46; 20: 1; 21: 37, 38; 22: 53). On into the early days of the church, Jesus' disciples also gathered there (24: 53; Acts 2: 46; 3: 8; 5: 20; Paul too, 22: 17). That Jesus will destroy the temple comes out only in the charge against Stephen (Acts 6: 13–14); Paul is charged with profaning it (Acts 24: 6). Thus the temple brings continuity as a 'holy place' to Luke's story of 'the word God sent to Israel, preaching good news by Jesus Christ' (Acts 10: 36).

Luke never uses the noun 'gospel' in his first volume, but favours the verb (to 'bring or preach good tidings'; Luke uses this verb ten times, compared with just once in Mark and Matthew, and that in a quotation from Isaiah 61 at Matt. 11: 5). See Luke 2: 10; 4: 18, 43; 8: 1; 16: 16, for examples. He keeps the kingdom of God as the theme of Jesus' proclamation (4: 43; 6: 20; 8:1) and of the kerygma announced by the twelve (9: 2) and the larger group of 70 who (only in Luke) form a second wave of missionary preachers in Jesus' lifetime (10: 9). That message will echo in Acts at times, even after the resurrection, which then becomes the chief theme (Acts 8: 12; 14: 22; 28: 23, 31).

Eschatologically, the kingdom is spoken of as future (21: 31; 22: 16, 18) but also present (6: 20; 11: 20). Only Luke reports the enigmatic saying: 'The kingdom of God is in the midst of you' (the Greek in context suggests a sudden appearance or that it is 'among you' (plural), not an inwardness within the individual). It is possible that Luke, with his view of the unprecedented 'time of Jesus', in contrast to the ages of Israel and of the Church, regarded the kingdom as present when Jesus was among us on earth, something that Israel could only await (1: 33) and that Christians after Easter could look back to (in the time of Jesus) and wait to enter at the end of all things (Acts 1: 6–7; 14: 22).

The Christology of Luke carries over the titles already seen in the other synoptics. Jesus is the Christ or messiah, announced by angels at his birth (2: 11). This honorific from the Old Testament is often used (4: 41; 22: 67; 23: 2, among some two dozen cases). Luke will later report the name 'Christians' for Jesus' followers (Acts 11: 26), which comes from 'Christ'. But for a Gentile audience it was not an entirely clear title without knowledge of the Hebrew Scriptures and the practice of anointing; hence for clarity Peter's confession becomes in Luke 'the Christ *of God*' (9: 20). Luke uses the title in Acts as a proper name for Jesus (2: 38; 10: 36). Peculiar to Luke is an emphasis on a 'suffering Messiah' (Luke 24: 26, 46), a concept not found in earlier biblical or Jewish literature ('suffering *Servant*', yes, but not messiah). Perhaps in keeping with the knowledge of a basically Gentile audience, Luke rarely refers to the title 'Son of David' (18: 38–9; 20: 41), although David and his house are spoken of in the 'Israel' sections (1: 27, 69; 2: 4).

Luke's most frequent title for Jesus is 'the Lord'; indeed, the Greek term *kyrios* is often used by the evangelist in narrative (7: 13, 19; 10: 1), a sign that the post- Easter exaltation is being read back into Jesus' earthly life. 'Son of God' and 'Son of man' continue in use, the former especially in light of the virginal conception of Jesus (1: 30–5), the latter in a phrase unique to Luke as part of an ongoing eschatology, the 'days [plural] of the Son of man' (17: 22). Luke alone of the synoptics calls Jesus 'saviour' (2: 11; Acts 13: 23). Acts will add other titles to the list concerning the man whom Luke depicts as 'a prophet mighty in deed and word before God and all the people' (Luke 24: 19), yet in very human terms (2: 40, 52) and as a person of prayer (3: 21; 4: 16; 5: 16).

One matter that has often called forth comment is the failure of Luke to relate the Cross of Jesus to forgiveness in the way that Mark 10:45 does, so that 'Christ died for our sins' (1 Cor. 15: 3). Even the words of the centurion at Jesus' death (23: 47), 'This man was innocent' (a statement that speaks to any Roman worries over Jesus or Christians as political rebels), should be contrasted with the awe-stricken confession in Mark 15: 39 and Matthew 27: 54, 'This man was the Son of God.' It has been argued that Jesus' death in Luke is depicted as that of a martyr, like Stephen (compare Luke 23: 34 and 46 with Acts 7: 60 and 59 respectively). Or that Luke presents the Cross as the noble death of a wise and righteous teacher, much as can be found in Graeco-Roman biographies. Some counter-evidence can be adduced (Luke 22: 19; Acts 20: 28; and possible application of the Suffering Servant verses to Jesus, Isaiah 53: 7–8 at Acts 8: 32–3—though the crucial details of 53: 6 and 8d are missing). A better explanation is simply that Luke has a different theology from that of Paul or Mark: no crucifixion was needed to bring about forgiveness, for God was always like that, forgiving sins. That is why, during Jesus' ministry, there could be 'greater pardons' for sinners. In some ways, God (and the Holy Spirit) loom so large in Luke–Acts that Christology seems diminished, compared with the books by the other evangelists.

Luke's ecclesiology is best seen in Acts. His gospel is more oriented to soteriology and discipleship, to specifics such as repentance (5: 32; 13: 3, 5), prayer (11: 1–13), and right use of wealth (19: 1–10) with good news for the economically poor (6: 20, 29; 16: 19–31). But Luke lays the groundwork for a comprehensive Christianity by his well-known concerns for women (8: 2–3; 10: 38–42; 13: 10–17; 24: 1–11), children, the poor, and outcasts, as part of a 'universalism' (3: 6; 4: 25–7; 13: 29 east, west, north, and south—the last two compass directions are added only in Luke). Luke never says that all will be saved; cf. Acts 4: 12; 2: 21; 'universalism' in Luke–Acts means a divine mercy for people of all possible sorts and conditions who repent and believe. Within the movement surrounding Jesus, 'the twelve' are regarded by Luke as 'apostles'; he uses the term with great frequency during the lifetime of Jesus (9: 10; 11: 49; 17: 5; 22: 14; 24: 10). Thus Jesus and the twelve become 'the Lord' and 'the apostles'. Looking toward the developments to be presented in Acts, Luke's Gospel at the very end depicts the eleven and others 'gathered together' in Jerusalem (24: 33) and blessing God in the temple (24: 52).

While faith will become very prominent in Acts, with 'believers' a name for Christians (Acts 2: 44; 4: 4, 32, etc.), Luke's Gospel carries over the common synoptic sense of 'faith' from Jesus. There are inherited miracle story references to faith that saves at Luke 8: 48, 50 and 18: 42, plus new ones at 7: 50 and 17: 19, as well as the mustard-seed analogy (17: 5–6). Already in the infancy narrative Luke strikes the note of faith in a beatitude about Mary, 'Blessed is she who believed that there would be a fulfilment of what was spoken to her from the Lord' (1: 45). Disciples can be asked, 'Where is your faith?' (8: 25) and may need (even Peter) Jesus' prayer for them individually (22: 32).

Luke relates faith to salvation in a statement that the devil 'takes away the word . . . in order that people may not believe [the Christian message] and be saved' (8: 12–13; cf. 12: 46 about the unfaithful). If only they believed the prophets (24: 25, cf. 16: 31) and continued to believe the word (8: 13)! Acts will describe Christianity not only as 'the way' (9: 2) but also as 'the faith' (Acts 6: 7; 13: 8; Luke 18: 8).

Luke–Acts is a work rich in themes. The story of Jesus is here set forth winsomely, with some links to Israel but even more to Hellenistic–Roman culture. It is above all the gospel that connects Jesus with the church that resulted, and with the Spirit as the vehicle for the next stage of God's ongoing salvific activity. Synoptic in heritage, Luke's Gospel also has certain affinities with the Fourth Gospel. Above all, it is an account of Jesus for a longer future, not just for the crisis period around 70 when Mark wrote. Jewish antecedents and audience are not as prominent as in Matthew. Luke–Acts helped establish Jesus and the kerygma in the Gentile world. It gave us a chronological, calendrical outline that includes the events of Christmas, Ascension, and Pentecost, flanking the Good Friday/Easter core.

John: written for believing and life

The Johannine corpus is in itself an example of unity and variety. The Gospel of John has long been associated with three New Testament epistles and the Apocalypse or Book of Revelation, all traditionally said to be by one of the twelve, the 'Beloved Disciple', John, the son of Zebedee, though at different points in his long lifetime. (Even the ancients recognized differences in tone and content among the books, which they accounted for by appealing to changed conditions in the apostle's situation.) The title 'Lamb (of God)' for Jesus, for example, seems to unify the books, occurring in John 1: 29, 36 and twelve different chapters of Revelation (5: 6; 6: 16; 13: 8, etc.). But the Greek words are not the same (*amnos* in the gospel, *arnion* in Revelation), and the connotations vary even more (paschal, sacrificial lamb; the wrath of the lamb, etc.). The term 'Paraclete' refers in the Fourth

Gospel to the Spirit whom Christ will send (John 14–16) but in 1 John (2: 1) to Christ as our advocate with the Father.

Nowadays the separate histories of each of these documents are widely recognized, with very few scholars holding to the direct apostolic authorship of any of them. There is some tendency to speak of a 'Johannine circle' or 'school' responsible especially for the Fourth Gospel and 1 John. We shall treat the letters and the Apocalypse in their individuality in Chapters 13 and 14, the Johannine Gospel here, with some reference to 1 John.

But even for the Gospel of John there is an increasing tendency (cf. Brown, *Origins of Christianity*, 114–17) to see a history of communal development, with the stages of literary composition reflecting, first, existence within a Jewish synagogue, then expulsion from it (9: 22; 16: 2); after that, feelings of isolation, with identity and solace coming from the exalted Christ, until the Christian community itself, alas, divides, with some 'going out from us' who never really were 'of us' (1 John 2: 19).

The Christianity of the Fourth Gospel represents a radical type when we grasp what is really said and not simply the domesticated sense later often given it. While some of the stories are akin to those in the synoptics, like the feeding of the five thousand (6: 1–14, the only miracle found in all four gospels), John makes this narrative different by calling the miracle a 'sign' (*sēmeion*, 6: 2, 14, 26, 30; the term is used repeatedly in the Fourth Gospel) and by concluding with an attempt on the part of the people to make Jesus king (6: 15). Then follows a long discourse (6: 25–65), not like those in Matthew or the parables (a term John never uses). Instead, Jesus presents a Midrash on himself as 'bread from heaven', reflecting Israel's wilderness experience (Exod. 16; Ps. 78: 22–5). As so often in John, the speech is built around a first-person statement, 'I am . . . ' in this case 'I am the bread of life' (6: 35; for other 'I am' claims, cf. 8: 12; 10: 7, 9; 10: 11, 14; 11: 25; 14: 6; 15: 1, 5). There are thus tantalizing similarities with, but annoying differences from, the other gospels.

Quite possibly John shares a pool of oral tradition with the synoptists, particularly Luke. But the finished gospel—if it really is completed, for there is evidence of incomplete editing; compare 14: 31, 'Let us go hence', and the fact that the discourse in the upper room goes on for three more chapters—the somewhat finished book is the product of meditation amidst great pressures. 'The Jews' and 'the world' (which the Jews sometimes symbolize) are hostile forces. Jesus' disciples, though sometimes torn asunder by defections from Jesus (6: 66; 7: 5), cling all the more fervently to the Word and his words (8: 31, 51; 14: 23–4).

The very surface structure of the book differs markedly from that of the synoptics. Jerusalem is not simply the goal of a final journey that leads to the Passion (or of a childhood trip, as in Luke 2: 41–51). Instead, Jesus goes there four or five times, always at a Jewish festival (2: 13–17; 5: 1; 7: 2; (10: 22); 11: 55). Usually there is a confrontation during these trips to Jerusalem, for Jesus is no Jewish pilgrim but himself replaces the temple festival (e.g. at Tabernacles, when he claims, '*I* am the light of the world', 8; 12). Indeed, he replaces the temple itself (2: 13–22). There is no messianic secret in the book; people know from the outset who Jesus is, and he keeps making new 'I am' assertions. The kingdom of God is spoken of only at times (3: 3, 5; cf. 18: 33, 36, 37, where Jesus' kingship, not God's, is at issue). A new way of expressing the good news is far more frequent: 'eternal life', i.e. the life of the new age, which Jesus brings. Examples of John's different tone could be multiplied. Jesus prefaces statements, as in the other gospels, with 'Amen (truly) I say to you', but in John it is always doubled, 'Amen, amen'. There are words from the Cross, three as in Luke, but all of them are different from those in the synoptics (John 19: 26, 28, 30).

Oddly, John's 'gospel' never uses the term 'gospel', noun or verb. A feature of the book seldom noted is the Fourth Gospel's emphasis on its *written* nature. Here, even Jesus writes (in the fragment at 8: 6). Cf. also 1: 45, where it is stated that Moses and the prophets wrote of the messiah. By and large, early Christianity was a matter of oral proclamation, telling others by word of mouth. Paul's letters began as emergency substitutes for his apostolic presence, to answer questions, comfort, or chastize. The gospels grew up as a way of fixing, often artfully, the good news for community situations or needs. While Theophilus in Luke (1: 3) could represent a reading public, more likely the synoptics, at least Matthew and Mark, were for internal church use. John can be said to have grown out of expositions and addresses at the community's gatherings for worship (not necessarily eucharistic, given the long years the group seems to have stayed within the synagogue and the general Johannine emphasis on the word and faith, not sacraments). But note the stated purpose of John at 20: 31,

> these signs have been written up
> in order that you may [continue to] believe that
> Jesus is the Christ, the Son of God,
> and that, by believing, you may keep on having life in his name

The ultimate goal, life, through faith in Christ, is precisely furthered by this book. The previous verse (20: 30) grants that the many other *sēmeia* which Jesus did are not written in this book, implying that there could be other volumes about his miracles. A later verse adds, 'I suppose that, if the many other things that Jesus did were, every one of them, to be written down, the world itself could not contain the books that would be written' (21: 25). The matter is important enough for the penultimate verse to contain a sort of community certification about the disciple who is bearing witness to these things and who wrote them down: 'we know that his witness is true' (21: 24). Probably nowhere else in the New Testament, even in the classic verses cited on 'inspiration' (2 Tim. 3: 16; 2 Peter 1: 21), is so high a tribute paid to the power of what is written to evoke faith and hence life. Is all this a Christian counterpart to the Jewish view of the Scriptures, that in them is life (John 5: 39)? If 'they bear witness of me', as Jesus says, is the Fourth Gospel and its witness to Christ, then, in its own view, regarded as 'Scripture'?

The Christology of John is a high one. At the outset, in the prologue (1: 1–18), Jesus is presented as 'the Word' (*logos*), a concept that had a rich Old Testament background, especially in wisdom thought (Prov. 8: 22–30; cf. Blenkinsopp, *Wisdom*, 136–40), but also was meaningful to Greeks. The Jewish Targums substituted 'word' (Aramaic *memra*) for Old Testament references to God. Philo built bridges via the term *logos* between Greek philosophy and the God of the Scriptures acting in the world. The prologue, after outlining how this logos which was '*vis-à-vis* God and was God' (1: 1) had acted in creation and in Israel's history (1: 3–4, 9–12), makes its most shocking statement when it says this divine word 'became flesh' and 'tented among us' as the man Jesus (1: 14, 17). References to John the Baptist as forerunner and witness help make clear that it is the Jesus we know from the synoptic tradition who is the 'only God' (1: 18 in the now preferred manuscript reading). Thus John presents a real incarnation in a way no other gospel does. This glimpse of Jesus' 'godness' is the first prong of a bracket which encloses the story of the earthly ministry in the Fourth Gospel. The second one is 20: 28, Thomas's post-Easter confession, 'My Lord and my God!' The *logos* title is not used after 1: 18.

The Jesus who appears in John's Gospel is often presented, during his ministry, in most human terms. He grows weary (4: 6) and thirsty (4: 7; 19: 28), he weeps (11: 5), and can be troubled in spirit (11: 33). Most of the titles used in the synoptics reappear in John. He is the Christ (11: 27; 20: 31) and, in the parlance of Samaritan expectations, 'the "Messiah" that is coming' (called by Samaritans *Taheb*). 'Son of God' also appears, at 20: 31 and elsewhere (1: 34, 49) and more especially 'the Son' in relation to 'the Father'. The Son gives life (5: 21). 'Son of man' occurs some 13 times, often with the Johannine verbal phrase, 'be lifted up' (3: 14; 8: 28; 12: 32), i.e. on the Cross, which turns out to be the revelation of his 'glory' (12: 23; 13: 31; 21: 19). The 'I am' sayings and the signs or miracles he does enhance the picture of who Jesus really is.

A particular feature of John is the way the parousia is handled. That term of Matthew and Paul is never used in the Fourth

Gospel. But Jesus does speak of 'going away' and 'coming again' (14: 3, 28); disciples will see Jesus no more and then will see him again (16: 16–19). And he does go away, in death, but comes again—on Easter day. He also promises that he (or God) will send another Paraclete, who will witness to Jesus (14: 16; 15: 26). This he does on Easter evening, breathing on the disciples the Holy Spirit (20: 22). And while the risen Christ refers to ascending to God (20: 17), there is no ascension scene such as Luke 24 and Acts 1 provide. Does all this mean that the Fourth Gospel regards Christ's (second) coming as having already occurred, at Easter? We are really, then, in the new age! Childs (*The New Testament as Canon*, 142) sees 21: 23 as pointing to a *future* second coming, which, although different from the 'major eschatological emphasis of the book itself', provides 'canonical' context.

Such matters reflect, of course, the eschatology in John. It is definitely on the 'present' side. Eternal life is now; believers have already passed from death and judgement into this life (5: 24; 1 John 5: 11–12). Yet side by side with such statements are some more futuristic ones, as at 5: 28–9, about resurrection to life or resurrection to judgement at the last day. What John has done is to claim the whole vast present time for the life of the new age, somewhat at the expense of future expectations. Links to the past are kept not so much by references to Israel and its history but by writing a gospel, about Jesus who once ministered on earth but who for John is now the life, resurrection, good shepherd, the door, bread of life, the true and living way, and the vine in whom alone disciples have and retain life.

This gospel of eternal life is also one about love (Greek, *agapē*). God is love (1 John 4: 16) and, amazingly, loves the world that as a whole and in every part, each one of us, rebels against this God (3: 16; 1: 10–11). Yet love is also enjoined on believers (13: 34) in a 'new commandment' which is really God's will of old (1 John 2: 7). Ethics in the Johannine school is not developed into a host of prescriptions. Love, walking in the light, and practical sharing of this world's goods with those we claim to love (1 John 3: 17) are tirelessly reiterated in opposition to living in the darkness selfishly. But the scope of loving extends only to the community of faith, not to those outside it or to enemies. The community is a compact island of light in a world of darkness; to it one must be drawn by the Father (6: 44) through the Cross of Jesus (12: 32).

Ecclesiology in John is thus virtually nonexistent in any institutional sense. The community consists of a band of sisters and brothers, loving one another. Outside the figure of the Beloved Disciple, there is no authority structure or trace of officialdom. All share in the Spirit as children of God. The disputed textual reading in John 20: 31 is pertinent here; it is indicated by brackets in the rendering above (cf. NIV and its textual note; it is a matter of a single letter in Greek). While 'in order that you may believe', indicating an evangelistic purpose for the book (i.e. 'come to initial belief'), is possible, continuance of belief on the part of those who have already come to faith is even more likely, in view of the community's history: its members must be built up and preserved in the world (17: 11, 14–19).

It is not surprising that faith plays a major role in Johannine thought. Always the verb is used, never the noun. At times, faith is said to be the result of Jesus' miracles (2: 11; 4: 54; 20: 30–1). The 'signs' move people to believe. But the Fourth Gospel can also be quite critical of such 'signs faith' (as at 4: 48). The story of Thomas is a test case. Ostensibly he confesses Jesus, moving from faithlessness to believing, because he had asked for certain conditions to be met (20: 25) and Jesus encourages him to see and examine his wounded hands and side (20: 27). But there is no statement that Thomas actually did this. Jesus' final beatitude in 20: 29 is on 'those who have *not* seen and yet *believe*'; they are blessed. This seems to be John's ultimate word, in contrast to all possibilities of 'seeing and believing', seeing and not believing, or not seeing and not believing (9: 39–40). Faith brings life (20: 31).

The long discourse in ch. 6 on the manna can likewise be read as teaching faith. The 'work of God' here is 'that you believe' in Jesus; the person who comes and believes does not hunger or thirst; those who believe have eternal life (6: 29, 35, 47; note the contrast in vv. 64 and 69 between those who believe and those who do not have faith). Even 6: 52–8, in the words about 'gnawing the flesh' and 'drinking the blood' of the Son of man—the words, impossible in Old Testament thought, are deliberately offensive, in order to shock one into truth—can be read as a vivid way of repeating v. 35: to believe is to eat and drink. The expressions have good Old Testament precedents in the tradition about a banquet which wisdom spreads for the needy (Prov. 9: 1–5; cf. Isa. 55: 1–3, contrasting 65: 11–13; in the Apocrypha, Sirach 24: 19–22 extends the figure, 'Eat me, drink me', never hunger and thirst; cf. also Jer. 15: 16; Ezek. 2: 8–3: 4). The final truth in ch. 6 is that it is the Spirit that gives life, through the words Jesus speaks (6: 63). 'Believe—and you have eaten' (Augustine). No wonder John has been called 'the maverick gospel'!

6

✔ *Pauline Theology*

THIS phrase is itself ambiguous, and opens up the question of the historical approach as against canonical criticism (see Chapter 2).

On the one hand, 'Pauline theology' can mean the theology of the whole Pauline corpus, from all 13 letters in the canon that claim to be by Paul. At times, evidence from Acts has also been drawn in, especially to provide a chronological framework for the epistles. For many centuries, Hebrews was also attributed to Paul. On the other hand, the phrase can mean, historically, the theology of Paul himself. In that case, one works only with the letters one is sure come from his hand (or voice, for they were regularly written by a secretary or amanuensis, like Tertius, Rom. 16: 22). Today, Hebrews is recognized as a separate kind of early Christian thinking and Acts as reflective of Luke's theology (although Acts may preserve valuable traditions about Paul). These books not by Paul will be treated in Chapters 11 and 16.

Within the Pauline corpus, the pastoral epistles have a clear profile and, because of their differences from the acknowledged letters, will also be taken up separately (in Chapter 9), even though some would find Paul's hand or at least fragments from his genuine letters in their production. Colossians and Ephesians form a subclass of Pauline thought, either later in his career (if the letters are genuinely his) or the work of the Pauline school, probably in the decades after Paul's martyrdom. The arguments for the latter position seem more convincing to me, and 2 Thessalonians may also be the work, not of Paul, but of an apocalyptic wing of his followers, likewise later. These works by Paulinists will be treated in Chapter 8. For fuller discussion in this series, see Ziesler, *Pauline Christianity*, rev. edn. especially 6–7, 122–35.

Influences on Paul's thought and letters

In addition to the question of how many more than the seven 'sure' letters (Rom., 1–2 Cor., Gal., Phil., 1 Thess., Philemon), if any, should be considered in sketching Paul's teachings, there has long been debate over how these letters should be interpreted.

Should Paul himself be viewed in the light of Palestinian Judaism, perhaps of the rabbinic variety? (He does use rabbinic teaching devices, as at Romans 4: 3–8, where the word 'reckoned' in Gen. 15: 6 is interpreted by means of Ps. 32: 1–2, so that 'not reckoned' means to forgive. The statement in Acts 22: 3 that he studied in Jerusalem under Rabbi Gamaliel strengthens this contention.) Or was he a Jew of the diaspora, more Greek in his outlook? (Paul can employ Greek poets like Menander, 1 Cor. 15: 33, and Stoic themes as at Phil. 4: 8. Acts makes him specifically a citizen of Tarsus, 21: 39; 22: 3.) Still others insist that, although Saul of Tarsus did not know Jesus of Nazareth, his confrontation with the risen Lord was the decisive element. (Gal. 1: 15–16 alludes to Paul's calling, Phil. 3: 7–8 to its personal effects for him. Acts thrice recounts what has been called a conversion experience, 9: 1–22; 22: 4–16; 26: 9–18).

These background questions have also given rise to discussion over whether what Paul writes is best understood by drawing on the Hebrew Scriptures, Pharisaic rabbinic thought, Qumran ideas, apocalypticism, Greek rhetoric, or mystery religions. It is assumed in our presentation that all these factors were of some importance, especially the biblical-Jewish for Paul himself, but his audience was more clearly of pagan background, and so a Graeco-Roman component may enter in.

Data about the congregations Paul addresses have also been sifted to help modern interpreters. What Paul writes may respond specifically to their questions (1 Cor. 7: 1, 25; 8: 1; 12: 1; 16: 1, 12, the topics arise out of a letter or oral contacts from

Corinth). His advice hinges often on situations in the local congregation (a dispute between Euodia and Syntyche, Phil. 4: 2; attitudes toward a runaway slave in the note to Philemon and the debt Onesimus owes Paul, Philem. 19). The racial temperament of the Galatians was a factor in the ardent reception they once gave Paul and now in their quicksilver swing to new teachers (Gal. 3: 1; 4: 13–20; 1: 6–9). Paul must adjust what he says or does not say about a congregational collection project for the saints at Jerusalem to each local situation and, indeed, to rapidly changing situations (1 Cor. 16: 1–4; 2 Cor. 8, 9; in Galatians, only by the reference at 2: 10).

In recent years, attention to the situations Paul addresses has moved from preoccupation with the opponents (Gal. 2: 4, 12; 4: 21; 5: 7–10; 6: 17; Phil. 3: 2, 18–19; 2 Cor. 11: 12–15, 20, 22–3) to sociological analysis of the community and city involved. How do social divisions in Corinth, for example, play into disorders at the Lord's Supper (1 Cor. 1: 26–8; 11: 18–34)? More recently, rhetorical analysis, preferably along the line of Graeco-Roman rules for oratory, has come into prominence. Thus one looks for 'narrative' (*narratio*, Greek *diēgēsis*) where Paul, following current practices for plausible presentation of the case, arranges facts (Gal. 1: 12–2: 14) to support his thesis in 1: 12 about the origin of his gospel (not from humans but from Christ).

A final area of influences on Paul, besides his personal heritage and congregational situations, would include the apostolic kerygma with which he works, its expression in certain formulas, knowledge and use of Jesus traditions, and Paul's employment of the Old Testament. (The latter term is not improper in speaking of Paul, for he thinks of old and new convenants or dispensations, 2 Cor. 3: 5–18; 'Hebrew Scriptures' is inaccurate because Paul usually works with the Greek Septuagint.) While he can speak of his kerygma with personal accents (1 Cor. 2: 4) like 'Christ crucified' or 'the word of the Cross' (1 Cor. 1: 18, 23), Paul shared a general message about Jesus' death and resurrection with other apostles (1 Cor. 15: 3–5, 11; Gal. 1: 18). He used existing credal slogans (Phil. 2: 11; Rom. 10: 9), hymns (Phil. 2: 6–11), cultic recitations (1 Cor. 11: 23–5), and at times appealed to what Jesus said (1 Cor. 7: 10, cf. Mark 10: 2–9; Rom. 13: 8–10, cf. Mark 12: 31). He could use the Scriptures by direct citation (Rom. 15: 9–12), allusion (Christ as 'the last Adam', 1 Cor. 15: 45), typologically (1 Cor. 10: 1–13), and on occasion allegorically (Gal. 4: 21–31).

It is of some importance to keep these varied influences in mind—Paul's own make-up, the congregations, and factors within Christianity—for they help to explain the variety in Paul: variety of expression, emphasis, and ideas. Given his own intercultural heritage, the plethora of ideas with which he worked, and the contingent factors (those dependent on specifics like the presence of opponents) in situations to which he spoke, it is surprising there is much unity at all to his many letters. Even the seven allowed by historical criticism break down into parts of as many as thirteen, on partition theories—so that, for example, 2 Cor. 10–13, parts of 1–7, chs. 8 and 9 represent four separate notes to Corinth as the circumstances in that city, the circumstances of Paul (in Asia Minor), and relations between them changed.

The centre of Paul's Christianity

It is no new question to ask whether at the heart of Paul's life in Christ there was some master theme, or to seek to locate the centre of his theology as it emerged in missionary and pastoral work. Marcion in the second century saw such a centre in terms of 'antitheses', contrasting the gospel of Christ and the Jewish law (Tertullian, *Against Marcion* 1. 19). Augustine saw it as grace. The *Acts of Paul and Thecla* (late second century) made Paul a model of asceticism, teaching 'Blessed are those who have kept the flesh pure, for they shall become a temple of God' (sect. 4; cf. Matt. 5: 4–9 and 1 Cor. 6: 19 for this assertion, which is impossible for Paul, who understood 'the flesh' to denote human beings as they are by nature, in contrast with God). The Reformation found in Paul the principle of justification by grace through faith. Albert Schweitzer championed 'Christ mysticism'. Others have quarried from Paul's writings such things as predestination, charismatic gifts, freedom, and the impact of sin as his contribution to theology and life. Protestant liberalism dismissed him contemptuously as the 'second founder' of Christianity who ruined Jesus' simple teachings. Neo-orthodoxy revelled in Paul's thought. Black, liberation, and feminist theologies give him varying receptions.

In recent years at least, three main lines of interpretation have appeared, often as rivals. One, championed by Bultmann and his pupils, reads Paul in existentialist terms. Anthropology, or Paul's understanding of the human situation, becomes the key. The 'new being in Christ' is one way of expressing Paul's meaning for our day. A second approach, continuing earlier emphases, especially in the nineteenth century, on *Heilsgeschichte*, sees salvation history as the overarching theme in Paul. Oscar Cullmann and his followers have depicted as Paul's great contribution what he said about Christ as the turning-point, definitively, for salvation, in the sweep of history. A third approach has more recently regarded apocalypticism as the flaming centre of Paul's thought (Beker). Paul employed, it is said, this Jewish type of thinking to set forth the triumph of God through the resurrection of Jesus. Not only 1 Thessalonians, at the outset of Paul's writing career, but also Romans at its end make use of such categories (cf. Rom. 1: 17 and 18 about the saving righteousness and wrath of God being revealed, *apokalyptetai*).

The attempt in all these approaches to Paul is to find 'the centre'. Sometimes 'a centre' is spoken of, as if there were several, or as if they change from letter to letter. A current way of putting this is 'coherence' as against the 'contingency' in the individual letters (Beker). Is there something that 'coheres', an amalgam of points, around which all or almost all of what Paul says can be intelligently understood, in contrast to the varying incidental, local factors in each letter? One advance in recent discussion may have been to impress on students of Paul that the centre or what coheres cannot be static, but develops or shifts with circumstances.

All this can be illustrated by the theme or complex of themes in Paul of 'justification' (or righteousness) by 'faith'. It has been held by many that this topic leaps into prominence, in Galatians, only when Paul is confronted by the Judaizers, who teach justification by works of the law, and circumcision as well. Because Paul crafted Romans about the same time as he wrote Galatians, the argument goes, that letter takes up this same theme, although with less passion and in more tranquillity. Even if one holds that righteousness/justification has a broader background than the polemic with the Judaizers (see below), the point is scarcely to be denied that the theme 'by faith' came to prominence only in the course of Paul's long use of righteousness terminology.

The complexity of sketching Pauline thought on such matters can be further illustrated by asking to what extent his meaning for faith (*pistis*) and the way his audiences understood it could vary. Did it denote belief and trust in God's power, providence, and justice, as in the Old Testament? Was there influence from the tendency in Hellenistic Judaism to psychologize faith, stressing the individual's inner nature? Or was there a connection with Graeco-Roman ideas, at least on the part of Paul's audience? There the Aristotelian ethic of 'friendship' provided a context for relating justice (righteousness), as one of the four cardinal virtues, with fidelity, and there the legal formula 'to believe in what is right', and to trust to the court for hope of delivery, was commonplace. Given such backgrounds, there would, of course, be variety in what Paul says about righteousness/justification and faith.

Can there be one centre, or even coherency, in all Paul says? Unity amid variety is a matter of many decisions about the scope of the Pauline collection of letters to be considered, judgements on the situation for each one and the background involved, and conclusions on the relative weight to be given to certain ideas and topics. There are also considerations concerning us, the interpreters. For denominational background (or lack of it), personal experiences, and even prejudices or the times in which we live may dispose us more toward one theme than another. Underlying everything is the question of whether we think Paul thought and worked with some consistent coherence to his ideas or *ad hoc* and as the Spirit or his own spirit moved him.

It is also possible that points of similarity that seem to unite Jesus and Paul, for example, may, upon closer examination, turn out to be due to happenstance or simply to like reactions to the same situation, rather than to direct influence. To illustrate, the ministries of both Jesus Christ and Paul were characterized by (*a*) deprivations (homelessness, hunger), (*b*) commitment to humble service, (*c*) persecution and suffering, and (*d*) celibacy. The second of these may for Paul have sprung from his imitation of Christ (the pre-existent One who became the incarnate Lord) more than from any acquaintance with the historical Jesus (2 Cor. 8: 9). (*a*) and (*c*) arise out of similar situations in the lives of Jesus and Paul (cf. 1 Thess. 2: 14–16). (*d*) may be inaccurate if Paul was a widower. The gospels are utterly silent on Jesus and this question. It is doubtful if an unmarried Jesus influenced Saul of Tarsus here. What seems a point of agreement may thus, on examination, turn out to reflect a certain diversity.

The summary of selected Pauline themes which follows below, each of which has sometimes served as the centre for Paul's thought, rests on the view that Paul did work with a certain logical consistency, and that what he said made sense and hung together in his own mind, if not always for his converts. It should be remembered, too, that all these themes interrelate in Paul's theology, and that some are virtually interchangeable. In them we find a unity for Paul's message.

Some major themes in Paul

To preserve objectivity, we shall take these up roughly in the order of frequency of occurrence for the key phrase in Paul's letters. There are, however, certain topics in Paul which, while statistically frequent, like 'the law' (119 times), no one would ever propose as integrative or central because Paul wrote primarily of their negative function. There are others that we might suppose or wish would be more common, like the Lord's Supper or evangelism, which are dealt with but briefly in the letters, although they must have been part of the life of Paul and the Pauline churches. The list that follows of what some term 'dominant perspectives' is suggestive of patterns for unity and variety. For details, larger treatments (Ziesler, *Pauline Christianity*; Fitzmyer, *Pauline Theology*; or the New Testament theologies) ought to be consulted.

1. *God*. Not often considered thematically (perhaps because what Paul says here is not always new or distinctive), the Greek word for God, *theos*, occurs more than 500 times in the Pauline corpus (over 425 times in the acknowledged letters). The 'one God' of Israel's *shema* (Deut. 6: 4, cited at 1 Cor. 8: 6) is now the Father of our Lord Jesus Christ (2 Cor. 1: 3) and of a new people (Rom. 1: 7). This God demonstrated love for us in Christ's death (Rom. 5: 8), predestines, calls, justifies, and glorifies (Rom. 8: 29–30), but also judges (2: 16).

2. *Christ*. The Greek word for 'messiah' occurs over 350 times in the Pauline corpus, with some 270 of the examples in seven acknowledged letters. This title for 'anointed one' in Greek has, in Paul, often become a proper name. He can say, 'Christ died for our sins' (1 Cor. 15: 3, a pre-Pauline formula) or 'I have been crucified with Christ' (Gal. 2: 19, Paul's own testimony). There are dozens of other statements about Christ's love (2 Cor. 5: 14) and relation to all sorts of divine functions (judgement, 2 Cor. 5: 10) the kingdom of Christ, 1 Cor. 15: 24–5). Ziesler's *Pauline Christianity* devotes a chapter to 'The Centrality of Jesus Christ' (rev. edn., 24–48, including a number of christological titles).

3. *'In Christ'*. This phrase can be considered next because it is so closely related to the previous one. Some 165 cases of 'Christ' (or 'Lord', or some equivalent) in the Pauline letters occur in this prepositional phrase, *en Christōi* in Greek. Deissmann and others argued for its centrality as 'Christ mysticism', the result of Christ's work and the response of believers, so that they are 'sanctified in Christ Jesus' (1 Cor. 1: 2), live in unity in Christ (Gal. 3: 28), and obey 'in the Lord' (Phil. 4: 2, 4). But in some of these examples 'in Christ' means simply 'as a Christian' (Rom.

16: 7; Paul never employs, and perhaps did not know, the adjective 'Christian'); at times it is used in an ecclesial sense (Gal. 1: 22); and other instances mean 'by Christ', instrumentally (so 1 Cor. 1: 2). Our being 'in Christ' (only Gal. 2: 20 speaks of 'Christ in me'), which also is paralleled by being 'in the Spirit', means belonging to Christ's sphere of power and influence (Ziesler, *Pauline Christianity*, rev. edn., 49–52, 60–5).

4. *Faith*. The noun, the verb 'to believe', and the adjective 'faithful' are found over 225 times in all the Pauline letters (over 140 in the 'genuine' letters), though with a variety of meanings. It emerges as a characteristic Pauline word. Paul brought faith to deeper meaning, beyond the Old Testament sense found in Jesus' words and even beyond the post-Easter sense of belief in the apostolic kerygma. 'Faith' will be further considered below, as one of the themes we have been examining in every segment of the New Testament, as part of our quest for its unity.

5. *The Spirit*. While it is not always possible to distinguish whether a reference is to the Holy Spirit or to the human spirit (e.g. Phil. 1: 27), the Holy Spirit of God (Rom. 8: 14) or of Christ (Rom. 8: 9) is referred to in Pauline letters some 100 times. This Spirit becomes God's means for communicating with believers since the Christ event. Many of the functions of Christ are now also attributed to the Spirit. 2 Corinthians 3: 17–18 has encouraged some commentators and systematic theologians further to identify and even to equate Christ and the Spirit. But 'the Lord' there mentioned (v. 16; cf. Exod. 34: 29–35) is Yahweh, who is now among us (the believers) as Spirit (cf. NEB). It is characteristic of Paul to think of the Spirit always in the light of Jesus Christ. Some especially relate this theme of the Spirit to such functional aspects as sanctification or *holiness* (a dozen times in Paul; 1 Thess. 4: 7–8), 'holy ones' or saints (over 75 times), and spiritual gifts (1 Cor. 12). Because the Greek term for the Spirit is *pneuma*, the adjective 'pneumatic' is sometimes used, in Paul and other New Testament writers, to describe Christians and their life—that is 'marked by or filled with God's Spirit'.

6. *Grace*. This characteristically Pauline term for God's love

in action can be mentioned next. If *charis* (literally, 'gracious-ness, favour'; Old Testament 'loving kindness, mercy'), noun and verb, and related terms are included, there are similarly about 100 examples. Among the related terms is *charisma*, 'grace gift' (1 Cor. 12: 4 ff., spritual 'gifts'). Paul is the great New Testament exponent of this theme of grace, followed next in frequency by Luke.

7. *Justification/righteousness*. The single Greek term that is behind both these renderings in English occurs over 80 times in Paul, and in his letters ranks highest in frequency among the several metaphors for how human beings experience God's saving actions. A major theme in the Hebrew Scriptures, righteousness/justification leaps to prominence in early Christianity prior to Paul, to help expound the meaning of the death of the Righteous One, Christ, for us (1 Peter 3: 18; Rom. 3: 24–5; 4: 25). Paul develops this law court theme (about sinners under divine judgement) especially in Galatians, Philippians, and Romans. It can also be used of the response called forth from believers—they are to be just/righteous (Phil. 1: 11, possibly Rom. 14: 17).

8. *The church*. Rather surprisingly, *ekklēsia*, the Greek term for 'community', including the church community, turns up in the Pauline corpus 62 times (out of 114 in the entire New Testament). (Of these 62, 39 are in the letters commonly acknowledged to be by Paul, so the usage cannot be said simply to have been developed after Paul's death by his pupils.) Most letters are addressed to 'the church' in a particular house, city, or region. Even those written to an individual include an ecclesial setting (Philem. 2). The term is a Greek word that need mean only an assembly. Perhaps Christian use was conscious of its application in the Septuagint to the Hebrew *qahal*, Israel in the wilderness, possibly with the nuance of Israel at worship. Paul applies *ekklēsia* to the local congregation (1 Cor. 11: 18), usually a house church, meeting in someone's home (1 Cor. 16: 19), and the term is often found in the plural (Gal. 1: 22). At times there is a world-wide sense (1 Cor. 15: 9; 12: 28). His image of the church as the 'body of Christ', as in 1 Cor. 12: 12–27, connects

ecclesiology with Christology, but there are many other terms like 'household' (Gal. 6: 10), 'commonwealth' (Phil. 3: 20), and above all *koinōnia* ('fellowship, participation in what God has granted', 1 Cor. 1: 9; 2 Cor. 13: 14).

9. *Gospel.* Because the noun *euangelion* is found some 60 times in Paul (compared with only ten in all four gospels) and the verb on 21 more occasions ('Christ . . . sent me . . . to preach the gospel', 1 Cor. 1: 17; cf. 9: 16, 18), and because Paul links his very identity to the good news about Jesus Christ (Gal. 1: 11–12, 15–16), some term this *par excellence* 'Paul's . . . way of summing up the significance of the Christ-event' (Fitzmyer; *NJBC* 82: 32; cf. 31–6 and *JBC* 79: 27–34). It is both objective, with content about Christ, and personal, with deep meaning for Paul (Gal. 2: 20; Rom. 2: 16; 16: 25). We shall also treat it in the list of themes common to most New Testament authors, in the next main section, below.

10. *Salvation.* The noun for 'salvation', *sōtēria*, crops up some 18 times in the Pauline corpus, 'saviour' 12 more (especially in the pastoral epistles, but cf. Phil. 3: 20, of Christ), and the verb 29 times. The sense is regularly religious: to be delivered from sin, death, and this age or world, for the life God bestows in Christ. It may denote a state (2 Cor. 7: 10) or a process or activity now going on (Rom. 8: 24, past tense; 'those being saved', 2 Cor. 2: 15; and future, Rom. 5: 9, 1 Thess. 2: 16). Salvation is often directly linked with God's power, especially as righteousness (Rom. 1: 16–17) and with believing (1 Cor. 1: 21; Rom. 1: 16), and once at least with hope (1 Thess. 5: 8). Cf. Ziesler, *Pauline Christianity*, rev. edn., pp. 73–4, 114–15.

11. *Promise.* In this field of words, the noun 'promise' (*epangelia*; cf. *euangelion* or gospel) occurs some 25 times in the Pauline corpus, plus the verb five more times and 'promise beforehand' at Rom. 1: 2. Examples appear especially in Gal. 3 and Rom. 4 and 9, where Paul takes up God's dealings with Abraham and Israel. 'Promise' stands particularly in contrast with the law of Moses (see Gal. 3: 21–2; Rom. 3: 21 on how they are and are not contrary). Christ represents promise fulfilled (2

Cor. 1: 20). Christians are 'children of promise', heirs on the basis of God's promise (Gal. 4: 28; 3: 29).

12. *Jesus' death and resurrection.* From here on, in any list, figures become more difficult to establish. Paul with some frequency speaks of how 'Jesus (Christ) died and was raised (by God)' (1 Thess. 4: 14; 1 Cor. 15: 3–5). 'Death' and 'resurrection' may be referred to separately or together. Paul himself prefers to refer to Jesus' specific death by the graphic terms 'Cross' (1 Cor. 1: 18) or 'crucify' (1 Cor. 2: 2, 8) altogether some 18 times in the Pauline letters. The topic is deeply significant to the apostle (Gal. 6: 14). The term 'blood' is found especially in phrases Paul takes over (e.g. 1 Cor. 11: 25; 10: 16; Rom. 3: 25). There are also key terms about the meaning of Jesus' death (see sect. 13 below). For Jesus' resurrection there are all sorts of implications drawn out for believers, about life now and life to come. On baptism and ethics, for example, consult Rom. 6: 3–11. Depending on how one counts references and what is grouped under this heading, it can be rated quite highly in significance. The problem is that there is no single term or phrase, occurring a large number of times, to which one can refer for study.

13. *Expiation* (AV 'propitiation'). This is the place, statistics to the contrary, where vivid imagery in Paul about Christ's death deserves mention, a theme emphasized in both medieval Catholic piety and Evangelical thought since the Reformation. Although the word *hilastērion* occurs only at Rom. 3: 25 in all the Pauline corpus, and although its meaning there is disputed (as to whether it should be translated as expiation for sin or, less likely, propitiation (of an angry God); see Ziesler, *Pauline Christianity*, 87–91; Morris, *New Testament Theology*, 34–5, 73, seems to defend the latter rendering along with the 'wrath of God' p. 63), the Old Testament background lies in references to the Mercy Seat in the Day of Atonement ritual in Leviticus 16. Not only has Paul taken over such imagery and developed the sacrificial aspect of Christ's death 'for sins' or 'in our behalf', but his letters also speak in other related imagery. There is, for example, the 'sin offering' of Israelite cult, reflected at 2 Cor. 5: 21 and Rom. 8: 3. This theme, often called 'atonement' (Rom. 5: 11 AV), has had

immense influence, especially if 'the Cross', 'blood' and statements about how and for what 'Jesus died' be added. It readily connects also with justification ((7) above) and reconciliation ((14) below) as the basis for these metaphors of salvation.

14. *Reconciliation.* Although this concept has been amazingly popular in recent years, it has a relatively small data base in the Pauline corpus. There are only 13 occurrences for *katalassō* and derivatives, three of them in Colossians–Ephesians and one referring to the reconciliation of a couple who separate from each other (1 Cor. 7: 11). It is a figure drawn from human relationships. There is no Old Testament background. In Jesus' sayings, only at Matt. 5: 24 (concerning reconciliation with another disciple) does the verb occur. But Paul's use in 2 Cor. 5: 18–21 and Rom. 5: 9–11 has made a powerful impression concerning what God did in Christ and what Christians receive and are to proclaim. In each of these passages Paul, after speaking of reconciliation, reverts to justification language. Sometimes 'reconciliation' is augmented by references to 'forgiveness', but such terminology appears in Paul rarely.

15. *Redemption, liberation.* The statistics for a theme which has been used at times as an umbrella term in Pauline theology to cover a number of topics listed above, and which, of course, suggests 'liberation theology', are 'redemption' (*apolytrōsis*), seven times in the Pauline corpus (notably 1 Cor. 1: 30; Rom. 3: 24; 8: 23); to 'buy (back)' or 'purchase', four times (1 Cor. 6: 20; 7: 23; Gal. 3: 13, 4: 5); and 'rescue', eleven times (e.g. 1 Thess. 1: 10; Rom. 11: 26; Col. 1: 13). Some speak of 'redemptive liberation' from sin, death, the law, self, and the tyrannical 'principalities and powers' that control human life. To employ such an image helps carry one back to the thought-world of Paul's converts. Moreover, it is a theme that avoids debates in the later history of theology, such as have sometimes raged over justification or reconciliation or expiation versus propitiation as rival themes. But one must be careful not to read today's current, often political, meanings into 'liberation', especially given Paul's verses on the citizen's obligations to the Roman State (under Nero!) in Rom. 13: 1–7. See also Ziesler (*Pauline Christianity*,

rev. edn., 85–7), who, while making 'liberated from' a constant theme, points to faith, grace, reconciliation, and justification, and ultimately Christ's death as the means of liberation. A fruitful avenue in Pauline thought is 'freedom' as the result of liberation (2 Cor. 3: 17). The Greek terms for 'set free' occur some 27 times as Paul (never in the pastorals) discusses the freedom of the Christian (Gal. 4: 22–5: 1; Rom. 6: 18; 8: 21).

16. *Salvation history*. Readers may wonder why this theme, so widespread and favoured in much modern discussion, has not appeared earlier. One reason is that there is no single Pauline term to cite. One might refer to God's will or purpose ('plan' is not a word he uses in the way Acts does). There are Pauline references to election (being chosen, Rom. 8: 33, 9: 11) and predestination (Rom. 8: 30). Passages about Abraham (Gal. 4; Rom 4, often using 'promise' language) and Israel have often been battlegrounds for the debate whether there is *Heilsgeschichte* or a sketch of the history of salvation according to Paul. The approach has also been used of enquiring into what Paul says about great pivotal figures in the history of salvation, figures like Adam (Rom. 5: 12–21) and Eve (2 Cor. 11: 3), Abraham, Moses (2 Cor. 3), Christ, and the Adam to come (Rom. 5: 14). Perhaps the word 'mystery' (Greek *mystērion*), in its Semitic sense of 'divine secret' now openly revealed through Christ, as at 1 Cor. 2: 7, suggests that Paul had a salvation-historical way of thinking. But it is up to the modern interpreter to put together scattered references.

To these 16 chief themes can be added others (referred to above), such as holiness, the body of Christ (ecclesially, on the Cross, and in the Lord's Supper), love (*agapē*), *koinōnia*, hope, forgiveness, or freedom, each of which some have championed as keys to Paul. To this list could certainly be added 'covenant', which is popular with those who stress the Old Testament where it is a major theme. But in Paul there are only nine references, chiefly in Gal. 3 and 4: 21; 2 Cor. 3: 6–14; and 1 Cor. 11: 25, in the upper room. Sacraments, which some today, out of their experiences, might expect to be central, are, however, rarely mentioned. Baptism (1 Cor. 12: 13; Rom. 6) is referred to more than the Lord's Supper (1 Cor. 10: 16, 11: 17–34), but even baptism is something Paul argues from, not for. In Paul's letters, we must remember, with regard to topics like evangelism, we hear, not the kerygmatic, missionary advance of the gospel into new fields, but the pastoral, hortatory words of the apostle to those who are already in Christ.

It is also possible to cluster certain of these themes, as no doubt Paul did in his mind, even using some of them interchangeably, for example, gospel, Christ, salvation, justification, reconciliation, although each had particular nuances of its own, not covered by the other rough equivalents. At times we can see such combinations cohering in his letters, for example, justification, grace, and faith (Rom. 3: 24–5; Gal. 2: 20–1) or reconciliation, righteousness, faith (2 Cor. 5: 20–6: 1). More light will be shed on some of these themes if we summarize, in relation to Paul, aspects of Christian thought which we have been considering for all segments of the New Testament.

A summary comparison of Pauline thought with the gospel traditions

Gospel clearly is a topic of major importance for Paul (see theme 9, above). But in contrast to Jesus himself and, to a lesser extent, the four gospels, *euangelion* in the Pauline letters has to do not so much with the kingdom as with Christology and the effects of what God has accomplished in the Christ event. These results are often exhibited in some of the metaphors of salvation, listed above, like justification or reconciliation. Paul knew the gospel to be revealed by God as a dynamic power working salvation (Rom. 1: 16–17, where the form it takes is 'God's righteousness . . . through faith for faith'). There is, of course, a content to the gospel, above all the death of Jesus on the Cross for us. The gospel is for all potentially. For those who believe this news it serves as norm for belief and life (Gal. 2; Rom. 2: 16). It is truth (Gal. 2: 5, 14), which one obeys (Rom. 10: 16, an aspect of faith). Promised beforehand (Rom. 1: 2), the good news is about Jesus

Christ, the Davidic descendant who died on the Cross and was raised as Son of God with power (Rom. 1: 3–4). It is now being 'gospelled' throughout the world by Paul and others (1 Cor. 15: 1; Rom. 15: 15–20).

Jesus' great theme of the kingdom of God was not lost in Paul. He speaks of it in terms of power seen in his own ministry (1 Cor. 4: 20). God calls people to his kingdom (1 Thess. 2: 12). Paul presents it to his hearers as 'righteousness and peace and joy in the Holy Spirit' (Rom. 14: 17). Some of his references are future in their eschatology (1 Cor. 15: 22–8). A number of them seem to be common sayings among the earliest Christians about moral conduct, as to who will or will not 'inherit the kingdom of God' (1 Cor. 6: 9–11; Gal. 5: 21). But if the incident described at Acts 17: 2–9 was at all typical, when people in Thessalonica understood Paul to be preaching Jesus as 'another king' against the decrees of Caesar, it is understandable why Paul would have muted the kingdom theme in a pagan world that knew nothing of the Old Testament 'reign of God'.

Among the alternate expressions of the good news that Paul found more helpful for his audiences was 'life'. The Johannine idea of 'eternal life', which has some roots in the synoptics (cf. Mark 9: 43, 45, 47 in its paralleling of 'life' and 'the kingdom'), has an echo in Paul, right down to the adjective about life 'of the age to come' ('eternal life', Rom. 2: 7; 5: 21). Romans 5: 17–21 and ch. 8 are the two great Pauline passages on 'life'. It is connected in both instances with Christ's 'act of righteousness' leading to 'righteousness which means life' (5: 18; 8: 10).

In the case of righteousness/justification, which provides the content of the gospel being revealed, according to Rom. 1: 16–17, Paul takes up a scriptural theme that had been little developed by Jesus. But it was a theme employed quite naturally after Easter in early Christian slogans to present the meaning of the Christ event (above, theme 7; cf. also 1 Tim. 3: 16; 1 Cor. 1: 30; 6: 11; 2 Cor. 5: 21). Paul makes some references to 'righteous(ness)' in almost every letter, but it is in Galatians, Philippians, and Romans that he elevates it to a dominant level. His particular contributions were to make clear that God's justifying of sinners is a matter of faith, not performance of works commanded by the law, and that the experience of being declared 'justified', which had in Jewish thought been expected at the Last Judgement, takes place here and now, so that there is 'no condemnation' to those in Christ, who now have peace, access to God, hope, and endurance for the sufferings they may face (Rom. 8: 1; 5: 1–15). Further, the indicative statement that 'we are justified by faith' undergirds all the imperatives in Paul which direct the living of the Christian life.

Many terms cohere with justification. Behind it is Christ's Cross, as expiation. Received by faith, justification/ righteousness leads by grace to life 'in Christ' and the gift of the Spirit (Gal. 3: 2, 5). The church is a community of justified sinners (1 Cor. 6: 11). Other expressions of salvation, like reconciliation, overlap with it. 'Faith righteousness' (Rom. 9: 30; 10: 6) was Paul's own experience, and became emphatically his apostolic assertation.

If Paul's ways of putting the good news differ somewhat from that of Jesus and the gospels, his Christology shows great similarity with that in the four gospels. Obviously, Christ was the major figure in his life, and to die meant being even more intensely in Christ (Phil. 1: 21, 23; see themes 2 and 3 above).

It is widely held that the exalted titles which were increasingly used of Jesus after Easter in the New Testament writings went through a series of stages, often taking on new meanings. Jesus himself used 'Son of man' in one sense or another, was regarded as at least a prophet, and had a filial consciousness as 'son' of the *Abba*-God. The early church moved through Palestinian, Hellenistic–Jewish, and then Hellenistic–Gentile phases in working out fuller assertions about Jesus. In the first stage, Aramaic-speaking followers in Galilee and Jerusalem focused on the earthly ministry (including Jesus' death) and the imminent parousia. Next, Greek-speaking Jewish Christians (like Stephen and his circle, Acts 6–8) extended the range to include God's sending of the Son (Gal. 4: 4; Rom. 8: 3) and Jesus' present reign as exalted Christ. It was in the third phase, when Greek converts with no real Old Testament–Jewish background came into the church, that 'pre-existence' and a role in creation began to be assigned to Christ (1 Cor. 8: 6; Phil. 2: 6–8), as well as 'incarnation' (cf. 1 Tim. 3: 16 and 2 Cor. 8: 9, though not in the specific terms of John 1: 14). All these phases were *prior* to Paul's letters, and all these types of Christology crop up in his writings.

On this reading, then, Paul is not original in the area of Christology, for he shares most of the titles with predecessors. Yet he uses the titles, if somewhat interchangeably, at times with new contributions of his own (cf. Ziesler, *Pauline Christianity*, 27–44 (rev. edn., 28–46)).

'Christ', for example, Paul develops through the use of prepositions. 'In Christ' has personal (2 Cor. 12: 2; Gal. 6: 14), ecclesiological–sacramental overtones (Rom. 6: 11, 23), as well as those of future hope (1 Cor. 15: 22; Phil. 3: 9, 11). 'With Christ' refers both to the baptismal experience of being united to Christ's death and resurrection in the past (Rom. 6: 3–11) and to the future fulfilment, when believers will be united with Christ in their own resurrection (Rom. 6: 5; 2 Cor. 5: 8). 'Lord' emphasizes Jesus' present rule, especially with regard to daily life in the church. Many imperatives in Paul are spoken 'in the Lord' (1 Cor. 7: 10; 1 Thess. 4: 1; Phil. 4: 1, 4). 'Son of God' helps connect Jesus with God but also with believers as 'sons of God' (Gal. 4: 4–7). 'Wisdom' is an emphasis of Paul (1 Cor. 1–4), as is Christ as 'second' or 'last' Adam (1 Cor. 15: 45, 47).

Some claim, however, with good reasons, that Paul's real contribution christologically is his doctrine of justification. If Christ is what Christ does, then for Paul justification is 'functional Christology', that is, it shows how Christ works in the experience of believers, to save.

Paul's eschatology, it has been suggested above, was of the 'both present and future' variety. This can be seen in the fact that, although justification is a present experience, yet there remains a future judgement even for believers. The Cross was definitive, but there will be a parousia. Paul could at one point triumphantly write, 'The person who is in Christ is a new creature; the old has passed away, behold the new has come' (2 Cor. 5: 17) and at another say, 'We wait for adoption as God's children, . . . we hope and wait in patience' (Rom. 8: 21–5). The Spirit is the down-payment that God has made to us, guaranteeing future salvation (2 Cor. 1: 22). This paradox eschatologically fits with Paul's view of faith as 'having yet not having' (1 Cor. 7: 29–31; 2 Cor. 4: 7–12). Paul's eschatology with its twin aspects is akin to that of Jesus.

The prominence of the church in Paul (theme 8, above) distinguishes him from Jesus and the gospels. But the gap is in part bridged when it is remembered that, while Paul wrote *to* congregations, each gospel is reflective *of* a community or church. The type of writing (genre) and the fact that the gospels remain true here to Jesus' own times help account for some of the differences. The gospels picture discipleship; the letters assume membership in Christ, i.e. in his body, the church.

This changed situation from the time of Jesus to the decade or so when Paul wrote his letters also accounts for the greater emphasis, though still a fluid one, on structures of leadership in Paul's communities. Beyond the apostle himself, we read of prophets and teachers and a host of ministerial functions (1 Cor. 12: 28–30; Rom. 12: 6–8). Once there is reference to 'overseers and ministers' (Phil. 1: 1, in Greek *episkopoi* and *diakonoi*), but never in Paul to elders (presbyters). There were also congregational 'apostles', people sent on a mission for the group, like Epaphroditus (Phil. 2: 25, 'your messenger'). Yet the community, for all the need to have leadership and authority under Christ, is egalitarian, with regard, for example, to divisions of the times like 'slave and free' and 'male and female' (Gal. 3: 28; Rom. 4: 16–17).

Faith has been alluded to as statistically the most frequent theme in Paul after God and Christ (theme 4, above). A major Old Testament concept, demonstrable in Jesus' teachings, faith was foreign neither to Paul's Jewish nor to his Greek listeners. Briefly, it is basically the response of commitment to God, and the means for making the gospel and its benefits one's own and thus living in Christ (Ziesler, *Pauline Christianity*, rev. edn., 83–5).

Faith was for Paul the means of participating in what Christ offers. When the kerygma is preached, with its displays of power and the Spirit (1 Cor. 2: 4; 1 Thess. 1: 5), hearers believe and obey (Rom. 1: 5). 'Faith comes by hearing', but the event involves the Spirit (Gal. 3: 2, 5). The ensuing confession of faith (Rom. 10: 9–10) brings one into the community of Christ via baptism—all by faith (Gal. 3: 26–9). The object of faith is in particular the expiating death of Jesus (Rom. 3: 25), which produces forgiveness of sins (1 Cor. 15: 12–19). The emphasis on faith or believing as righteousness/justification is strengthened, for Paul, by use of Gen. 15: 6 and Hab. 2: 4 (Gal. 3; Rom. 4, on Abraham; Rom. 1: 17). For Paul, Christians stand by faith (1 Cor. 16: 13; Rom. 11: 20), in hope (Rom. 4: 18), living in love (Gal. 5: 6). They need to grow in faith by God's power (2 Cor. 10: 15).

The attempt has been made to take the ambiguous Greek phrase 'the faith of (Jesus) Christ', which has usually been understood to mean faith in Jesus Christ (objective genitive; NRSV text), to mean Jesus Christ's own faith (subjective genitive; Gal. 2: 16, 20; Rom. 3: 22; Phil. 3: 9; NRSV notes). Such an interpretation is excluded in some instances by the fuller context. Gal. 2: 16 explains the phrase in question, *pistis Iēsou Christou*, by the words 'we have believed in [*eis*] Jesus Christ'. Any uncertainty in Phil. 3: 9 about 'righteousness which is through the faith of Christ' (a literal translation; RSV 'faith in Christ') is clarified by the further phrase, 'righteousness that depends on faith to know Christ and the power of his resurrection and having a share in his sufferings' (3: 10). It also runs into the general use of 'faith' by Paul (sketched above) and his frequent references to 'believers' (Rom. 1: 16; 3: 22; 1 Thess. 2: 13; 2 Cor. 2: 13, faith like the psalmist at Ps. 116: 10).

For some later theologies and theologians, it would be a happy conclusion to be able to say that the faith involved is that of Jesus, just as the Cross and grace that save are the death and gracious favour of Jesus. This interpretation, as a subjective genitive, would clearly make of faith a divine gift, something wrought for sinful human beings by Jesus, not acceptance, trust, and obedience on the part of each person who hears the kerygma about Jesus. One may see as laudable the aim of stressing the historical Jesus' fidelity to God and 'obedience unto death'. For believers, faith includes obedience (Rom. 1: 5; 16: 26). But when Rom. 5: 19 talks of obedience, it uses another term, not 'faith'. Moreover, does Paul ever include a clear statement that 'Jesus believed . . .' or had faith? Abraham is Paul's great example of believing (Rom. 4, especially vv. 5, 17, 24–5). It is speculation to see in Paul a reference to 'the faith Jesus exercised historically and now exercises', and credits Paul with more interest and knowledge of what we call the historical Jesus than he probably had. At best, one may wish to appeal to Jesus' fidelity to God's purposes, including the Cross, and then stress the crucial need for hearers to believe in Jesus as the crucified and risen One.

The 'trajectory' of faith from Jesus to Paul and the gospels

The term 'trajectory' came into biblical studies in the 1970s, probably from the language of space rocketry, to denote the chronological course of an idea or theme in the early decades or centuries of Christianity. The term, however, is susceptible, on the one hand, to an overemphasis, in conservative interpretation, on notions of God at the launch-pad aiming and then guiding the trajectory; whatever happened becomes endowed with a divine aura. On the other hand, in liberal interpretation, the term becomes susceptible to manipulation of the trajectory, redefining directions, adding new twists, and making what data exist from ancient times palatable to our directions and tendencies today; the interpreter seems to direct the claimed trajectory. It is therefore better to speak of charting a course of developments, with their ups and downs (usually not a smooth evolution), over the decades, moving in and out of Jewish Christianity into the Gentile Churches. One must recognize here the contingencies of history and variety of situations, before making judgements about uniformity of course and direction, let alone about where the divine hand is to be seen most clearly or what the implications are for today.

In looking at Jesus, the three synoptic gospels, the single

Johannine one, and Paul's acknowledged letters, we move from the man of Nazareth who spoke of faith, for example, in a way quite consonant with Old Testament belief in Yahweh, to Christianity as belief in Jesus, as 'the faith' (Gal. 3: 23; Acts 6: 7), a new and growing religion in the Mediterranean world. These lines of development might be charted in many ways. The kingdom of God, for example, waxes as the theme of Jesus' preaching, continues in the synoptics, but wanes in Paul and John. Jesus spoke of 'preaching good news', but 'gospel' as a term came to the fore only in Paul and Mark, less so in Matthew and Luke, not at all in John.

Christology, which can be spoken of with regard to the period of the earthly Jesus only in a limited way, exploded into prominence after Easter. As a result, Paul works with it in elaborative ways (e.g. via justification/righteousness). Paul perhaps even speaks of Jesus as God—cf. Rom. 9: 5 and the punctuation problem, to be seen in RSV or NEB and their notes. Certainly, functions of God are attributed to Jesus. The synoptics think in ways more reflective of the historical Jesus. John is the one who most of all escalates Christology (Jesus as God, 1: 1, 18 in the RSV note; 20: 28).

Eschatology is rather consistently of the present-and-future variety. What was new in Jesus' teaching was the imminence of the kingdom, if not its actual presence in advance of the consummation. But this realized aspect brought with it even more intense expectation of the fullness God would soon bring about. Therefore future eschatology emerges. Paul and the synoptics generally are true to this double emphasis of 'now' and 'not yet'. John's Gospel has to do much more with 'realized eschatology'. Luke saw the time Jesus was on earth as one of realization, but for the unfolding present period, the church lives between the times of Jesus and a distant parousia.

In community terms, we may speak, for Jesus' day, of disciples and a movement around him. After Easter the church develops, but is not structurally elaborate in any of our documents. Paul's letters take up aspects and problems of community life together and of leadership in the 50s of the first century, but with fluidity. Ten to 40 years later, the gospels all reflect or even address a community of Jesus. Of the four, only Matthew overtly uses the term 'church'. For the rest we must read between the lines, although with Luke much more emerges in the second volume, Acts.

This general picture of a certain unity to all these writings about Jesus, and yet of their inevitable variety, can be glimpsed most vividly with regard to faith. Jesus, in the light of this major Old Testament theme, talked of, and must have, for followers, exemplified, faith in God, especially in connection with prayer and miracles. Faith means believing, trusting encounter with the God (*Abba*) who can do all things (Mark 9: 23). The Easter faith meant belief in God as the one who raised Jesus from the dead and hence in Jesus as risen Lord. Creeds (1 Cor. 15: 3–5), hymns (Phil. 2: 6–11, perhaps with 3: 20–1 continuing the story with the parousia hope), and formulas about the meaning of the Christ event like Rom. 3: 24–6 were common property for all subsequent Christianity.

Paul is the one who deepened the sense of the term beyond 'faith in the kerygma about Christ', so that faith in Christ and 'faith righteousness' became both the objective content and personal experience for preaching and all life. Indeed, it is by faith exclusively that one stands before God (Rom. 3: 28; 11: 20) and lives in the world with love and hope. Abraham is our great paradigm (Gen. 15: 6; Gal. 3; Rom. 4). But Paul is to be imitated here too (Phil. 3: 4–17).

Mark, as do some of the Q sayings, preserves Jesus' own view of faith and adds that of belief in a kerygma about God preached by Jesus (1: 14–15). Matthew, too, is true to Jesus' usage, but heightens the concept by relating faith to understanding and by using miracle stories to teach what faith is. Matthew presents disciples as those who do have (some) faith and understanding but who possess all too little faith. In Luke, too, faith saves, in miracle-story encounters with Jesus. More of the post-Easter atmosphere of believing in Christ (24: 24–5) and of holding on in faith until the parousia (8: 12–13; 18: 8) that will be apparent in

Acts may be retrojected into Luke's Gospel. Mary exemplifies faith as a model believer (1: 45; Acts 1: 14).

The Gospel of John goes its own way, as so often, with regard to faith. True, the concept is still connected with miracles (called 'signs'), but there is criticism as well as assertion of a faith built upon miracles. The Fourth Gospel does not refer to believing in the kerygma or gospel, as had Paul and Mark, but more directly to believing in Jesus' word (4: 50; 5: 24), keeping his words (14: 24), and abiding in what he says (8: 31). Jesus' word which is to be believed is closely connected with (Old Testament) Scripture (2: 22) and with what is written in the Fourth Gospel itself; to believe it means life (20: 31).

In these speakers and writers—Jesus, each evangelist, and Paul—the major voices in the New Testament are heard, in their variety and unity. It is with their witness that the shorter, so-called minor writings discussed in Chapters 7–16 are to be compared.

PART III

The Many Other Voices of Faith Within the Chorus of the New Testament Canon

Beyond the 'epicentre' of the gospels and Paul . . . . Jesus' singular story was conveyed in the gospels, directly and for new times, in a Christological way. Paul and his letters were epoch-making. Beyond these 'epichristian' sources, some of the 'profounder conceptions were not grasped by average Christian thought'. As 'the first enthusiasm began to fade', a tradition took shape, often with a 'lower level of conviction' and 'less exclusive of influences from outside', the literature 'embodying the Theology of the Developing Church' (Kennedy, *Theology of the Epistles*, 9–10). Is this so? What of the other New Testament books and the implications from their great variety for canonical unity?

Introducing the Other New Testament Books

THE New Testament writings apart from the four gospels and Paul's acknowledged letters—a dozen to 16 books, depending how one counts, among the 27 in the canon —are often looked on as the '*et cetera*' of Christian Scripture. The so-called 'catholic epistles' (James, 1 and 2 Peter, Jude, 1, 2, and 3 John), plus Hebrews, the single apocalyptic book in the New Testament (the Revelation to John), and the pastoral epistles (1, 2 Timothy, Titus), and finally the letters that are often denied by historical and literary criticism and theology to Paul himself (namely 2 Thessalonians, Colossians, and Ephesians) have often been treated as orphans. To such a list may be added the Acts of the Apostles, for that second volume by Luke, about Christian beginnings, has been separated from Luke's Gospel by the very arrangement of the canon, and by a tendency to study this gospel for its witness to Jesus, while Acts is ignored, or serves simply to provide a framework for Paul's letters and thus becomes the earliest church history.

Numerous textbooks, university and theological college or seminary courses, and Bible studies concern themselves with Jesus and the gospels, or with Paul as a person and apostle and with his theology. There is seldom similar treatment of the 'other' New Testament books. Where the epistles are treated, Paul dominates, and serious attention is often limited among the other books to Hebrews and 1 Peter (as in Kennedy, *Theology of the Epistles*) and sometimes James, at the expense of the 'little letters'. Yet these, while brief, open windows on many aspects of early Christianity.

An analogy between the New Testament writings and the

threefold Old Testament canon of the law, the prophets, and the sacred writings (cf. Luke 24: 27, 44) is suggestive. The gospels, like the Pentateuch, are foundational. The epistles of Paul are like the prophets in applying and advancing the significance of the great redeeming event, the exodus in the one case, Jesus' Cross and resurrection in the other. But the many other books or writings in the canon get only partial and sporadic attention.

It is an aim of the Oxford Bible Series, having treated *The Gospels and Jesus* in one volume and *Pauline Christianity* in another, also to provide proportional attention to every other book in the New Testament. Such is the intent of this volume, but within the context of 'variety and unity' in early Christian thought generally. We shall touch below on all the 16 documents mentioned above, even if for some, like Acts, 1 John, and Pauline letters that are disputed, reference has already been made in Chapters 5 and 6.

There are reasons, of course, why these 12–16 are often snubbed. For one thing, many are quite brief. Jude, 2 and 3 John are typical papyrus notes, in length like Philemon. Such brevity is frustrating for recovery of the historical circumstances addressed; there are few data on which to build. For another, it is difficult to identify the authors or to ascertain much about their lives, even on traditional views. If it is granted that the author of Jude 'the brother of James' was one of the brothers of Jesus (Mark 6: 3), we still know next to nothing about him. On the most conservative and traditionalist estimates, there were seven different authors for these 16 documents. This makes it difficult to develop a profile for these varied writings.

The situation is no different with regard to date. Many investigators nowadays place all or most of these writings between AD 70 and AD 100. But it has been claimed that James is the earliest writing in the New Testament, before AD 50, and some critics put 2 Peter around AD 140, as the last book to be written that came into the New Testament canon. There have been efforts to date all the 16 prior to AD 70. The majority of critics would put most of them in the 80s, but some in the second century. The documents surely fit into no compact period, as, say, Paul's unquestionable letters do, between 50 and 60, give or take a few years.

The geographical settings in these books likewise vary. The references make one look up atlases of the broader Mediterranean world. While James and Hebrews may smack of Palestine and Jerusalem, the latter also refers to '(those of) Italy' (Heb. 13: 24). The Apocalypse addresses seven city-churches in Asia Minor, while the author is incarcerated on the Aegean island of Patmos (Rev. 1: 9; chs. 2–3). 1 Peter refers to 'Babylon' (Rome? 5: 13) and addresses five Roman provinces in modern Turkey. The pastorals talk of mission work in Crete (Titus 1: 5), Epirus on the Adriatic (Titus 3: 12), and in the eastern Mediterranean generally, following what some have inferred as a 'fourth missionary journey' to Spain (assuming Paul's plans in Rom. 15: 28 came to fruition). This outlook is 'world-wide' for its day, but it does not help our focus in a unified way.

Much the same result follows when one asks about the 'genre' or the type of writing each of these 16 documents represents. They turn out to reflect everything except the gospel-book form.

Some of the epistles were real letters. Others are more like sermons, homilies, or treatises (Hebrews, 1 John), to which features of letters have been appended. In Hebrews, for example, there is a thirteenth chapter full of ethical admonitions and the 'news notes' one often finds at the close of a papyrus letter. James has the barest of epistolary beginnings, just a verse of greetings, but thereafter reads like a treatise. Colossians, Ephesians, and 2 Thessalonians are much more like Paul's acknowledged letters, but none is without difficulties. For example, in major early textual witnesses to Ephesians 1: 1, the key phrase 'at Ephesus' is missing, and the tone of this writing is remote for addressees among whom Paul had presumably spent several years, according to Acts 19: 8–10. The three documents addressed by Paul to his missionary assistants (Titus, and the two 'letters' to Timothy) read more like church constitutions or handbooks for administrators.

Although Revelation contains letters to seven churches within its second and third chapters, it is generally identified as an 'apocalypse' (see Chapter 14). And Acts, of course, is ostensibly a history book, recounting the advance of the gospel from Jerusalem to Rome, with biographical emphasis chiefly on Peter and Paul.

This great variety in the literary nature of these writings compels the reader to 'shift gears' in moving from one to another. For apocalyptic material (as in 2 Thess. ch. 2 or Rev. 6–22) calls for an attitude different from that appropriate for historical narrative such as one has in Acts. It will not do to read Hebrews or James as a letter to a specific community, since there is a general character to the contents (hence the name sometimes used of 'general epistles'), as if one were listening to an address or oration on a radio station, the location and target audience of which are not clear. Even the Pauline letters exhibit enough differences from Paul's proven style to prompt categorizing into subgroups, such as 'imprisonment epistles' (where Paul is in jail) or 'the pastorals' (for they are more about other pastors caring for those in their charge than about Paul's direct relations with his own converts). Thus no single literary profile emerges for this miscellany of writings which makes it easy for the reader to grasp hold of a genre, like 'gospel' or 'the letter form', and keep reapplying it.

Finally, the canonization process has not dealt kindly with the intentions of the original authors. Luke penned his gospel and Acts as a pair of scrolls, to be read together. The history of manuscript transmission separated them, so that the Gospel according to Luke circulated with three other gospels and Acts circulated by itself. In the eventual arrangement of New Testament books, John intrudes between Luke and Acts. Clearly the Fourth Gospel (as we call John's Gospel, based on such an arrangement) went originally with 1 John in content and historical associations. The canon has severed this connection, and 1, 2, and 3 John are isolated from the gospels collection by Acts and by 17 Pauline and other writings.

In fact, the three Johannine letters have been combined with two by Peter, and one each by James and Jude to make up a sevenfold sub-collection of 'catholic epistles'. This term, *katho-*

likē in Greek, meaning 'universal', was first used, by Dionysius of Alexandria in the mid-third century, for the epistle written by John, the son of Zebedee, who was also said to have written the Gospel according to John (see Eusebius, *Church History* 7. 25. 7). But Eusebius, by AD 310 or so, applied 'catholic' to all seven writings (*Church History* 2. 23. 24–5). The seven may have been grouped together by analogy with the letters to the seven churches in Revelation and the view outlined in the Muratorian Canon (second century or later) that Paul wrote to seven places (Corinth, Ephesus, Philippi, Colossae, Galatia, Thessalonica, and Rome). The idea was that the catholic letters were addressed to the universal church, not to individual communities. But the name is inaccurate, in that 3 John is addressed to an individual, Gaius, 2 John to a particular community, and 1 Peter to a region and its churches. The name 'church epistles', which some apply, is not much better for these seven, in that individuals as well as churches are addressed.

Finally, within the canon, the Apocalypse has been hauled from its often isolated position in Greek manuscripts—it regularly circulated alone, perhaps with less scribal care—and has been made the conclusion of the New Testament collection. For some Christians, it is thus its crown. This move has definitely had the effect of encouraging readers to extend to the entire New Testament (or all the Bible) the warning in the last chapter of the Apocalypse to 'every one who hears the words of the prophecy of this book: if any one adds to them, God will add to him the plagues described in this book, and if anyone takes away from the words of the book of this prophecy, God will take away his share in the tree of life and in the holy city, which are described in this book' (Rev. 22: 18–19). The canonical location has had the effect of encouring some readers thus to regard Revelation as a 'guard's van' for the entire canon, of allowing other readers to ignore this 'caboose' to the New Testament train, and of permitting others to view it as the climax toward which all other books point.

In such ways canonical arrangement has broken up historical patterns or authorial design in favour of new patterns of varying worth, by inserting disparate documents into a sevenfold grouping of 'catholic letters'.

All these factors have meant that the '*et cetera*' books of the New Testament have seldom been given their due. The Sunday readings, for example, which over the centuries developed as pericopes in the Roman Mass, the *Book of Common Prayer*, and Lutheran liturgies ignored completely some of these books, especially the little ones, and let others be heard only seldom.

More recently, however, in three-year lectionaries related to the *Ordo Lectionum Missae* (1969) that grew out of the Second Vatican Council, it was a principle that every book in the Bible should, if possible, be heard by the people of God at Sunday worship; further, that there be sequential lessons from the New Testament books. Thus James is to be read in excerpts from all five chapters over five consecutive Sundays, Hebrews over seven or eight weeks, and the pastorals for seven weeks. Acts is assigned for the first lesson in the post-Easter season, and Revelation as the second reading on Sundays after Easter in one year. A number of churches, Anglican, Lutheran, and Protestant, especially in the USA, have adapted this structure of readings to their own needs. In this way, neglected New Testament books are being heard and proposed for preaching, even if Titus, 2 Peter, and Jude, for example, get little or no attention.

While the New Testament books we shall take up below have thus come to fuller usage in the churches, they also call for greater attention on the part of even the casual New Testament reader because they are intrinsically interesting. Acts and Hebrews contain some of the best literary Greek in the entire canon. James provides blunt, programmatic wisdom for believers. The pastoral epistles have helped set the style for how Christianity came to terms with the world and culture of the day and encouraged Christians to live in society. Jude 24–5 provides one of the most beautiful benedictions anywhere, and 1 Peter an unforgettable interweaving of Christology and ethics for pilgrims in an often hostile world. In the Johannine letters we discern what has been called 'the life, loves, and hates of the community of the Beloved Disciple'. The Revelation to John, with its apocalyptic devices, has armed Christians facing martyrdom to hold on and endure, looking to a promised New Jerusalem.

We would be the poorer without these books in their incredible variety. Here alone, in Hebrews, out of the whole New Testament, one encounters Jesus as 'the Great High Priest', in an epistle that also sets forth the 'people of God' theme. We enter into fierce disputes over faith and works (James 2) and encounter heresies (2 Peter 2: 1; 1 John 2: 19) involving 'antichrists' (1 John 2: 18, 22; 4: 1–3) and mysterious figures of evil, like 'the beast' whose number is 666 (Rev 13: 18). We hear a full chorus, with counterpoint, dissonance, and new melodies of great complexity. Even if one speaks of a 'canon within the canon', as Luther did, it is within these 16 often neglected books that we find some of the most highly rated epistles (Ephesians and 1 Peter), not just books that were regarded as marginal (Hebrews, James).

In examining each of these writings in its original setting (insofar as that can be recovered), we must therefore be prepared to deal with the extraordinary variety these books add to the New Testament picture. They make the question of unity as difficult as it needs to be. For while appreciating each book in its own right, we must also be alert to ask what footholds for future directions each offered (for better or for worse), within the whole canon of Christian Scripture.

8

---

*The Pauline School: Colossians, Ephesians, and
2 Thessalonians, Paulinists during and after Paul's
Lifetime*

SIX letters which carry the name of Paul as author (Ephesians
and the pastorals) or co-author (Colossians, 2 Thessalonians)
have, although interspersed with his acknowledged writings
in the canon, been questioned by critics for more than a
century and a half. J. A. Ziesler, in his *Pauline Christianity* in
this series (rev. edn., 127–40), reflects these doubts. Usually
the issues about genuineness have to do with style and
content, and where they fit into Paul's known career as
missionary. At the least, the six exhibit development in his
views or variations from his usual emphases. They thus create
problems in discussing a unified Pauline theology. The
fluctuations are especially great in eschatology, ranging from
fervent apocalypticism in 2 Thessalonians to a timeless
emphasis in Ephesians on the church which, as Christ's body
(1: 23), replaces earlier emphasis on Jesus' coming again.
Other areas of change from (as well as agreement with) Paul's
views in the letters noted above (Ch. 6) will be presented
more fully below. In all likelihood, none of the six is by Paul
himself, but the evidence is more compelling in some
instances than in others. They are all part of the Pauline
heritage in the New Testament. There are ways in which 1
Peter also closely related to themes in the 13 Pauline letters,
so that some have termed it, too, 'Pauline'. 1 Peter will be
taken up in Chapter 10, directly after the six documents from
'the Pauline School'.

Colossians and Ephesians: advances in Christology, Church, and life in the world

In each case, Paul is presented as writing a medium-sized letter from prison (Col. 4: 3, 10, 18; Eph. 3: 1; 4: 1; 6: 20) to cities in the province of Asia. There are distinct connections with the little note to Philemon, which also stems from a time of imprisonment. These links are especially close for Philemon and Colossians, in that Timothy is mentioned as co-author of each and there is emphasis on how Paul takes pen in hand to write a few words himself at the end (Philem. 19; Col. 4: 18), a practice also found at 2 Thess. 3: 17; Gal. 6: 11–17; and 1 Cor. 16: 21. Above all, five or six of the same missionary colleagues appear in both Philemon (2, 10, 23–4) and Colossians (4: 9–10, 12, 17), namely Archippus, Onesimus, Epaphras, Mark, and Aristarchus. In addition, 'Jesus called Justus', mentioned at Col. 4: 11, can be conjectured behind the present text of Philem. 23, as the name of a Jewish Christian, rather than as a second name with 'Christ': 'Epaphras, my fellow prisoner in Christ; Jesus, Marcus, Aristarchus, Demas, Lucas . . .'. Through references to Tychicus at Col. 4: 7 and Eph. 6: 21–2, there is also a link to Ephesians.

What is to be made of these data? Some respected scholars continue to defend Paul's authorship of all three letters, but there are different views as to where Paul was imprisoned. Traditionally, it was in Rome, but the date could have been during the imprisonment mentioned in Acts 28 or during a second, later and fatal imprisonment there. The second possibility is a seaport in Palestine. The more than two years Paul spent in custody at Caesarea (Acts 23: 33–27: 1; note 24: 27) would have been earlier than the voyage to Rome. Thirdly, a conjectured imprisonment at Ephesus (Acts 19: 1; 20: 1) would have been still earlier. Equally good scholars hold that all three letters stem from the 'school' or circle of Paul's disciples a decade to 30 years after the apostle's death. (The imprisonment, then, is a reflection of the one during which Paul wrote Philippians and/or Philemon.) Still others assign Colossians to Paul but not

Ephesians. All kinds of theory have been proposed, including that Ephesians was put together by Onesimus (after he became a bishop) to introduce the collection of Pauline letters he had gathered. It has even been argued that Colossians was produced during Paul's lifetime, but by others for him, Paul from prison simply appending 4: 18 as 'proof of warranty'.

Colossians

Our understanding of Colossians would be immensely aided if there could be certainty about the opponents against whom the letter lashes out at 2: 8–23. The 'philosophy' they propose, using words like 'tradition' (2: 8), 'fulness' (vv. 9, 10), and 'rule and authority' (v. 10), conjures with a world of 'principalities and powers' (v. 15). Believers need more than the Christ Paul preached, and so circumcision (v. 11), legal demands involving food, drink, and festivals (vv. 11–16), and a series of ascetic, mystical practices (vv. 18–19a), perhaps also including sexual abstinence (v. 21) are recommended for full salvation. It is no longer possible to determine exactly what the opponents meant by their pentad of practices, involving stages of 'wisdom', namely (1) 'will-worship' (AV) or 'forced piety' (NEB), perhaps 'initiation' rites; (2) self-abasement; (3) severity to the body; (4) 'value' or (AV) 'honour', perhaps deification; and then (5) 'fulness'. The amalgam is a mixture of Jewish and other ideas, some possibly gnostic. While the profile of the heretics probably fits a real group in the author's day, some think it a composite picture of heresy that the writer warns against in one encompassing polemic.

It is a reflection of our poverty in terms of facts, and of the wealth of possibilities, that historical criticism cannot command wide assent on any one reconstruction of the 'original situation'. (This outcome will again and again obtain in study of the documents treated in Part III, and so the illustration with Colossians will be developed further here.) At one extreme, it is possible to homogenize a number of New Testament references and claim that Paul, from prison, sent off four letters at once: 'Philemon', to Onesimus' master; 'Colossians', to be read aloud in the church there and then be shared with the church at nearby Laodicea (Col. 4: 16); a (lost) letter to Laodicea, to be read also at Colossae (Col. 4: 16); and a circular letter which we know as 'Ephesians' to Hierapolis, which was also in the Lycus valley, and to other churches. At the other extreme is the view that one Paulinist wrote Colossians, another Ephesians, drawing on data from Philemon and other letters, after Paul's death, in order to address new situations in 'the spirit of Paul'. In between lie many proposals, including that Timothy wrote Colossians about AD 70, to meet a genuine threat to faith; it is, then, the first example, not of 'pseudonymity' (writing under a false name), but of 'deuteronymity', or second-level use of Paul's name to state what he would have said, in the face of later needs.

Two things are clear about Colossians, however. (1) The letter seeks to rescue the Pauline understanding of Christ and salvation from a syncretistic onslaught. (2) This restatement of Paul's gospel is carried through in a way that comes to terms with the Gentile–pagan world in which those addressed were living. We may expand on each point.

1. The letter depicts how Epaphras, the Pauline missionary at Colossae (1: 7; 4: 12–13), had encountered, in the opponents, a philosophy that stressed the cosmos—forces 'in heaven and on earth', including 'thrones, dominions, principalities, and authorities' (1: 16; cf. 2: 8, 'elemental spirits of the universe'). How then do Christ and Paul's gospel of 'justification by grace through faith' suffice for the universe? Are further cultic acts, practices, and heavenly mediations needed? Colossians, in response, stresses the sole sufficiency of Jesus Christ and his Cross (2: 8–15).

2. The Pauline answer is developed under new influences from the world of the day, such as had not appeared in Paul's (own) earlier letters. The developments in thought that are often pointed out as causing doubt about Paul's authorship (Ziesler, *Pauline Christianity*, rev. edn., 128–31) illustrate the point. Involved is more than a shift away from the Jewish–Christian setting characteristic of Paul himself and many of his letters. (This shift

is exemplified in Colossians by the virtual absence of Old Testament citations, reference to the Mosaic law, promise, or righteousness/justification). It is, rather, a shift toward categories of the Graeco-Roman environment and world religions of the day, as two illustrations will show.

2(*a*). In speaking of the community as the 'body of Christ', for example, Colossians introduces a different way of employing this image (1: 18, 24; cf. 2: 19). In 1 Corinthians 12: 12–27 and Romans 12: 4–5, Christians form the entire body, including the head, eyes, ears, and all. In Colossians, Christians are the body, Christ the head. A different background is to be assumed in the hymn quoted at 1: 18. There, in the stanza on Christ and creation (1: 15–18a), the whole created world or cosmos was envisaged as 'the body' of which Christ is the head. The background lies in the notion of the universe as the body of Zeus or of heaven, as Greek philosophers and Orphic hymns put it. The Colossians passage thus distinguishes 'the head' (Christ) and 'the body' (in v. 18 explicitly said to be the church, not the world). This shift has implications for both Christology and ecclesiology (see below). The major point is, however, a shift in the 'body of Christ' metaphor from Christ's identification with each Christian in the body (1 Cor. 11: 27) to Christ's pre-eminence as Head. That emphasis fits in turn with the point to be made against the opponents—Christ's sufficiency as the Head (2: 10, 19).

2(*b*). For the first time in a New Testament writing, Colossians introduces at 3: 18–4: 1 a set of guidelines for life together in households of the day. Such *Haustafeln*, as they are termed in German, or tables of duties for husbands and wives, parents and children, or masters and slaves, do not occur in Paul's prior letters but will be found also in Eph. 5: 22–6: 9; 1 Pet. 2: 13–3: 7; and Titus 2: 2–10, 3: 1–2. They are thus a feature in literature of the Paulinist school. The format is well known. Oriented around the verb 'be subject' (Col. 3: 18) or 'obey' (3: 20, 22), a 'superior' (husband, parent, master) is admonished in one way, the 'inferior' in another, usually in terms of subordination.

While causing difficulty for any society where freedom and equality are stressed, and in need of theological analysis (see below), the *Haustafeln* have come into Christianity, beginning with Colossians, from a Greek background. Such ordering of relationships between husband and wife, master and slave, parent and child, can be traced back to Aristotle and other writers on 'household management' (*oikonomia*). As developed in the popular philosophers, including the Stoics, the theme became part of societal organization (*politeia*), often rooted in the idea of God's ordering of the universe. Jews like Philo and Josephus took up the ideas in connection with God, country, and friends as well as family and the household (which was often also the primary economic unit). It has been conjectured that Christians took up *Haustafeln* as a way of asserting to the Roman authorities, in contrast to impressions rampant about other Eastern cults like those of Dionysus and Isis, that Christians were not dangerous to civil order and society (see below, under 1 Peter, on 2: 13 ff.). Christians are thus shown to be a dependable part of the social order.

But in all the letters involved, these codes for Christians in their homes and society serve a more particular purpose: as paraenesis or instructions on living in the married state, with children, and with the current practices of society such as slavery. Christianity is here coming to terms with the 'real world' of the day and affirming values of an ongoing existence in the world, such as marriage, home, and work. We, today, may not always like what these codes said (but see below under ethics). They did, however, represent an affirmation of current social structures, a Yes to being Christian in the society of the day. Such rules may also have been necessary to check excesses (such as Paul had experienced in Corinth) arising from the equality asserted in Christian baptism (Gal. 3: 28). In Colossians the verses further speak against the asceticism of the opponents by suggesting how Christians ought to live between extremes of libertinism, on the one hand, and rejection, on the other, of marriage, having children, and working within the institutions of society. .

How does Colossians, then, shape up in relation to the features sketched above in Chapter 6 for Paul's unquestioned letters, features in regard to which we have been comparing all New Testament documents?

The gospel is spoken of directly just twice, once as 'the word of the truth, the gospel which has come to you' (1: 5, a phrase which in Greek reflects Paul's polemical stand and the standard he envokes at Gal. 2: 5 and 14 about 'the truth of the gospel'), and once at 1: 23, about 'the hope of the gospel' which the Colossians have heard. But synonyms abound, all familiar from Paul's theology: the 'word of God' which Paul preaches (1: 25) or 'word of Christ' among the Colossians (3: 16); the 'mystery' now revealed, which is Christ (1: 26; 2: 2; cf. 1 Cor. 2: 7; God's plan of salvation); and Christ proclaimed to all (Col. 1: 28). Since Christ's achievement of 'reconciliation' (1: 20, 22; cf. 2 Cor. 5: 18–20) came through the Cross (Col. 1: 20; 2: 14–15), the Pauline gospel of 'Christ crucified' (1 Cor. 1: 23) thus continues in Colossians.

The kingdom, Jesus' own great theme, appears in a reference to three Jewish Christians as 'workers for the kingdom of God' (4: 11). A more remarkable formulation occurs in the lyric passage in 1: 12–14, which is perhaps a short quotation from a liturgy or hymn, about the Father 'who has delivered us from the dominion of darkness and transferred us to the kingdom of his beloved Son'. Here, as in 1 Cor. 15: 23–8 (cf. also Matt. 13: 41, 43), it is the kingdom *of Christ* in which Christians dwell. The metaphor echoes the deliverance from Egypt in the exodus and transfer to the promised land. But any hint of spatial terms is absorbed within the imagery of 'darkness' (for the domain of Satan; cf. 2 Cor. 6: 14–18; Acts 26: 18) and 'light' (for the realm of the saints; cf. 2 Cor. 4: 6; 1 Thess. 5: 5). And then the good news of the kingdom is further explained in 1: 14 as 'redemption' (cf. 1 Cor. 1: 30; Rom. 3: 24; 8: 23) and then, for the kind of world and situation in which the Colossians live, as 'the forgiveness of sins' (cf. Rom. 3: 24–5, otherwise a note Paul's letters do not strike).

The references at 1: 13 and 21 to 'darkness' and 'evil deeds' serve as a frame, in terms of 'redemption' (1: 14) and 'reconciliation' (1: 22), for the great hymn about Christ in 1: 15–20. These verses are the centre for the Christology of Colossians. The structure of the hymn's two stanzas is well brought out in the Jerusalem Bible or in Ziesler's *Pauline Christianity*, rev. edn., 128–9. They speak (1) of Christ, 'the Image of the invisible God', as the one in whom, by whom, and for whom all creation took place, who, pre-eminent, holds all things together, as Head (vv. 15–18a), and then (2) of Christ as the Beginning also of the new age, as First-Born from the dead, who, indwelt by God (cf. 2: 9), has reconciled all things to himself by giving his life on the Cross to make peace possible for those estranged and hostile (vv. 18b–20).

Employing categories drawn from the wisdom tradition and phrases current in world religions of the day, this great Christology sets forth Christ in creation and upholding the world, incarnate, crucified, yet reigning as Head of the church. The soteriological cast cannot be missed, to reconcile and make peace. One should not overlook, however, the interpretative application in the verses that follow (1: 21 ff.). What Christ accomplished is applied to the Colossians (1: 21–3, 'you . . . Christ has now reconciled') and the mission, theirs and Paul's, to proclaim Christ in the world (1: 24–9).

The Christology in the letter is thus directed toward the redemption of the Colossians and all who hear the message about Christ, their maturing (1: 28), and living in Christ (2: 1–7, especially v. 6). It passes over into an appeal to become what they already are, recognizing their new identity as the redeemed and translating this status into how they live 'in the Lord' (2: 6–7). Out of Christology the ethical imperatives develop. Christ, who is 'among us' and is 'our life' (3: 4), is already Lord at God's right hand (3: 10), but the future aspect continues, concerning his coming and glory (1: 27; 3: 4).

The eschatology in Colossians is of the 'both present and future' variety, with an inclination toward present fulfilment. This latter aspect can be seen in references to how God 'has transferred us into God's kingdom' so that 'we have redemption'

(1: 13–14), being 'now reconciled' (1: 22) and to some degree already 'mature' (AV 'perfect', 1: 28; 4: 12). Above all, it appears in the description of baptism. Here Colossians goes beyond the pattern of Rom. 6: 1–4 ('baptized into Christ's death' to 'walk in newness of life') by stressing that believers are already 'raised' and 'made alive' with Christ 'above' (2: 11–13; 3: 1–2). However, any notion that Christians possess heavenly status is deflected by references to 'hope laid up for you in heaven' (1: 5; cf. 1: 27), a future presentation before God (1: 22), and Christ's future appearance in glory (3: 4). Although there is little talk of judgement (perhaps at 4: 1 only), there is more said about God's wrath (3: 6) and reward (3: 24). For final salvation the condition is: 'provided you continue in the faith' (1: 23). The gift of 'life' that Christians now possess is 'hid with God in Christ' (3: 3).

Ethics in the letter dare not take the form of rules such as the opponents inflict (2: 20–2). But the call is to 'things above', i.e. Christ and God (3: 1–2). The imperatives are exemplified in five 'virtues' (3: 12), in contrast with five 'vices' (3: 5). Life in the Christian community is to be marked especially by love, harmony, peace, and thanksgiving, grounded in praise of God (3: 13–17; cf. 4: 2–6). The *Haustafeln* in 3: 18–4: 1 have already been discussed above. These Greek commonplaces for society are no longer grounded in God's cosmic rule but are modified by reference to the Lord (Jesus) (3: 18, 20, 22, 23, 24; 4: 1 'Master'). The admonitions to wives, children, and slaves are an advance over Greek codes, where such subordinates were not considered capable of being addressed in ethics. The worship setting which recalls the equality of Christian baptism also urges believers to 'admonish *one another*', and so a seed is planted that could demolish the code—eventually—by mutuality. But the accommodation to society that the *Haustafeln* represented obviously also carried seeds for disastrous oppression of inferiors. To come to terms with culture or social structures may demand a price.

Ecclesiologically, Colossians, while addressed to a local congregation (1: 2) which was closely related to a neighbouring church (4: 15–16), thinks universally. From the Christology of a Lord who is Head over all (1: 18; 2: 10) flows a concept of a world-wide Church of all who are delivered into the kingdom of God's Son (1: 13). 'Every creature under heaven' is the object of the preaching of this missionary church (1: 23, 28). Little is said about ministerial leadership. Paul's own office as apostle (1: 1) is to preach to all (1: 23b, 25–9; the Gentiles are envisaged, 1: 27). This may also involve the participation of the imprisoned apostle in a quota of eschatological sufferings (1: 24). Epaphras (1: 7; 4: 12) and Tychicus with Onesimus (4: 7–9) minister in the Pauline tradition. Every Colossian believer is to teach the others (3: 16) as they live the faith (3: 17). The gospel as 'word of truth' stands over them all (1: 5–7a), growing and fruitful.

Faith is mentioned five times (always the noun, never the verb 'to believe'). The Colossians' faith in Jesus Christ is well known (1: 4; 2: 5). It has christological content (e.g. 1: 15–20). They are to live in Christ, 'established in the faith, just as you were taught' (2: 7), and are to 'abide in it' (1: 23). All these are instances of what the Latin phrase in classical dogmatics called *fides quae creditur*, 'the faith which is believed' (see Ch. 3), i.e. the content of faith (in contrast to *fides qua creditur*, 'faith by which or with which one believes', the subjective side). Only Col. 2: 12 may incline in the other direction: by baptism the Colossians were also raised with Christ 'through faith in the working of God, who raised him from the dead'. God's activity is the object of faith, but the new life of baptism is itself here a matter of faith.

Overall, the achievement of Colossians—important beyond the size of its four chapters—was to show how Paul's message could come to grips with new situations. It offers an example of translating his theology into new terms and a warrant for adapting to the world of culture, society, and even the religions of the day with flexibility and firmness.

Ephesians
The epistle 'to the saints who are also faithful in Christ Jesus' (Eph. 1: 1 RSV) has, for centuries, been taken to have been Paul's, 'written from Rome unto the Ephesians by Tychicus', as later manuscripts and the colophon (scribal note) reported at the end in the AV have it. Almost everyone would agree that it is the

greatest epistle about the church in the entire New Testament. But its ecclesiology needs to be unpacked to discern what it really says, as distinct from later doctrines of the church. And for each of the other statements above—about author, place of writing, and even destination—certainty has been eroded in the last 400 years of study and new discoveries.

The beginning of Chapter 8 discussed certain facts relating to Ephesians as an imprisonment epistle, with a link to Colossians through Tychicus. There are also substantial connections in phraseology with Colossians (cf. 1: 1–2 with Col. 1: 1–2; 6: 21–2 with Col. 4: 7–8; 6: 18–20 with Col. 4: 2–4), as well as through the *Haustafeln* form (5: 22–6: 9, cf. Col. 3: 18 4: 1) and ethical instructions (4: 22–5: 21, cf. Col. 3: 5–17, e.g. 'the old nature' and 'the new', 4: 22, 24, or 'psalms, hymns, and spiritual songs', 5: 19). Phrases paralleled word for word in Colossians often turn up in Ephesians, such as 'in whom we have redemption through his blood, the forgiveness of our trespasses' (1: 7; Col. 1: 14, 'forgiveness of sins') or 1: 15–16, which combines ideas from Col. 1: 4 (faith, love toward all the saints) and 9 (do not cease to give thanks or pray). But the same words may be used with different meanings. The 'mystery' in Colossians was Christ (1: 26–7; 2: 2; 4: 3); in Ephesians (1: 9; 3: 3–6, 9–11) the term refers more to God's plan and how the Gentiles partake of the promise in Christ, or to the husband–wife relationship and its reference to Christ and the church (4: 32).

It can also be shown how Ephesians reflects but differs from terms and ideas in the unquestioned letters of Paul. To 'imitate' Paul or Christ is enjoined in 1 Cor. 11: 1 and Phil. 3: 17, but Eph. 5: 1 urges, 'Be imitators *of God*.' To 'stand against the wiles of the devil' (6: 11; cf. 4: 27) sounds Pauline, but only here and in the pastorals is the word *diabolos* employed; Paul's letters otherwise use 'Satan' (1 Thess. 2: 18; 1 Cor. 5: 5; 7: 5, etc.).

Example after example can be piled up, over which scholars have long argued, suggesting a different tone to Ephesians from Paul's acknowledged letters and Colossians. It can be agreed, for example, that Ephesians contains longer sentences (1: 3–14 is one sentence in the Greek), chains of genitive constructions, often repetitive (like 1: 19, 'the working of the power of the might of him'), and an expansive style (3: 7, 'the gift of the grace of God which was given me', cf. Col. 1: 25). Some of these features can be explained by appeal to use of hymnic, liturgical materials (which often tend to be verbose). Examples of hymns have been claimed at 1: 3–14 (with the refrain 'to the praise of his glory', vv. 3, 12, 14, printed as poetic lines in the Jerusalem Bible); 2: 4–10; 2: 19–22; or 5: 14 (cf. RSV). But the tone is not Paul's usual one.

The textual problem in 1: 1 has been alluded to above (p. 99) and by citing the RSV rendering (p. 114) which tries to make sense of the Greek where the words 'at Ephesus' are not included. The fact that the oldest Greek manuscripts lack the phrase, as do early church fathers (although Latin and Syriac versions include it), causes most recent translators to bracket this place-name or relegate it to a note.

If written by Paul to Ephesus, the letter ought to show reflections of the years the apostle spent there (Acts 19: 1–20) and their warm relationship (Acts 20: 17–38). Instead the tone is impersonal. What is more, the imprisoned apostle, while writing often in the first person ('I', 1: 15–16; 3: 1–14; 4: 1, 17; 6: 21–2), makes the odd statement, '*assuming* that you have heard of the stewardship of God's grace that was given to me for you' (3: 2); cf. 4: 21, 'assuming that you have heard about [Christ] . . .'. Of course they would have known of Paul's apostleship and teaching, if the historical Paul and Ephesus (cf. 1 Cor. 16: 8) were involved.

Furthermore, the letter is devoid of news about Paul's circumstances (in contrast to Phil. 1: 12–26 or even Col. 1: 5–7; 2: 1–5; 4: 3–4). There is only the promise that 'Tychicus . . . will tell you everything' (6: 21–2, apparently taken over from Col. 4: 7–8). Small wonder that many critics, echoing the queen's remarks in *Hamlet* (III. ii) about a play within the play, think the real author 'protests too much' that Paul is writing.

In such ways, destination, author, and the hypothesis of a Roman imprisonment have come to be placed in doubt. So also the claim that 'Ephesians' is a real letter. True, there is a salutation to some saints, but the usual first-person prayer ('I/we

thank God') has been replaced by a benediction or (Hebrew)
berakah, 'Blessed be God' (cf. 2 Cor. 1: 3–4; 1 Peter 1: 3–12). But
there are no greetings, nothing on how Paul may come to visit the
recipients (cf. Col. 4: 10–17; Philem. 22–3). Most startling of all,
there is no reflection of local conditions—no problems, no
opponents, little specifically to commend or rejoice over
(perhaps 1: 15 = Col. 1: 4; 3: 13). The document speaks
timelessly to perennial situations. Hence commentators have
preferred to call it a 'treatise' or 'tractate' or, using a term from
ancient rhetoric, an 'epideictic' epistle, showing forth praise and
exhortation, affirming God and the church in the present time.

The document we call the Letter to the Ephesians has also
called forth vigorous debate in recent years over its context in the
history of religions. While often rooted in traditions from Paul
and general apostolic Christianity, Ephesians has, in the minds
of some, evoked associations with the gnostic movement. There
is emphasis in Ephesians on *gnōsis* (3: 19) and *epignōsis* (1: 17; 4:
13, RSV 'knowledge') and enlightenment (1: 18; 3: 9; 5: 8–9,
13), but enough similar uses of these terms can be documented in
unquestioned letters by Paul to make the emphasis a heightened,
rather than a new, one. More pertinent is the 'sacred marriage'
theme of Christ and the church at 5: 32. Some read it as a
reflection of the pairing of a heavenly figure with a mortal in
myth and cultic ritual, as in Justin the Gnostic's book *Baruch*
about the deity (Elohim) and Eden (Israel) (preserved in
Hippolytus, *Refutation* 5. 24. 2–27. 5) or the erring soul and her
bridegroom-saviour in the bridal chamber, as in the document
from Nag Hammadi, 'The Exegesis on the Soul'.

Others find sufficient background, however, for this passage
in the marriage imagery of God and Israel in Hosea (2: 14–20), or
in Paul's own reference to betrothing the church at Corinth to
Christ 'as a pure bride to her one husband' (2 Cor. 11: 2–3). The
'mystery' of Christ and the church at Eph. 5: 32 does grow out of
the verse quoted at 5: 31 from Gen. 2: 24 about man and wife
becoming 'one flesh'. The whole concept of 'mystery' has Old
Testament and Qumran pedigree. Numerous Semitisms occur
in Ephesians, like the genitive constructions noted above or 'sons

of disobedience' (5: 6). Finally, since the discovery of the Dead Sea scrolls, certain parallel concepts have been pointed out, like the community as temple (2: 20–2). So the precise religious roots of Ephesians remain debated: gnostic, Jewish, or some combination thereof.

Unfortunately, critics have not been able to agree on the purpose or even purposes of the document. No crisis is to be seen in Ephesus or elsewhere prompting the writing, and no local setting is apparent. (How could one attempt a sociological analysis of the community based on this letter?) Therefore we are at a loss to determine the writer's aim. To 'stress church unity' or to 'provide a comprehensive summary on doctrine and duties' is the best many commentators can come up with, short of positing some specific situation (see below).

The exhilarating or exasperating variety within Ephesians can perhaps best be seen by a profile of its theology in the crucial areas in which we have been measuring most New Testament writings.

Ephesians' gospel has to do with 'your salvation', and is defined as hearing 'the word of truth' and believing in Christ (1: 13; cf. Col. 1: 5). Through the gospel the Gentiles become 'partakers of the promise in Christ' (3: 6). It means 'good news of peace' (6: 15; cf. Isa. 52: 7; Eph. 2: 14–16). This gospel is once said to constitute 'the mystery' (6: 19). Christ came preaching or 'gospelling' peace (2: 17). Paul's task was to 'gospel' to the Gentiles 'the riches of Christ' (3: 8). Only once is the kingdom referred to, and that as 'the kingdom *of Christ and God*' (5: 5; perhaps a development of Col. 1: 13 together with the 'kingdom of God' theme).

The Christology of Ephesians is not built around any hymn like Col. 1: 15–20, but surely presents a towering, cosmic figure in whom God's plan has been set forth (1: 9). 'In Christ' or equivalent phrases are frequent (e.g. 1: 7, 9, 10, 11, 13). Christ's sacrificial death (5: 2, 25), blood (1: 7; 2: 13), and Cross (2: 16) are mentioned. His resurrection (1: 20) is not so prominent as the ascension theme that God 'made him sit at his right hand in the "heavenly places"' (1: 20; cf. 2: 6) or simply the phrase 'he ascended' (4: 9 = Ps. 68: 18). Jesus is now lord and 'head over all things' (1: 22) but specifically 'head of the church' (5: 23). New is the complex imagery of 2: 14–18, that he 'has broken down the dividing wall of hostility' between Jew and Gentile, God and humanity. The note of judgement is not heard. Instead, Christ is the saviour (of the church) (5: 23) who 'fills all in all' (1: 23), i.e. specifically, believers with the Spirit (3: 19; 5: 18).

Generally, the eschatology in Ephesians stresses present realization, not future expectations. The word 'parousia' is not used. Rather, 'we *have* redemption' in Christ (1: 7), have been raised with Christ (2: 6), both phrases already found in Colossians (1: 14; 2: 12; 3: 1). Ephesians goes beyond this by stating that believers have also been 'made to sit with Christ in the heavenly places' (2: 6). Instead of a second coming, there is the prospect of 'coming ages' where God is to 'show the immeasurable riches of his grace in kindness toward us in Christ Jesus' (2: 7), although 'the riches of God's grace' have also already been 'lavished upon us' (1: 7–8).

But the very idea of 'this age' and 'that which is to come' (1: 21) derives from Jewish apocalyptic thought. So do statements that 'the days are evil' (5: 16; cf. 6: 13) and 'the wrath of God comes upon' the disobedient (5: 6), and the concept of a titanic struggle with evil powers, for which only God's armour will suffice (6: 11–17). Present possession of salvation is also qualified by reference to a future 'inheritance' (1: 14, 18; 5: 5), for which the Holy Spirit serves as 'down-payment' or guarantee 'until we acquire possession of the inheritance' (1: 14). All of the 'growth' language, like 2: 2 and 4: 15–16, suggests, too, that full attainment is yet to come. The statement that the 'building up' of the body of Christ 'until we come to' the 'Perfect Man', Jesus Christ, refers, it has been suggested, to meeting Christ at the parousia (4: 13; cf. AV).

What is the ecclesiology in Ephesians? It concerns the world-wide church. The local community is never mentioned (although what is said of the church as a whole can refer to the individual congregation in each place). The outlook in Ephesians is the result of a cosmic Christology, especially when references to 'church' are no longer tied to local needs or a specific situation, as was still true in Colossians. In the opening salutation of Ephesians, no specific 'church' is addressed (1: 1), but rather 'the saints (who are also faithful)', a term that will continue to inform the ecclesiology ('saints' occurs at 1: 15, 18; 3: 8, 18; 4: 12; 5: 3; 6: 18, although some references, like 2: 19, may be to the 'holy ones' of Israel or the angels).

Christology, in our document, controls ecclesiology. Christ is the church's head and lord (5: 29, 23), who loves her (5: 25, in the husband–wife analogy), gave himself for her, and nourishes and cherishes the church (5: 29). The church, as Christ's body, gets its growth (to violate all human analogy) from the head down (4: 16, an image even clearer in Col. 2: 19), although Ephesians can also talk of the church as a temple growing 'in the Lord', its cornerstone (2: 21). This church accords with God's purpose and design for the ages (3: 11; cf. 1: 11). Eschatologically, the church is to make known God's wisdom even to the 'principalities and powers in the heavenly places' (3: 10). It is a church of Gentiles and Jews, a new household exhibiting the meaning of reconciliation and peace (2: 11–22). Redeemed and ruled by Christ, chosen and destined in love by God (1: 4, 5, 12), sealed (baptized) with the Spirit, the community is depicted as holding within itself 'the fulness of him [Christ] who himself receives the entire fulness of God' (cf. Col. 2: 9) or as called 'to be all that he himself is who fills the universe in all its parts' (NEB text and note for 1: 23; cf. the parallelism of 'in the church' and 'in Christ Jesus' at 3: 21). But even this ecclesiologically grand vision does not lose sight of the individual believers: you (plural) are to be 'filled with all the fulness of God' (3: 19) via the Spirit (5: 18), as 'we . . . grow up in every way . . . into Christ' (4: 15–16).

Much has been made of the fact that, unlike 1 Cor. 3: 11, where Christ is the only foundation for 'God's building', in Ephesians the temple is 'built upon the foundation of the apostles and prophets, Christ himself being the cornerstone' (2: 20). The imagery is different. Christ remains crucial (and the NEB note may be correct in translating 'keystone', as in an arch, a parallel to Christ's role as 'head'). But 'the-apostles-and-prophets' (one group) are important. To call them 'holy' (3: 5) may suggest a later time, looking back with veneration. But Paul is an apostle (1: 1), even if 'the very least of all the saints' (3: 8; cf. 1 Cor. 15: 9 and 1 Tim. 1: 15–16).

For all this ecclesiology, Ephesians, remarkably, never mentions bishops, elders, or 'deacons' (although Paul is a 'minister'—in Greek, *diakonos*—3: 7, as is Tychicus, 6: 21). There is almost nothing on 'church structure'. But among the 'gifts' the ascended Christ gives 'to equip the saints for (their) work of ministry, for building up the body of Christ' were that 'some should be apostles, some prophets, some evangelists, some pastors and teachers' (4: 11). The 'gospelling', shepherding, teaching functions are indispensable for the growth of the whole community. In context, that involves doctrine and 'speaking the truth in love' (4: 14–15), especially the 'seven unities' of 4: 4–6, the 'Apostles' Creed in reverse': one body, one Spirit, one hope (the Third Article, including ecclesiology and eschatology); one Lord, one faith, one baptism (the Second Article, Christology); one God and Father (the First Article). For all the emphasis in Ephesians on unity (4: 3, 13), under the banner of 'One God, One Church' (4: 4, 6), 'truth' is the church's other guiding star (1: 13; 4: 21; 6: 14). (The relation of truth to unity remains a tension to this day in the ecumenical movement.)

Faith, accordingly, has content in Ephesians. The 'one faith' of 4: 5 suggests a system of belief. The Lord Jesus is the object of faith (1: 13, 15). Believers, however, are those who have experienced God's great power (1: 19). They are 'saved through faith' (2: 8), know access to God through faith (3: 12), and pray that Christ may dwell in their hearts by faith (3: 17). Love goes with faith (6: 23; cf. 1: 15), and faith is part of their essential equipment for the battles of life, along with the gospel, salvation, the Spirit, and the word of God (6: 15–17). All this suggests that Ephesians' high view of Christ, church, and present blessings still rests on faith, not sight.

One passage excellently exemplifies how Ephesians resembles Paul's unquestioned letters but also uniquely differs. The hymnic lines at 2: 4–10 present the good news of God's gift to us in Christ, in contrast to a background picture of human beings dead in sins (2: 1–3, 5). The stress on grace (2: 5, 7, 8) or mercy (2: 4) and on faith (2: 5), in contrast to works and boasting (2: 9), is almost more Pauline than Paul. But 'justification' by grace through faith has been replaced by 'salvation' by grace through faith. This terminological shift results from loss of the 'last judgement' or law court setting of Old Testament righteousness, and from the fact that the verb 'to save' spoke more clearly to Greek hearers. In vv. 5–6 the present aspect of fulfilment is the focus; the future is only vaguely seen in v. 7. 'Works *of the law*' are no longer the concern. Indeed, our 'new creation' is 'for good works' (2: 10). But any tendency to boast of these is removed by saying that they are the result of God's destining them, for God 'prepared them beforehand' as our way of life. This is Paul with a new accent.

How, historically, is the document we call Ephesians to be explained? In the fifth century, Theodore of Mopsuestia suggested, in order to account for the vagueness about a city and its people where Paul had laboured for several years, that the apostle wrote the letter *before* he was in Ephesus. No one agrees. Over a thousand years later, Theodore Beza and then Hugo Grotius suggested that 'Ephesians' was a general letter, an 'encyclical' to several churches. This theory can take the form of a single letter (without address to a specific place) passed from church to church, or of several copies, each with a different place name. Perhaps the surviving copy came from the archives 'in Ephesus'. Those who still defend authorship by Paul invoke this theory, often along with the supposition of a new secretary given a great deal of freedom. But Tychicus has been proposed as author, as has Luke.

The most romantic theory is that Onesimus, the former slave of Philemon and later bishop of Ephesus (according to second-century tradition), was spurred by Luke's writing of Acts to contact places Paul had visited, in order to collect letters which his benefactor and mentor Paul had written. Onesimus, it is suggested, then wrote Ephesians as an introduction to the resulting Pauline corpus. This theory about how Ephesians originated as a cover letter for a little canon cannot be said to command broad support today, however, and there is no evidence that Ephesians ever stood first in a collection of Paul's letters.

There thus remains no wide agreement on historical origins, though the view that Paul did not write Ephesians is widespread. The effect of this Pauline work has been to let new ages hear Paul's gospel in transmitted form, and to extend his Christology (or especially that of Colossians) to a vision of the universal church.

2 Thessalonians: new directions in apocalyptic eschatology

The shorter letter of the two in the Pauline corpus addressed 'to the church of the Thessalonians' has traditionally been read as a follow-up to the longer epistle. The assumption, then, is that it was written shortly after 1 Thessalonians, in order to amplify points in that letter about 'the times and seasons' until Christ comes again (1 Thess. 4: 13 5: 11). Because the day of the Lord was regarded by some as having already come (2 Thess. 2: 2) and because that notion had an effect on conduct, the subject of the letter is eschatology and ethics (2 Thess. 1: 5–10 and 2: 1–12; then 3: 6–15, respectively). Numerous prayer-wishes are also interspersed (1: 3–4, 11–12; 2: 13–3: 5; 3: 16, 18), as well as a concluding assertion that Paul's personally written greeting at 3: 17 is a mark of 'every letter of mine'.

Much of 2 Thessalonians is very like 1 Thessalonians. There are almost verbatim similarities in 2 Thess. 1: 1–2, 3–7, 11; 2: 1, 13–17; and common phrases or words in 3: 1, 6, 7, 10–12. Yet 1 Thessalonians is never explicitly mentioned in the way a former letter was at 1 Cor. 5: 9. Moreover, the tone is sharper in the second letter. Paul commands (3: 4, 6, 10, 12) rather than exhorts (1 Thess. 2: 12; 3: 2; 4: 1).

Even where phrases are repeated from the first letter, usage may be somewhat different. For example, whereas 1 Thessalonians referred to God, the second letter often speaks of 'the

Lord', and that with reference to Jesus. Compare 'brothers and sisters beloved by God' (1 Thess. 1: 4) with 'beloved by the Lord' (2 Thess. 2: 13), or 'the glory of our Lord Jesus Christ' (2: 14) in contrast to the more customary 'kingdom and glory of God' (1 Thess. 2: 12). Descriptions of the Lord Jesus are expanded by use of Old Testament phrases about God. 2 Thess. 1: 12 thus employs Isa. 66: 5; 1: 7–10 use Isa. 66: 4 and 15, along with Jer. 10: 25, as well as the refrain from Isa. 2: 10, 19, 21 about terror before Yahweh and the glory of his majesty, together with Pss. 68: 35 (67: 36 LXX) and 89: 7 (88: 8 LXX). 1 Thess. 3: 13 had spoken of Christ's parousia in a positive way with regard to believers; 2 Thess. 1: 7–9 speaks in negative tones concerning those who do not obey Jesus' gospel.

Parallelism, often antithetical, abounds in 2 Thessalonians: for example,

repay with affliction those who afflict you,
grant rest with us to you who are afflicted   (1: 6–7)

or 1: 12, Jesus 'glorified in you and you in him'. But the triads which were common in 1 Thessalonians (such as faith, love, and hope, 1: 3 and 5: 8) disappear, although dyads continue, exemplifying parallelism (1: 3, faith and love; 1: 4, steadfastness and faith, persecutions and afflictions). The considerable use of the Old Testament in 2 Thessalonians (1: 8–10; 1: 12, as noted above; 2: 4, 8) is surprising, since 1 Thessalonians reflects the Hebrew Scriptures scarcely at all.

The heart of 2 Thessalonians and the nub of interpretative problems is an account at 2: 1–12 about what will happen before the 'coming [parousia] of our Lord Jesus Christ and our assembling to meet him' (2: 1). According to 2: 5, Paul had instructed the Thessalonians when he was with them about how first there must be 'the rebellion' and then 'the person of lawlessness, the son of perdition' would be revealed, an anti-God, sitting in 'the temple of God' and claiming to be God (2: 3–4). 1 Thessalonians had spoken often of the parousia of Christ (2: 19; 3: 13; 4: 15; 5: 23). Now Paul takes up the topic in more detail (2: 1–12), including the parousia of 'the lawless one' (2:

8–9), whom the Lord Jesus 'will slay with the breath of his mouth' (cf. Isa. 11: 4). This account of future activity is termed 'revelation' (2 Thess. 1: 7; verb at 2: 3, 6, 8) and involves 'the appearing' (*epiphaneia*) of Christ (2: 8).

Paul himself had painted a picture in 1 Thessalonians 4: 14–17 about how, at Jesus' parousia, the 'dead in Christ' would rise and the living saints would 'be caught up together with them' so as 'to meet the Lord in the air'. (This is the closest the New Testament ever comes to the idea developed in the nineteenth century of 'the rapture'.) It is widely agreed that the passage in 1 Thessalonians may have contributed to further speculations among Christians in that community. Now the apostle writes in 2 Thessalonians to quiet the panic over the claim that 'the day of the Lord has come' (2: 2). This new crisis may have been encouraged by a forged letter or 'word' or prophet speaking 'in the spirit', claiming new insights from Paul and his companions (2: 2).

Whatever the source, the apostle deals with the problem by describing, according to conventional apocalyptic jargon, the things that must take place before it really is 'the day of the Lord', the parousia of Christ as judge (1: 7–9). Although 'the mystery of lawlessness is already at work', there are inhibiting factors, namely 'that which restrains' (2: 6, neuter) and 'he who restrains' (2: 7, masculine). While Satan is and will continue to be at work, the decisive events have not occurred as yet. The implication might be drawn, as in 1 Thess. 4: 18 and 5: 11, that Christians should comfort and exhort one another with these words. But 2 Thessalonians moves instead to a thanksgiving for the fact that, with Paul's readers, God has been at work to save. The exhortation is, 'Stand firm and hold to the traditions . . . taught by us, either by word of mouth or letter' (2: 15). This last listing of sources for 'valid revelation' forms a framework with 2: 2 for the entire passage. Pauline word and letter (not 'spirit', or Spirit, which is pointedly omitted) are the norm for 'the traditions'. This is the sort of evidence that has been pointed to as a sign for a post-Pauline period: it is tradition, oral and written, that provides the norm for revelation.

The scenario of expected events in 2: 3–12 is filled with allusions no longer understood today. 'The restraining hand' at 2: 6 and 'the Restrainer' (2: 7 NEB) were known to the original readers (2: 6, 'you know'). This pair of terms has been taken subsequently to refer to God and the divine plan; or to Paul and the preaching of the gospel; or to the Roman emperor and empire; or to a myth about an angel like Michael and some divine power detaining Satan (cf. the imagery of Rev. 20: 1–2). Another proposed solution argues that the references are to what the readers have already experienced in Thessalonica: some charismatic figure, seized by 'the divine' in the way followers of the Greek god Dionysus were possessed, has posed a threat to the faith of the Christian community there. This 'seizing power' that has shaken the Thessalonians (v. 2) will in the future cause further deception in the world (vv. 8–12). But God is also at work, delivering those who believe in the gospel, and will condemn those who do not believe the truth (2: 11–14).

So run the theories, but no one knows the original, historical meaning in the apocalyptic source, the Thessalonian situation, Paul's intent, or a Paulinist's endeavour. Ironically, what seems to have been intended to calm eschatological excitement has again and again, over ensuing centuries, aroused attempts to identify 'for our day' the 'man of lawlessness' or 'the restrainer'. It must be remembered that the whole presentation was to confront the false notion 'that the day of the Lord has already come'. In 2 Tim. 2: 18, false teachers hold 'that the resurrection is past already', not that of Jesus but our resurrection, so that true Christians are already raised. Such a view in 2 Thessalonians could have grown out of the phrase in 1 Thess. 5: 5, 'You are all . . . sons of the day', interpreted as 'the Day of the Lord' (cf. also the presentation of 1 Cor. 4: 8 that believers already 'reign as kings').

While it has traditionally been maintained that Paul himself and his colleagues wrote 2 Thessalonians (1: 1 and 3: 17 frame the contents), recent commentaries, including those by Catholic scholars as well as Protestants, have moved toward the explanation of pseudonymity: a later Paulinist is writing. In between these extremes are various half-way houses, like the suggestions that Paul wrote 2 Thessalonians *prior* to 1 Thessalonians, or to a *Jewish*–Christian segment within the congregation there, or to another place, such as Philippi; or that we have a composite, made up of fragments from several Pauline letters; and that Timothy or someone else wrote, perhaps under Paul's direction, with the apostle 'signing' it (3: 17). Those who use the approach of canonical criticism (see above, Ch. 2) vary in their reactions. They take the document either as a second response by Paul the pastor 'to stages in a community's panic' (Johnson, *The Writings of the New Testament*, 267) or as a serious test case because the 'canonical construal' is in tension with the process which produced the letter (Childs, *The New Testament as Canon*, 371–2).

The issue has to do especially with the shift in eschatology. In 1 Thessalonians, the problem was the *delay* of the parousia (4: 13–5: 11: Christians die but the end is not yet); in 2 Thessalonians, it is that the End is *already present* (2: 2). Or worse, 2 Thessalonians may have been written by a Paulinist to correct or replace 1 Thessalonians and so forestall henceforth the sort of results to which it led; then the famous warrant of authenticity at 3: 17 is a trick to gain acceptance of the document. Or, it has been argued, 2 Thessalonians is a very late work by someone in the Pauline school bent on correcting or refuting the direction of the theology in Colossians and Ephesians.

It is often said that 2 Thessalonians 'makes little contribution to Pauline theology' (Ziesler, *Pauline Christianity*, rev. edn., 128). 'Gospel', we may note, has become the criterion for salvation or condemnation (1: 8; 2: 14). God's kingdom seems future (1: 5), as is most of the eschatology. The Christology stresses Jesus as Lord, primarily a figure of glory and vengeance (1: 8). Comfort is offered to those who hold the traditions fast (2: 15–17). The ethic is stringent: those who, in the face of apocalyptic day-(of-the-Lord)-dreaming, do not work shall not eat (3: 10). To hold the faith and hold to faith is frequently commended (1: 3, 4, 11; 2: 13). But to have faith is, although the Lord is faithful (3: 3), admittedly not 'everyman's thing' (3: 2).

Believers stand in contrast with those who have not so responded to the truth, the gospel (1: 10; 2: 11, 12).

Second Thessalonians makes one exceedingly important contribution to Pauline theology, however. The letter moves Paul's eschatology in a more apocalyptic direction, even while seeking to calm panic speculations over the day of the Lord. If Paul wrote the letter, we are forced to ask how much his views fluctuated in the face of changing circumstances. If 2 Thessalonians is only indirectly Pauline, the document makes us consider how a later writer amplifies, corrects, or even tries to displace an earlier one: it has become, as *Second* Thessalonians, a kind of commentary on 1 Thessalonians. Among the deutero-Pauline letters, it shows that not all Paulinists tended toward a realized eschatology, one where the fruits of fulfilment are already harvested, for in 2 Thessalonians the future aspects of 'not yet' are vividly presented. Overall we are reminded, as in the Jewish proverb, that 'This and that too are part of Scripture'. That is, both points of emphasis are found in the New Testament.

The Pauline School: Three 'Pastoral' Epistles to Timothy and Titus, to Further Faith and Order in the Household of God

FIRST and Second Timothy and Titus 'give us a valuable glimpse of what happened to Pauline Christianity about the end of the First Century' (Ziesler, *Pauline Christianity*, rev. edn., 140)—or, others have maintained, late in Paul's career in the middle 60s, or, others claim, in the second century. But what glimpses do they show?

The three documents appear in the canon, after Paul's letters to congregations, in a sub-collection of four letters to individuals. They are arranged in order of decreasing length, with little Philemon coming after Titus. The three 'pastoral letters'—so named in 1726–7 by Paul Anton, a Pietist who was Professor of Exegesis, Polemics, and Practical Theology at Halle, even though the term 'shepherd' or pastor never appears in them—are ostensibly from Paul, 'an apostle of Jesus Christ', to assistants in the Pauline mission who are known from other New Testament books.

The pastorals pose the question of variety and unity in two ways: first, with regard to the other letters of Paul, and second among themselves. The first question has been discussed since the early nineteenth century, when first 1 Timothy and then the other two letters were dismissed from the ranks of genuine writings by Paul himself. The second is masked by a tendency to treat the pastorals as a unit.

The tradition over most of the centuries has been to accept at face value the assertion in the salutation of each letter: Paul wrote them. No co-author or scribe is mentioned. But some church fathers in the second century rejected one or all of them. Questions about contents, style, historical setting, and theology have caused a swing in the twentieth century to the view that they are pseudonymous, that is, written by a Paulinist to say to a later age what Paul's message implied for that new day. In between these extremes have been proposals that secretaries employed by Paul account for some of the variation from his own letters, or that fragments of genuine letters have been woven together by a later editor. Usually the fragments attributed to Paul are identified as passages in Titus (e.g. 3: 12–15) or 2 Timothy (1: 16–18; 3: 10–11; much of ch. 4) and are (auto)biographical.

The claim of pseudepigraphy in early Christian literature has been explored most in connection with the pastorals (and 2 Peter). While to some the practice of writing under the name of another person amounts to forgery, recent discussion, especially by German Catholic scholars, has moved far beyond claims that 'imitation is the sincerest form of flattery' or that 'people practised it in antiquity with no qualms'. The evidence suggests that the device was widespread in the Hellenistic world, with varied functions, some religious. In the case of the pastorals, this includes the possibility that the writer employing the device may have felt that God was using that writer's efforts to say what the apostolic voice implied for the present situation. There is also the suggestion that the Pauline school saw new letters as a way of personalizing the tradition of Paul, or of continuing his own practice where letters were a substitute for the apostle's presence. Just as Moses continued to speak in the synagogue through extension of his authority in later writings and traditions (cf. Acts 15: 21), so also did apostles in the church.

Very much involved in any discussion concerning the origins of the pastoral epistles are what they say about Paul and about the addressees. What is said about Paul? According to 1 Timothy, that he had gone from Ephesus to Macedonia (1: 3) and that now, in case he is delayed in coming back to Timothy, he writes instructions on aspects of church life and warns against false teachers. Woven in is first-person reference to Paul as once 'foremost of sinners', now experiencing God's mercy and grace (1: 12–17). 2 Timothy portrays Paul a prisoner in Rome (1: 8, 17; 2: 9), alone except for Luke (4: 11), facing death (4: 6–8). He has been in Miletus and Troas (4: 20, 13). Titus says Paul had left Titus in Crete (Titus 1: 5, implying that Paul had been there too). Paul wants Titus now to join him for the winter in Nicopolis (on the Adriatic Sea in western Greece), as soon as Paul sends Artemas or Tychicus to relieve Titus in Crete. In this letter, Paul appears very much the mission leader, whereas 2 Timothy depicted him suffering, near life's end, and 1 Timothy as the figure of authority representing orthodoxy and order.

A great difficulty is that these data in the pastorals do not fit with details about Paul's life as reported in Acts, or with references in his clearly genuine letters (e.g. the references to Ephesus in 1 Cor. 16: 8 and 4: 17). This has led to reconstructions of a further missionary career after the Roman detention with which Acts 28 ends, involving travels long after what is recorded in the unquestioned letters. Usually this reconstruction has Paul going from Rome to Spain and then back to the East (although others arrange the itinerary in reverse) before a second imprisonment in Rome and martyrdom as late as AD 68. On this reconstruction, the likely sequence of the pastorals is Titus, 1 Timothy, and 2 Timothy.

Addressees and opponents

What of the addressees? In Paul's letters, Timothy appears as co-author of three genuine letters (1 Thess., 2 Cor., Phil.) and two questioned ones (2 Thess., Col.). He played a role in Paul's relations with Corinth, as a person who could remind people of Paul's own 'ways in Christ' (1 Cor. 4: 17) but who may have lacked self-confidence and been easy to despise (1 Cor. 16: 10–11). He also played a role, this time more successful, with the Philippians (Phil. 2: 19–24). Earlier, Timothy had been sent from Athens to Thessalonica 'to establish and exhort' their faith (1 Thess. 3: 2). Cf. also Rom. 16: 21. Acts 16: 1–3 states that he came from Lystra (or Derbe) in Asia Minor, the son of a Jewish–Christian woman and Greek father. Paul is said in Acts to have 'circumcized him because of the Jews' before the young man joined Paul and Silas in mission work (16: 4). The two pastoral letters to him reflect this knowledge of Timothy. He is young, and people may despise him (1 Tim. 4: 12). He teaches and exhorts (1 Tim. 6: 2b; 2 Tim. 4: 2) and is an example (1 Tim. 4: 11–12). His faith is traced back to his mother and grandmother, both of whom are named (Eunice and Lois, respectively, 2 Tim. 1: 5). Circumcision, however, is never mentioned.

Such details can, of course, be taken as proof either that 1 and 2 Timothy are historically accurate or that a later author was using information from Acts and Paul's other letters to create these documents. Indeed, the verisimilitude seems strained and mechanical when Timothy, who by now must have been a missionary for almost 20 years, is told to 'flee youthful passions' (2 Tim. 2: 22); the claim that he had been acquainted 'from childhood' with 'the sacred writings which are able to instruct you for salvation through faith in Christ Jesus' (2 Tim. 3: 15) can be squared with Acts 16: 1–3 only by assuming that his mother and grandmother had helped him to the Scriptures (cf. 2 Tim. 3: 14) but did not have him circumcized.

With Titus the matter is somewhat different. He is never mentioned in Acts. He was a Greek who went along to the meeting in Jerusalem described in Gal. 2: 1–10 but 'was not compelled to be circumcized'. Titus played a major role in healing the stormy relations or breach between Paul and the Corinthian Christians (2 Cor. 2: 13; 7: 6–16) and a key role in the financial collection being gathered in Corinth for the 'saints' at Jerusalem (2 Cor. 8: 6, 16–17, 23; cf. 12: 18). Although Titus seems thus to have been a more successful leader than Timothy, in Paul's unquestioned letters praise of Titus is not so frequent or fulsome as for Timothy. (Perhaps such praise was not needed.)

The same impressions hold in the Letter to Titus. He is Paul's 'true child in a common faith' (1: 1), who is to teach and exhort

(2: 1, 15, 'let no one disregard you'). The most personal note is, 'Do your best to come to me at Nicopolis' (3: 12). A cross-reference to Titus 3: 12 in 2 Tim. 4: 10 says that Titus, at the point of Paul's final imprisonment, had gone 'to Dalmatia' (Albania, southern Yugoslavia). It is stretching the Greek to see connections with Titus' fund-raising experience at Corinth in the admonition, 'Our own people must be taught to engage in honest employment to produce the necessities of life; they must not be unproductive' (Titus 3: 14 NEB; RSV 'apply themselves to good deeds'). The verse sounds more like social-economic advice for Cretans, who were described as 'lazy gluttons' (1: 12–13)

The difficulty, to repeat, with all the quite specific details in the pastorals about Timothy, Titus, and Paul is that these can be read as historical fact (guaranteeing authenticity) or as fictional touches by a writer who knew Acts and Paul's own letters and had a good imagination—or (still others would say) as genuine fragments or traditions embedded within what later hands have written. The portrait of Onesiphorus, for example, is quite vivid: he is said to have rendered service to Paul in Ephesus and to have sought out the imprisoned apostle in Rome (2 Tim. 1: 16–18; 4: 19). The detail that Paul, in his last days, craves the cloak, the books, and the parchments left at Troas (1 Tim. 4: 13) is moving. The appeal that Timothy 'come before winter' (and Paul's imminent death, 2 Tim. 4: 21) is poignant (and the subject of later powerful sermons). But are they historical, or literary touches? The list of greetings in 2 Tim. 4: 9–21 is impressive (the only place in the pastorals where this epistolary feature occurs). But are they culled from other letters (e.g. Demas, Luke, Mark, and Tychicus from Philemon and Col. 4; Prisca, Aquila, and Erastus from Rom. 16: 3, 23) or simply new inventions (about Crescens in 2 Tim. 4: 9 nothing else is known)? To write that 'Luke alone is with me' (4: 11) and then have three other men, a woman, and 'all the brethren' send greetings (4: 21) seems inconsistent on any reading.

Another avenue of approach to the pastorals is through their genre. Usually all three are called 'letters' and are said to deal with 'church office' and false teaching, and with Paul's imminent fate. But contents vary. The instructions about church office occur primarily in 1 Timothy. Paul's fate is chiefly depicted in 2 Timothy. Opponents crop up in all three letters, though they are most prominent in 1 Timothy. But is there one consistent group of enemies?

Older analysis, taking the pastorals as a group, saw all three as letters of instruction to younger 'clergy' leaders by Paul. More critical treatment suggested that we have in 1 Timothy a 'church order', in 2 Timothy a 'farewell address', and in Titus instructions for a missionary church being planted, each document also including biographical and epistolary trimmings. Most recently, rhetorical criticism has seen personal 'paraenetic letters', especially in 1 and 2 Timothy, where the model teacher offers reminders and exhortations to pupils for their life and work (Johnson, *The Writings of the New Testament*).

A further attempt to solve problems in the pastorals has been made by analysing those against whom the polemic is directed. Are they Jews, gnostics, or schismatics who have broken away from the Church of Paul, Timothy, and Titus? Controversies do loom large (1 Tim. 1: 4; 6: 4; 2 Tim. 2: 23; Titus 3: 9). It is often stated that the author of the pastorals simply blasts away at these opponents as liars and deceivers who 'must be silenced' (Titus 1: 11), in contrast to Paul's method of refuting by appeal to the Old Testament, credal statements, or Christian experience.

A closer look at 1 Timothy suggests that those 'certain persons' who teach different doctrines (1: 3, 19) are Christians who 'have made shipwreck of their faith'; among them two are named, Hymenaeus and Alexander. The deviance of such teachers seems now Jewish ('to become teachers of the law', 1: 7), now gnostic (forbidding marriage and foods God created, 4: 3), their characteristics sometimes capable of interpretation in either direction (the 'myths' and 'genealogies', 1: 4, could refer to rabbinic Haggadah or gnostic speculations about aeons). The attempt to find behind 6: 20 ('contradictions (Greek *antitheseis*) of what is falsely called knowledge') a reference to the book called

Antitheses by the great but ultimately heretical theologian Marcion in the mid-second century does not attract much support today. For the opponents in 1 Timothy, the author takes time to correct their views on law (1: 8–9), creation's gifts (4: 4–5), and proper 'training' in faith (1: 4) or godliness (4: 8–10).

In 2 Timothy one meets again with Hymenaeus who, together with Philetus, is said to teach that 'the resurrection is past already'. This probably means that they held that they were already raised, into the full new life. Thus they are Christians who 'have swerved from the truth' and are now 'upsetting the faith of some' (2: 17). Is the picture in ch. 3, about those who 'in the last days' will 'make their way into households and capture weak women' (3: 1–7), concerned with the same deviants or with a different group? Or is it a composite warning about a stereotyped apocalyptic endtime? In Titus, the section (1: 10–16) on 'all too many . . . who are out of all control' (1: 10 NEB) seems to reflect conditions peculiar to Crete and especially the circumcision party (RSV; Jews? or 'Jewish converts', NEB).

It is, of course, possible to blend together data from all three letters to make a composite profile of the opponents. But it is also possible to see a variety of opposition groups, either in Paul's day or as a device by a Paulinist to warn against all sorts of later synergistic trends. What cannot be said is that conclusions emerge about the false teachers which make the setting of the letters very precise. Perhaps the sheer amount of polemic is what is most striking (a feature also to be seen in Jude and 2 Peter). Invective is sustained over several verses, rather than in a single angry outburst like Gal. 5: 12 or Phil. 3: 2 (with its word-play in Greek about circumcision and mutilation).

None the less, attempts to reconstruct the historical situation in which the pastorals emerged continue to be advanced. For instance, the pastorals contain anti-feminist passages, like 1 Tim. 3: 11–15 ('I permit no woman to teach . . . Adam was not deceived but the woman was deceived') or 4: 7 (about 'old wives' tales', AV). It has been urged by some scholars that a portion of a later document in the New Testament apocrypha, the Acts of Paul, was written in the late second century AD in opposition to this view. The sections in these Acts concerning Thecla tell of a woman who was converted by Paul's preaching and, after many vicissitudes, sent by him to preach; she 'enlightened many with the word of God'. At the house of Onesiphorus in Iconium, she testified to how Jesus was her 'helper in prison' (cf. 2 Tim. 4: 16–17) and 'helper among the beasts' (2 Tim. 4: 17). More recently, the putative sequence has been reversed, with the claim that oral traditions and stories told by women preachers in Asia Minor antedate the pastorals and reflect the Pauline heritage of equality for women. The pastorals would then be a male chauvinist counterblast from another segment of the Paulinist movement, seeking to put women in a subservient place! On this analysis, the Acts of Paul deserves a place of authority that the three ecclesiastical letters in the canon have usurped. It cannot be said, however, that those involved in canonical criticism are impressed with this theory.

Theological themes

Recognizing that each letter is distinctive in some ways, can one find certain theological themes running through the three pastorals? How do they measure up concerning the topics by which we have been characterizing all the New Testament documents? Controversy, as has been noted, is reflected in each letter. As an antidote to wrong teaching, sound doctrine is again and again urged (1 Tim. 1: 10; cf. 6: 3; 2 Tim. 1: 13; 4: 3; Titus 1: 9). Often right teaching takes the form of hymns (1 Tim. 2: 5–6; 3: 16; 2 Tim. 1: 9–10, 11–13; Titus 3: 4–7), which are christological and about salvation, but also about God (1 Tim. 6: 15–16). But there is built in also a moral concern about remaining faithful (2 Tim. 2: 13), and conclusions are drawn about behaviour in the household of God (1 Tim. 3: 15), leading to 'good deeds' (or 'honourable occupations' in the world, Titus 3: 8 RSV).

The teaching of the pastorals is anchored by and finds its norm in the gospel (1 Tim. 1: 11), i.e. 'in accordance with the glorious gospel of the blessed God' with which Paul has specifically been entrusted (2 Tim. 1: 11). Hence Paul can speak of 'my gospel', referring to a formulation about Jesus' Davidic descent and resurrection (2 Tim. 2: 8). It is something God has entrusted to Paul, with a 'pattern' or outline (2 Tim. 1: 12–13), which brings life and immortality and the power of God, even as the apostle suffers for it (2 Tim. 1: 8, 10). Timothy's own ministry is also 'the work of an evangelist', i.e. one who spreads the gospel (2 Tim. 4: 5 NEB).

The kingdom of Christ is once mentioned (2 Tim. 4: 1). Reflecting Old Testament usage, however, God is twice referred to as 'the king' (1 Tim. 1: 17; 6: 15). The 'heavenly kingdom' for which 'the Lord will rescue me' (2 Tim. 4: 18) is probably God's. There is a similar overlap involving God and Christ with the use of the term 'Saviour'. As in the Hebrew Scriptures, God can be so designated (1 Tim. 1: 1; 2: 3; 4: 10; Titus 1: 3; 2: 10; 3: 4; cf. Ps. 27: 1, 9; Isa. 12: 2). When Jesus is given the same title (2 Tim. 1: 10; Titus 1: 4; 3: 6), it need not be a term from the Greek world. At Titus 2: 13 it is difficult to decide whether God or Christ is meant by the term, but that is because the Greek can be read to call Jesus 'our great God and Saviour' or to refer to 'the great God' and 'our Saviour Jesus Christ' (see RSV text and note).

Christologically, the pastorals thus reflect on Jesus as Saviour, Lord, and possibly God. He is the one mediator between God and humanity (1 Tim. 2: 5), who 'gave himself as a ransom for all' (2: 6; cf. Mark 10: 45). There are several references to how God's 'goodness and loving kindness' (Greek *philanthrōpia*, a good Hellenistic term) were manifested in Christ (Titus 3: 4; cf. 2: 11; 2 Tim. 1: 10). This is an 'epiphany' Christology, though it is not 'incarnational' in the same way as John 1: 14. But Jesus' Cross, death, and blood, as in Paul's acknowledged letters, and even 'reconciliation', as in Colossians–Ephesians, are absent. Harking back to Paul's own usage, however, Jesus is also mentioned as future judge of the living and the dead (2 Tim. 4: 1; cf. 4: 8).

While one might expect the eschatology in the pastorals to move in the direction of present realization of the final hope, that position is characteristic of the heretics Hymenaeus and Philetus in their extreme view that 'our resurrection has already taken place' (2 Tim. 2: 18 NEB). True to Paul's reservation about eschatological existence in the present, the pastorals hold doggedly to Christ as 'our hope' (1 Tim. 1: 1) who 'was taken up in glory' (1 Tim. 3: 16) and who will 'on that Day' appear as judge (2 Tim. 4: 8; cf. 1: 18). But instead of 'parousia', the word 'appearing' (literally 'epiphany') is used (1 Tim. 6: 14; 2 Tim. 4: 1, 8; Titus 2: 13). 'Eternal life' is not, as in John's Gospel, something present now but is a future eschatological hope (2 Tim. 1: 1; Titus 1: 2).

The concept of faith is heavily on the side of belief as something which has contents, 'that which one believes'. 'The faith' (1 Tim. 1: 2; 4: 1, 6; 6: 10, 12, 21; 2 Tim. 4: 7; Titus 1: 13) means faith in Christ (1 Tim. 1: 16; 2 Tim. 1: 12) and in God (Titus 3: 8), as Paul sets it forth. It is therefore a 'common faith' (Titus 1: 4), a 'sincere' faith (1 Tim. 1: 5; 2 Tim. 1: 5), which, however, some deny (1 Tim. 1: 19; 2 Tim. 2: 18). There can thus be 'counterfeit faith' (2 Tim. 3: 8). The personal or subjective side is suggested at 2 Tim. 2: 18 or 3: 15 ('salvation through faith'). 'The faith of God's elect' at Titus 1: 1 has sometimes been taken as a parallel to 'their knowledge of the truth'—that is, Paul furthers orthodox belief. But it may fit better with Paul's more usual use: the apostle is 'marked . . . by faith' (NEB), and faith is the way God's chosen people respond.

The term 'mystery' is applied in 1 Timothy in a new way—not to God's plan, Christ, or Christ and the church (cf. Colossians and Ephesians) but to the content of our faith; see 3: 9 and 16, followed by a credal summary. The 'faith' is associated with truth (1 Tim. 2: 7), love (1 Tim. 1: 14; 2 Tim. 1: 13), love and holiness or purity (1 Tim. 2: 15; 4: 12), and other virtues (1 Tim. 6: 11; 2 Tim. 2: 22; 3: 10), even 'a good conscience' (1 Tim. 1: 19). It can denote 'fidelity' (Titus 2: 10). The Greek term is on one occasion masked in English by reference to 'the first pledge' which widows took when placed on a community roll, in the sense of pledge of faith (1 Tim. 5: 12).

A special series of statements in all three pastorals is

introduced by the formula, 'The saying is trustworthy' (RSV 'sure'; NEB 'words you may trust'), perhaps a parallel to Paul's formula, 'God is faithful' (1 Cor. 1: 9). Found nowhere else in the New Testament, these 'faithful' sayings are about Christ (1 Tim. 1: 15; Titus 3: 8, with reference to 3: 4–7) and Christian living (1 Tim. 4: 9–10; 2 Tim. 2: 11–13). Use of the phrase at 1 Tim. 3: 1 is usually taken to refer to what follows about being a bishop, rather than the sentiments about women in 2: 11–15.

Other themes from Paul can be traced in the pastoral epistles for their continuity and fresh developments. Justification or righteousness by grace through faith is echoed as a Christian experience at Titus 3: 7, actualized in baptism (3: 5–6), and rooted ultimately in the fact that Jesus 'was justified' (1 Tim. 3: 16 RSV note). But the theme is more connected with living 'upright' lives now (Titus 2: 12; 1 Tim. 6: 11; 2 Tim. 2: 22). Reflecting Hellenistic use, the term 'holy' is associated with 'upright' (Titus 1: 8), and 'godliness' appears with it, or where Paul might have employed 'righteousness' (e.g. 1 Tim. 4: 7–8; 6: 3, 5–6, 11; Titus 1: 1).

It is ecclesiology, however, that often seems to dominate the letters to Timothy and Titus. Yet they are 'pastoral' epistles, to individuals, not to congregations. The word 'church' is rarely used. It appears only at 1 Tim. 3: 15 to explain what the more common theme of 'the household of God' denotes; at 3: 5, 'God's church'; and 5: 16, for the community. While the three letters contain *Haustafeln* material only at Titus 2: 2–10 (for older men and women, younger women, slaves and masters) and 3: 1–2 (rulers and authorities; cf. 1 Tim. 2: 2), they have taken over quite fully the old Greek idea of the household as the basic unit of society. Here all is to be well-run and orderly. In laying down requirements for a bishop or deacon, the list insists that 'he must manage his own household well' (1 Tim. 3: 4–5, 12). Children and grandchildren should first practise piety in their own household (1 Tim. 5: 4, RSV 'family').

From the household rightly run, it is but a step to the 'household of God' and proper behaviour there (1 Tim. 3: 5, 15). This image will also appear in 1 Peter and Hebrews. It could have associations with 'the house of Israel' or of David in the Old Testament, or the house of God (Gen. 28: 17), especially the temple sanctuary (Ps. 84: 10). Or one could recall that Ephesians spoke of church people as 'members of the household of God' and as a growing building or temple (2: 19–22). But the usage in the pastorals is a reflection of social setting in the Graeco-Roman world. The figure is one where Hellenistic believers could be 'at home', in church as well as in society. The patriarchal attitudes toward women and an emphasis on well-ordered structure for the church found in the pastorals probably came from the influence of this 'household' theme (Schuessler Fiorenza, *In Memory of Her*, 285–91).

The other description used at 1 Tim. 3: 15 to characterize 'the church of the living God' calls it 'the pillar and bulwark of the truth'. More than rhetorical imagery is involved in this phrase, which looks in two directions. The 'support beam' and 'fortress' for the house is first 'what we confess', the 'mystery' of the faith, summed up here in the christological assertion in v. 16. But in context the pillar has also been taken to be Timothy as a representative of the Pauline gospel (vv. 14–15 then amount to instructions on how Timothy is to behave) or, better, the local congregation, members of which are to conduct themselves in a way that exemplifies, supports, and defends the true faith. The image may be static, not dynamic, but it is meant to present the church standing solidly amid 'times of stress' (2 Tim. 3: 1), guarding, like the apostle, the truth which God has entrusted (2 Tim. 1: 12, 14). The church in the pastorals, it may be added, appears to be a regional one—in Crete (Titus) or the Ephesus region (1 Timothy), with little about local congregations or on a 'universal church' as in Ephesians. (The geographical references in 2 Timothy come closest to this world-wide interest, but that letter says little about ecclesiology.)

The ministry as an emphasis

It is on references to ministries found in the pastorals that the greatest interest and debates have focused, down to the present day. Some have seen a blueprint here for the 'threefold ministry' of bishop (monarchical episcopacy, an *episkopos* reigning alone in each church or region), presbyters (equated with pastors and later with priests), and deacons as a third order above the laity. On the other hand, modern critical studies have placed question marks against the supposed evidence, here and elsewhere, for such a view. One result of this scholarly work is that the major ecumenical statement in this century on the ordained ministry holds that 'the New Testament does not describe a single pattern' for ministry, and that 'a threefold pattern of bishop, presbyter, and deacon became established as the pattern of ministry throughout the Church' only 'during the second and third centuries' (*BEM* 'Ministry' 19). What do the pastorals say on such matters?

Paul appears in the salutation of all three letters as 'apostle', a title reiterated along with 'herald' or preacher and 'teacher' (1 Tim. 2: 7; 2 Tim. 1: 11). Other apostles, 'the twelve' (1 Cor. 15: 5, 7), and congregational 'apostles' like Epaphroditus (Phil. 2: 25, your commissioned 'messenger', RSV) are never mentioned in the pastorals. While the three pastoral epistles do not literally refer to Paul as '*the* apostle' (with the article), he is the one to whom the gospel has uniquely been entrusted (1 Tim. 1: 1), whose gospel and ways Timothy and Titus are in turn to follow, imitate, and transmit to 'faithful persons' who, in turn, will teach others. To this extent there is an 'apostolic succession'—to Paul's teachings.

Timothy and Titus are each described in the salutations as Paul's '(true) child in the (common) faith'. By following his 'words of faith' and 'good doctrine', each will prove to be a 'good minister' or 'workman' and 'evangelist' (1 Tim. 4: 6, 16; 2 Tim. 2: 15; 4: 5; cf. Titus 2: 7). In connection with the public reading of Scripture, preaching, and teaching which he is to do, Timothy is reminded of 'the gift' he has, given 'through prophecy together with the laying on of hands of the group of elders' (*presbyterion*, 1 Tim. 4: 14); cf. 2 Tim. 1: 6, 'the gift of God that is within you through the laying on of my hands', Paul writes. (The NEB note takes 4: 14 to mean 'ordination as an elder', and 1 Tim. 6: 11–16 has been seen as wording from an ordination service of the day.) But no other titles beyond 'person of God' (1 Tim. 6: 11) are used for Timothy or Titus. We do well to avoid later epithets like 'apostolic legates' or 'missionary vicars'.

A good deal of the paraenesis or exhortation and instruction in the letters is addressed directly to Timothy (1 Tim. 1: 18–19; 3: 15; 4: 6–5: 23; 6: 2b, 11–16, 20–1; 2 Tim. 1: 4–2: 16; 2: 22–3; 3: 1–4: 4; 4: 9–16, 19–22a) or to Titus (1: 5; 2: 1–10, 15; 3: 1, 8b–15) in the singular. Words like 'Be [thou] strong in the grace that is in Christ Jesus' (2 Tim. 2: 1) could, of course, apply to any Christian. Custom, carelessness, or scribal additions make each letter close with the words, 'Grace be with you [*plural*]', in spite of the previous 'you [*singular*]'.

There are surprisingly few allusions to 'rank-and-file' members of the Church. 'Saints' appears as a term only at 1 Tim. 5: 10; 'the elect' only at 2 Tim. 2: 10 and Titus 1: 1; 'brethren' (and sisters) a little more at 1 Tim. 4: 6; 6: 2; 2 Tim. 4: 21; 'believers' and 'beloved' ones, at 1 Tim. 6: 2; cf. also 'those who believe', 1 Tim. 4: 3, 10, 12; 5: 16 ('believing woman'). Is this because the letters are directed to leaders?

Much of the pastorals' paraenetic material instructing Christians has to do with family, social, civil, and even business life. Recall the *Haustafeln*, and consider 1 Tim. 2: 1–2, 8–10 (prayers for all, including kings); 5: 3–16; 6: 1–2; and especially Titus 2: 1–10; 3: 1–2, 8. 'Christian citizenship' implies 'courtesy toward all' and gentleness while applying oneself in an 'honourable occupation' (Titus 3: 2; 3: 8 RSV note), so that Christians are 'useful to their fellow-men' (as NEB renders 3: 8; cf. 3: 14). God seeks 'a pure people marked out for his own, eager to do good' (Titus 2: 14 NEB); but the rather obvious admonitions that older women should not be 'slaves to drink' or that young women should be trained to love their husbands and children (Titus 2: 3–4), and the minimal qualities of character sought in church leaders (below), have led to the observation that Christian teaching includes 'instruction in civility'. The pastorals are more than affirmation of the world. In Titus, it has been suggested, 'the gospel itself has a civilizing function: it teaches people how to become members of a society' (Johnson, *The Writings of the New Testament*, 404). Is the ministry of God's people therefore 'service in the world' in this sense?

The church community includes widows in sufficient numbers to necessitate guidelines (1 Tim. 5: 3–16) for distinguishing 'real ones' (without family) and providing for their enrolment (if over 60, after a life of piety), for church support, and for service by them (continuing in prayer and perhaps hospitality and relief of the afflicted). The problem of widows also appears in Acts 6: 1–7, in the account of the early community in Jerusalem, where the matter led to ethnic or language-background controversy.

The most disputed area involves passages in the pastorals about 'bishops', 'elders' (Greek *presbyteroi*), and 'deacons', to cite the RSV rendering. Even the translations have been debated for centuries. The Greek *episkopos* means 'overseer'. The AV, most translations influenced by it, and churches with episcopal structure have generally insisted on 'bishop' for the term. But now the NEB has 'leadership' and 'leader' alongside 'bishop' at 1 Tim. 3: 1–2. *Presbyteroi* could refer to elders in a Jewish synagogue or to 'presbyters' in Christianity (so NABRNT consistently). Paul in his acknowledged letters never uses this term; Acts and the pastorals do. Most translations settle on 'elders' as the rendering in 1 Timothy and Titus. The problem with *diakonos* is that, while it comes to refer to the 'office' of deacon (which has had a very chequered history of interpretations), the Greek could also mean 'minister' and be used also of Timothy (1 Tim. 4: 6; cf. 2 Tim. 4: 5), of Onesiphorus (2 Tim. 1: 18, verb), and of Paul's own service (*diakonia*, 1 Tim. 1: 12), and Mark's (2 Tim. 4: 11). It seems often in the pastorals a generic, not yet a technical, term.

In several passages in the pastorals, number (singular or plural) and gender (masculine and feminine) alternate. Were there 'deaconesses' or female elders/presbyters? The aspects listed for each group involve, not duties, but characteristics needed to hold position or play the role. (In 1 Tim. 3: 1 'office of bishop', in both AV and RSV, is an attempt to translate the

abstract noun anglicized in modern ecumenical discussion as
episcopé, as *BEM* 'Ministry' 53 spells it; there is literally no word
for 'office' in the Greek there.) To our surprise, liturgical
functions, above all at the Eucharist, are never mentioned in the
pastorals. That leaders be 'apt to teach' (what Paul taught) is not
surprising in the documents. A striking number of phrases
suggest administrative ability, something that would have been
well received in the Roman world.

A key issue is the relation of 'elders', the topic in Titus 1: 5–6,
and 'bishop' in what follows (1: 7–9). Some have viewed vv. 7–9
as a later interpolation to bring in the monarchical episcopate
such as Ignatius of Antioch championed in the second century.
Others see a traditional Graeco-Roman source applied here to
the *episkopos* and in 1 Tim. 3 to both bishop and deacons. Some
of the very same characteristics crop up also in commonplace
tables from antiquity, such as schoolboys might have memor-
ized, for 'qualities of a good general' or other leaders in the
Graeco-Roman sources. (Such terms are asterisked below.)
Titus 1: 5–9 also raises the question of whether a bishop was
chosen from among the 'presbyters', as indicated here, or out of
the ranks of 'deacons', as appears in other sources.

The evidence, which repays careful scrutiny, can be laid out as
follows:

1 Timothy 3: 2–7 (RSV):	*Titus 1: 5–9 (RSV):*
Overseer/Bishop:	Elders (5–6)/Bishop (7–9):
above reproach (v. 2)	cf. blameless (6, 7)
husband of one wife (2)	husband of one wife (6)
	not profligate (6)
	not insubordinate (6)
	God's steward (7)
*temperate (2)	cf. self-controlled (8)
*sensible (2)	cf. master of himself (8)
dignified (2)	cf. lover of goodness (8)
hospitable (2)	hospitable (8)
an apt teacher (2)	cf. hold firm the word as taught (9)
no drunkard (3)	not a drunkard (7)

not violent (3)
but gentle (3)
not quarrelsome (3)
no lover of money (3)
manages his own house well (4)
*children submissive and
   respectful (4)
not a recent convert (6)
well thought of by outsiders (7)

not violent (7)
cf. not arrogant (7)
cf. not quick-tempered (7)
cf. not greedy for gain (7)

children are believers (5)

upright (8)
holy (8)

1 Timothy 3: 8–13 (RSV):

Deacons:

serious (8); cf. 11
not double-tongued (8); cf. 5: 17 and Titus 1: 9 about 'the word'
not addicted to much wine (8); cf. 3: 3 and Titus 1: 7
not greedy for gain (8): cf. 3: 3 and Titus 1: 7
hold the faith with a clear conscience (9); cf. 3: 2 and Titus 1: 9
be tested first (10)
prove blameless (10); cf. Titus 1: 6, 7
husband of one wife (12); cf. 3: 2 and Titus 1: 6
manage children and household well (12); cf. 3: 4 and Titus 1: 6

The Women:

serious (11); cf. 8
no slanderers (11); cf. Titus 2: 3
temperature (11)
faithful in all things (11); cf. Titus 1: 6, faithful children

1 Timothy 5: 17–19 (RSV):   *Titus 1: 5–6 (7–9) (RSV):*

(see above on Elders/Bishop)

Elders:

who 'rule well' (governing
   elders); cf. 1 Tim. 3: 5
are worthy of double honour,
   especially those who 'labour
   in preaching [the word] and
   teaching'   cf. 1: 9, the 'sure word'; sound
cf. 1 Tim. 3: 2, apt teacher   doctrine

wages deserved (18)
charges heard only from 2–3
   witnesses (cf. Deut. 19: 15)

Such orderly but not quite parallel lists call for some orderly comments.

   1. In no letter are three groups clearly mentioned together. 1 Timothy has 'bishop and deacons' in ch. 3, 'elders' only briefly in ch. 5. Titus speaks of 'elders', then 'bishop' in ch. 1, with characteristics from the 'deacons' list' in 1 Tim. 3 cropping up to describe what elders/bishop should be (1: 6–9). 1 Timothy is enigmatic, in that the 'elders who rule well' (5: 17) do what 'the bishop' does at 3: 5, namely rule (RSV 'manage') a household (shifting in 3: 5 to 'care for God's church', perhaps because it is assumed the church is under not human but divine rule). Reading the texts as they stand, many scholars have opted for the view that elder and bishop are interchangeable terms in the pastorals (cf. also Acts 20: 17, 28; 1 Peter 5: 1–2, elders 'tend the flock').
   2. Stages in the still-fluid development of ministries are reflected. It is difficult to conceive of the threefold ministry in Paul's own day (but cf. Johnson, *The Writings of the New Testament*, 398–402), and one ought to be hesitant about seeing church orders and liturgies of later times even if the pastorals are dated in the second century. It is possible that the three letters are an attempt to conflate the structure of 'overseers and deacons' in Philippi (Phil. 1: 1), which may have grown into a 'Pauline model', with the model of 'elders' derived from the synagogue (Dunn, *Unity and Diversity*, 115–16). It is attractive to see much in the pastorals as reflecting how diaspora synagogues were organized for charitable deeds, education, learning, and worship, with a 'ruler of the synagogue', group of 'elders' (of senior years), and assistants.
   3. In spite of the pastorals' attitude that women should not teach or have authority over men (1 Tim. 2: 12), women probably were deacons (1 Tim. 3: 11, sandwiched between 3: 8–11 and 12–13 about male deacons), and widows had tasks

assigned to them of prayer and ministering (1 Tim. 5: 5, 10). As heads of households, women like Lydia (Acts 16: 14–15, 40) may elsewhere have been presbyter-bishops. Women might have even been part of a *presbyterion* or group of elders (1 Tim. 4: 14), with roles like men who were elders (1 Tim. 5: 1–2). But the pastorals exclude them, then, from the position of 'ruling elder' or 'bishop' (1 Tim. 5: 17; 2: 12 with 3: 1–7; cf. Schuessler Fiorenza, *In Memory of Her*, 288–91). In this case the Greek patriarchal idea of the household, more than the synagogue model, has taken over.

4. The distressingly minimal standards for all types of leaders—surely less than Paul called for from every believer—reflect the probable origins of such lists in the world of the day, putting emphasis on family, civic image, administrative ability, and some moral qualities. A growing church in the pagan world proved realistic in assessing possible leadership. But 'pagan'—a word often with negative connotations today—is not one the pastorals use. They employ the Greek word which *can* be rendered as 'pagan', to speak positively of Paul as 'teacher of *the Gentiles*' (1 Tim. 2: 7; 2 Tim. 4: 17; cf. 1 Tim. 3: 16). The pastorals thus reflect leadership in and for the Gentile world.

5. The point is well taken (Johnson, *The Writings of the New Testament*, 385, 401) that nothing the pastorals say on groups of leaders is rooted in 'God's will' or plan or in the gospel. Even if we translate as 'bishop, elder, and deacon', the names are not put into any hierarchical order. The focus is on practical tasks.

6. Often overlooked is the phrase introduced at Titus 1: 7, the bishop as 'God's steward' (*oikonomos*). The term again reflects the 'household (*oikos*, of God)' idea. It is to be related to the Pauline theme set forth at the beginning of 1 Timothy: 'God's plan for us, which works through faith' (1: 4 NEB). As the RSV's three renderings show, the word here (*oikonomia*) also carried with it connotations of 'order', 'training' in faith, or 'stewardship', here stewardship on God's part. The role which leadership plays must reflect God's dealings with us.

Developed in many subsequent directions, the sections on

ministers in the pastorals proved influential for later episcopacy, presbyterial governance, and threefold ministry. Another contribution of the three letters was to show how Paulinists could sustain the future aspect in eschatology, that Christ will appear, just as they also had emphasized present realization of eschatology (Colossians–Ephesians).

A single verse at 2 Tim. 3: 16 has also proved immensely significant for later doctrines of the inspiration of Scripture. Although the pastorals have relatively little to say about the Holy Spirit (cf. 2 Tim. 1: 14; Titus 3: 5; 1 Tim. 4: 1), this statement asserts, 'All scripture is inspired by God and profitable for teaching, for reproof, for correction, and for training in righteousness.' The context is the work of the person of God— here Timothy—who long knew the 'sacred writings' (the Old Testament) that can 'wise one up' to salvation. For the sense, it matters little where we insert the verb 'is' (cf. RSV note; NEB). It is the uses of inspired Scripture which are at stake. The uses do not surprise the reader of the pastorals: 'teaching the truth and refuting error, . . . reformation of manners and discipline in right living' (NEB) are aims of these books, as Paul speaks to a more Hellenized world.

In the final analysis, the contributions of the pastoral epistles to New Testament unity and variety turn out to be curiously akin to the title of the Chair of Professor Paul Anton at Halle, the man who first called them 'pastorals': Exegesis (of Paul's faith), Polemics (against false teachers), and Practical Theology (for ordering God's household in the world of the day, indeed, civilizing converts in society).

✓ *1 Peter: Apostolic Exhortation to Living Hope, Confidence, and Holiness, under Pressure*

'THE First Epistle General of Peter', as the AV called this letter of five chapters, addresses people who reside in what is nowadays Turkey who have newly come to faith (2: 1). Over the centuries, the document has received all sorts of interpretations, ranging from the view that it is first-hand encouragement about 'the true grace of God' (5: 12) by the prince of the apostles himself, Peter, to the suggestion that 1 Peter is or reflects a baptismal liturgy, addressed to victims of the persecution under the Emperor Trajan in the second century! Such diversity of opinions about setting arises from the contents themselves. One difficulty is that 1 Peter sounds now like Paul (cf. 2: 4–10 with Rom. 9: 25–33), now like James (cf. 5: 5–9 with James 4: 6–10), now like the Deutero-Paulinists (in use of *Haustafeln* material; cf. Ch. 8 above). What, then, characterizes 1 Peter in relation to other early Christian writings?

The document begins and ends like most New Testament letters. Peter addresses 'the exiles of the Dispersion' in five provinces of Asia Minor (1: 1–2). But little more is said about Peter than that he is 'an apostle of Jesus Christ' (1: 1) and 'fellow elder and a witness of the sufferings of Christ as well as a partaker in the glory that is to be revealed' (5: 1, something many Christians could say, unless we assumes '*eye*witness' is meant). No individual church is mentioned, for presumably the messenger went first to Pontus on the Black Sea, then south through Galatia and Cappadocia, and west to the provinces of Asia (where Ephesus was the chief city), and finally north to

Bithynia, if the sequence of 1:1 is to be taken seriously. The term 'Dispersion' could be a technical one for Jews living outside Palestine. But since the letter implies several times that those addressed were Gentile converts (cf. 1: 14, 18; 2: 9–10, 4: 3), it is widely agreed that the phrase is now being applied to Christians as 'God's scattered people who lodge for a while' in these areas (1: 1 NEB), perhaps a mixed group, but mostly Gentiles.

The closing greetings (5: 12–14) identify the place of writing as 'Babylon', a soubriquet for Rome in Jewish and early Christian usage; cf. Rev. 17–18. The community there ('she . . . who is likewise chosen') sends greetings, as does Mark. Silvanus the scribe is probably to be identified with the Silas of Acts 15–17. These two names connect the letter with Pauline mission work (Philem. 24; 2 Cor. 1: 19; 2 Tim. 4: 11; 1 and 2 Thess. 1: 1).

Contents in relation to other New Testament writings

Instead of Paul's usual prayer style, one finds in 1 Peter 1: 3–12 a formulation that begins 'Blessed be God' (as in 2 Cor. 1: 3 and Eph. 1: 3). The gist of these verses is to emphasize joy over the living hope to which those addressed have been 'born anew' (1: 3, 23; cf. 2: 3), through Jesus' resurrection and God's word proclaimed to them and actualized in baptism. (The term 'baptism' is not found until 3: 21, but the imagery in 1: 22–2: 3 is taken by many as baptismal.) There is frequent emphasis on a contrast between the past and the present of these converts (1: 18 and 21; 2: 10, 25; 3: 21). Yet already at 1: 6–7 there is allusion to suffering 'various trials'.

One characteristic of 1 Peter is that, instead of the pattern in Paul's letters—where indicative statements come first, spread over several chapters about what God has done to us, then imperatives or exhortations—here short kerygmatic statements are followed by exhortations, then another indicative declaration together with an exhortation. Thus, after reference to 'the grace that is yours' (1: 10), admonitions follow in 1: 13–17, including 'Set your hope fully on the grace that is coming to you at the revelation of Jesus Christ' (1: 13). After a reminder of how 'the precious blood of Christ' ransomed them (1: 18), there is admonition to 'love one another' (1: 22). This intertwining of kerygma and ethical teaching makes 1 Peter difficult to outline.

The body of the letter consists of assertions and admonitions about the Christian life. Because the verb 'I beseech (exhort)' occurs at 2: 11 and 5:1, these verses have been taken by some as turning-points. The result is, then, exhortations first to all the 'beloved', as 'aliens and exiles' in the world (2: 11–4: 19), and then exhortations to 'the elders' (5: 1 ff.). But 5: 5 is addressed to 'those who are younger' and 5: 6–11 to all, so the 'elders' section (5: 1–4) is disproportionately short. The transition at 2: 11 is better seen as a shift from the self-identity of God's people (2: 5–10) to their role in the world, 'among the Gentiles' (2: 12). Relations with the State (emperor, governor) then follow (2: 13–17), and tables of instructions for household servants (2: 18–25), wives (3: 1), and husbands (3: 7), before all Christians are again addressed (3: 8–4: 1). The appeals are constantly underpinned by christological statements (e.g. 3: 17–18; 4: 1).

Just as the document seems to be moving toward a conclusion at 4: 11 with a doxology and 'amen', there is suddenly a new beginning at 4:12. This is not simply a matter of the repetition of 'Beloved', the address also found at 2: 11, and a reiteration of what 1: 6 had said, about rejoicing amid sufferings. There is really a triple shift. (1) The *possibility* of suffering (1: 6; 2: 20; 3: 17, 'if it should be God's will') now becomes much more a reality (cf. 4: 12, 14, 19; 5: 6, 8) and specifically suffering 'as a Christian' (4: 16). (2) We no longer sense as directly that newly baptized Christians are being addressed. (3) The verses take on a more epistolary tone, with more ecclesial details. The focus is not on 'good conduct among the Gentiles' (2: 12) but on how those who, for all their 'doing good' (4: 19 NEB), suffer, are to entrust themselves to God. Indeed, the closing note at 5: 10 (before another doxology and 'amen', 5: 11) is the promise that the God of grace will, after your suffering, 'restore, establish, and strengthen you'.

Traditionally, the letter has been taken as a general exhortation which Peter wrote from Rome in AD 63–4 (or 67) before his own martyrdom. A short time later he was said, in 2 Peter (3: 1), to have referred to it with the words, 'This is now the second letter I have written to you.' But as critical scholarship came to look on 2 Peter as pseudepigraphical (see Ch. 15 below), questions were also raised about the excellent Greek of this first letter (could a Galilean fisherman use, for example, verb forms from classical Greek, employed to express mere possibility, in the optative mood, as found at 3: 14, 17?), and the fact that, contrary to the agreement reported in Gal. 2: 7, Peter would be addressing 'Pauline' territory (recall Galatians; Acts 16: 7). Furthermore, the letter is often seemingly indebted to Paul's thought (even the phrase 'in Christ', 3: 16; 5: 10) and reflects a type of persecution in 4: 12–5: 11 for the very name 'Christian' that fits the time when Pliny was ravaging church gatherings in Bithynia about AD 112, long after Peter's death.

To all these points there are possible replies. It can, for example, be allowed that Peter may not have written Greek so eloquently, but his scribe Silvanus (5: 12) could have been capable of it; then the epistle almost becomes '1 Silvanus'. One apostle being in another's 'territory' is no new matter, for it has been argued, on the basis of 1 Cor. 9: 5 and 1: 12, that during Paul's lifetime Peter was in the Pauline congregation at Corinth. Instead of debating whether 1 Peter borrows from Paul (or vice versa) or from James (or James from 1 Peter), a number of investigators have increasingly concluded that all these writings borrow from common apostolic traditions, hymns, and ethical teaching. And it can be claimed that 1 Peter, especially in 1: 3–4: 11, does not presuppose widespread official governmental efforts to stamp out Christianity, but merely reflects spontaneous local outbursts and malicious accusations (2: 12; 3: 15–16). None the less, a growing number of commentators have dated 1 Peter during the reign of Domitian (AD 81–96) or Trajan (AD 98–117), rather than under Nero in the 60s.

Because of all the references to being 'born anew', some scholars around 1910 claimed that 1 Peter reflected the entry of converts into Christianity from a mystery cult that stressed 'rebirth'; they dated the document in the second century. Others later used the same evidence to leap to a 'liturgical defence': the document reflects a baptismal liturgy or at least a homily at a service of baptism, or two homilies, before and after the actual baptism (the 'new birth'), which was assumed to have occurred between 1: 21 and 1: 22. A further solution was to say merely that language was being used which draws on Christians' recollection of their baptism.

Still others sought a Passover/Easter connection by linking the word for 'suffer' (Greek *paschein*) with the word for Passover (*Pascha*), a word-play later found in the homilies by Melito of Sardis in the second century. The difference in the picture of persecution in the letter before 4: 11 and after 4: 12 was ingeniously explained by the suggestion that a messenger carried two versions of the letter to be read. To Christians not yet under persecution, 2: 11–4: 11 would be read; to those already suffering, 4: 12–5: 11, with 1: 1–2: 10 and 5: 12–14 common to both recensions.

It cannot be said that any one of these theories dominates scholarship today. Versions of each still find supporters. The trends are away from Peter's own authorship and toward seeing 1 Peter as 'apostolic' in the sense of common early 'apostolic traditions'. Indeed, in its contents 1 Peter has ties with Pauline Christianity, Acts (see below, under Christology), and James ('faith tested by trials'; 1: 6–8, cf. James 1: 2–4). But on major points, where is it at one with other New Testament writings and where strikingly different?

Themes in 1 Peter

Although the noun 'gospel' is found in 1 Peter only once (at 4: 17, in a 'judgement' passage about 'those who do not obey the gospel of God'), there are references to 'those who preached the good news to you' (1: 12) and to 'the word of the Lord' (which abides for ever) as 'the good news which was preached to you'. The content of the good news is spelled out in hymnic excerpts about Christ (see 'Christology' below) and ransom by his blood (1: 18), living for righteousness (2: 24), access to God (3: 18), and future, final salvation (1: 5, 9, 10). The broad scope of 'gospelling' includes the statement that 'the gospel was preached even to the dead' (4: 6), which could mean simply that people are 'dead' (in sin) until they are confronted with the life-giving word. In view of 3: 18–20, however, it more likely involves an expedition which Christ made after his death to 'the spirits in prison' in Hades (see below).

The message of good news about Christ is a 'lively' one in 1 Peter, as one might expect with recent converts. The word of God is 'living' (1: 23). Christ is a 'living stone' (2: 4). Believers are to be 'living stones' built into the church (2: 5), with a 'living hope' (1: 3). The fact that the converts addressed live in a Gentile environment may account for the absence of any references to 'the kingdom of God', for Jesus' phrase would be misunderstood by the Roman authorities, the emperor and governors sent by that earthly king (2: 13). The closest 1 Peter comes to 'kingdom of God' language is the reference to the community as a 'royal priesthood' (2: 9), literally 'kingly body of priests', in a quotation from Exod. 19: 6.

The Christology of 1 Peter is extensive and intriguing. Much of it appears in poetic lines which, judging from their structure, must have been part of earlier hymns and creeds. This material deals especially with Jesus' death 'for you', a phrase occurring at 2: 21, and his suffering (or death) concerning sin 'for the unrighteous' (3: 18). As elaborated, the credo in 1 Peter tells how Christ

> was destined before the foundation of the world
> but was made manifest at the end of the times for your sake.
> His blood ransomed you, so that 'through him you have confidence
> in God who raised him from the dead and gave him glory'

(1: 18–21)

This message is reiterated in 2: 21–5 and 3: 18–22. In the first instance it is enriched by allusions to 'the Suffering Servant' of Isaiah 53: 4–9 (italicized below):

> Christ suffered for you . . . .
> He *committed no* sin, *no guile was found on his lips*. . . .

He himself bore our sins in his body on the tree. . . .
By *his wounds you have been healed.*
For you were *straying like sheep,*
but have now returned to the Shepherd and Guardian of your souls.

(2: 21–5)

The second passage is remarkable in that it introduces a 'mission to the underworld' between the time of Jesus' death and the day of his resurrection:

Christ died for sins once for all,
the Righteousness One for the unrighteous,
that he might bring us to God,
being put to death in the flesh
but made alive in the spirit,
in which he went and preached to the spirits in prison. . . .
Through the resurrection Christ has gone up into heaven
and is at the right hand of God,
with angels, authorities, and powers subject to him.

(3: 18–22)

This Christ 'is ready to judge the living and the dead' (4: 5, cf. 17). Christ's glory will be revealed (4: 5) when he, 'the chief Shepherd, is manifest' (5: 4; cf. 2: 25).

1 Peter 3: 19 (cf. 4: 6) became the main New Testament basis for the reference to Christ's 'descent into Hades' in later creeds. (Ephesians 4: 9 was also involved, but Christ's descent here 'into the lower parts of the earth' may mean merely 'the lowest level, down to the very earth', from heaven, not to 'regions beneath the earth'; cf. NEB text and note, where the descent to earth is preferred in the Ephesians context.) The allusion in 1 Peter means at the least to insist that Jesus really died (and went to the 'abode of Hades', as the ancients thought of Sheol or Hades). Opinions vary whether the verses are to be interpreted to mean that Jesus proclaimed doom to 'the imprisoned spirits' there who 'had refused obedience long ago' (3: 19–20 NEB) or 'preached the gospel' (good news of salvation) to them (4: 6). If mission is a leading theme in 1 Peter (cf. 2: 9, God's people are to 'declare the wonderful deeds of the One who called them out of darkness into God's marvelous light'), then Jesus led the way even by

approaching the generation of the flood in Noah's day, deemed a classic example of recalcitrants to God's call.

The Christology of 1 Peter goes further than many New Testament books in asserting the 'Godness' of Jesus. This is done by applying Old Testament verses, which were originally about Yahweh, now to Jesus as 'the Lord'. Compare 3: 14–15, 'Have no fear . . . , reverence *Christ* as Lord' with Isa. 8: 12–13, 'Do not fear . . . , but the Lord of hosts you shall regard as holy.' In this light, 1 Peter 2: 3, 'you have tasted that the Lord is good' (*chrēstos*, Ps. 34: 8), may, as word-play, intend hearers to conclude, 'The Lord is Christ (*Christos*)', but the text does not say this directly.

Among the new titles for Jesus in 1 Peter noted above are '(chief) Shepherd' (2: 25; 5: 4; cf. John 10: 11 and Heb. 13: 20) and 'Guardian (of your souls)' (2: 25, *episkopos*, AV 'Bishop'). The former term derives from Old Testament imagery of God's people as a flock (cf. 5: 2, 3), the latter from 'overseers' in the Greek world (cf. Acts 20: 28). Sometimes the five quotations from Isaiah 53 applied to Jesus in 1 Peter 2: 21–5 (see above) have led to the suggestion that we have here a 'Suffering Servant' Christology. Since Peter's sermons in Acts sometimes refer to Jesus as God's servant (or child; 3: 13, 26; cf. 4: 25, 27, 30; the Greek term *pais*, *paidos* can be translated either way), it has even been suggested that we have here a particularly Petrine way of speaking about Jesus—not a 'Christology' but a 'Paidology' (from the Greek noun for servant). Unfortunately, 1 Peter does not use the term *pais*.

'Living stone' is another title for Jesus at 2: 4. It stems from prophetic use of Ps. 118: 22 (quoted at 2: 7) and of Isa. 28: 16 (quoted at 2: 6) and Isa. 8: 14–15 (at 1 Peter 2: 8). The latter two images, of the chosen and precious corner-stone laid by God in Zion (2: 6) and of a stone that will make people stumble and trip them up (2: 8), are also combined christologically at Rom. 9: 33. We are therefore dealing here with what seems a common early Christian combination of 'stone' passages, applied to Jesus as 'corner-stone' (2: 6).

It is noteworthy also that 1 Peter, in stressing how Christ

suffered (1: 10, 19; 3: 18 RSV note; 4: 1), relates this to believers and their suffering. They are to follow 'in the steps' (2: 21) of their example, Christ, who suffered on their behalf. Their 'good conduct' (2: 12) for righteousness (2: 24) may lead, like Christ's, to suffering (3: 14, 16).

The eschatology of 1 Peter presents the 'already' and 'not yet' of Christian existence, between one's baptism and Christ's appearing, by means of a pair of terms characteristic of the writing. Believers already possess 'rebirth' (1: 3, 23). The term for future fulfilment is 'salvation' (1: 5, 9, 10), in heaven, to be revealed 'in the last times'. Something of 'the end of the times' is already revealed (1: 20) but not the full glory (4: 13; 5: 1). Meanwhile the Spirit is at work, sanctifying us (1: 2; 4: 14 NEB, the glorious Spirit of God), and especially through prophets (1: 11–12; early Christian prophets, not just Old Testament figures, may be meant).

The ecclesiology of 1 Peter unfolds without ever using the word 'church'. Once there is a reference to 'your brotherhood throughout the world' (5: 9 RSV; also at 2: 17; cf. 1: 22; 3: 8; 4: 8). That is not a term found elsewhere in the New Testament. There is no reference, however, to local congregations. In accord with this concept of the Church as a body of brothers and sisters marked by mutual love, there is little on structure. The 'Bishop' is Christ (2: 25). There are 'elders' (but also 'youngers'), and even Peter describes himself simply as an elder too (5: 1–5)

Phrases used originally of Israel in the Old Testament are applied in a remarkable way, in 2: 4–10, to the 'household of God' (4: 17, as in 1 Tim. 3: 15). The 'spiritual house' (2: 5) or world-wide church is based on Christ as corner-stone. To it are referred at 2: 9 a series of collective titles employed by God for Israel at Mount Sinai: 'royal priesthood', 'holy nation', 'a people for God's possession' (RSV note), all from Exod. 19: 5–9 and 23: 22 LXX ('you will be for me a "peculiar" people, . . . a royal priesthood, a holy nation', not in the Hebrew or in English translations). From Isa. 43: 20–1 come the words 'a chosen race' and a 'people . . . for myself'. Most of these phrases have been applied to the community of the Living Stone in previous verses.

This 'house' where the Spirit dwells is seen as people who have received mercy (2: 10; Hos. 1: 6, 9; 2: 1, 23), fulfilling the Mosaic hope for a community in which all might be priests, and declaring 'God's triumphs' in their witness in the world (2: 10 NEB).

In the very next breath, however, 1 Peter describes the addressees as 'aliens and exiles' (2: 11; cf. 1: 1, 17). Such language, coupled with the idea of 'an inheritance . . . in heaven' (1: 4) has often led to a view of Christians as 'pilgrims and strangers' on this earth, their true home being only in heaven (cf. Phil. 3: 20). Sociological analysis suggests, however, that the people addressed in 1 Peter might more literally fit into such a category in the Asia Minor of their day. Culturally, religiously, and socially, these Gentile converts had broken with their old environment, so that people think them strange in their new dedication to God (4: 3–4) and 'speak against' them (2: 12). Families are divided (3: 1–2, the pagan husband), and the world becomes a frightening place (3: 6b, 13–17). Hence the church must become 'home' for these aliens, people who are being built into Christ's house as 'living stones' (2: 5).

The ethics articulated in 1 Peter come especially in the 'household codes', noted previously, which grow in turn out of this 'household' imagery. (See the discussion above, in Ch. 9.) Christians are, as householders, to be 'good stewards of God's varied grace', each employing his/her gift for the sake of others in the community (4: 10–11). There is particular stress on holiness as part of the new life-style. The words of Lev. 11: 44–5 are cited to urge that, as the God who called you is holy, so you are to be holy in all conduct (1: 15–16). What it means to be 'sanctified by the Spirit for obedience to Jesus Christ' (1: 2) is suggested by an insertion on simplicity of life-style in the *Haustafeln* on women (3: 3–5) and the admonition to sanctify Christ even by the way one gently expounds one's faith to others (3: 15).

The treatment of faith begins with the fact that God is a 'faithful Creator' (4: 19). Christians are those who believe in Christ and love him without ever having seen him (1: 8). Since they believe in Christ the corner-stone, they 'will not be put to shame' (a reworking of Isa. 28: 16 in the LXX); this contrasts with those who disbelieve and stumble, destined to disobey, in contrast to the elect (2: 7–8; cf. 1: 2). Faith thus rests on God's power, in those 'guarded through faith for a salvation . . . to be revealed' (1: 5). Church members are to resist the devil, firm in their faith (5: 9), which probably involves both their personal trust and the Christian belief they espouse. Genuineness of faith gets tested, but its outcome is salvation as the result of faith (1: 7, 9). Faith makes people confident and issues in hope (1: 21, cf. RSV note; the reference to 'confidence' or in the NEB 'trust' is for a Greek phrase that means 'those who through Christ believe in or are faithful to God').

The chief contribution of 1 Peter may, however, lie beyond all these theological themes or, better, in the combination of them. This happens in the way 1 Peter makes possible a new note concerning Christian responsibility in the social world. There has been pointed out above a greater affirmation of the world in Colossians–Ephesians and the pastorals than in Paul. But the direction in those deutero-Pauline letters especially concerned the church internally, in its inward nature. The dynamics in 1 Peter, for all the threat of suffering, was different. The document often looks toward the world.

A commentary by a Continental scholar, Bo Reicke, in 1964 argued that the concern of 1 Peter (and James and 2 Peter and Jude) was with 'the right attitude of Christians toward their worldly environment'. The period of Nero and Domitian was one of political and social unrest. In the face of political Zealotism in Rome and strikes and sabotage by slave-workers against ruthless masters in Asia Minor, 1 Peter took pains, it was argued, to prevent Christians from getting caught up in such causes (cf. 4: 14–16). An American reviewer, at the time when the civil rights movement and war in Vietnam were heating up, faulted such an approach for concentrating on social behaviour, rather than theology or hermeneutics.

But subsequent study has put even greater emphasis on how 1 Peter stresses 'doing good' (RSV 'doing right', 2: 14, 15, 20; 3: 6, 17; 4: 19) as God's will in the world for Christians. The

Haustafeln were likely taken over into the church's ethics precisely as an apologetic defence against misunderstandings. In a day when Roman authorities looked with horror on the cults of Dionysus and Isis, and their sexual emancipation and revolutionary, destabilizing effects, as a threat to the body politic, civic, and cultural, not to mention home and family life, Jews and Christians seem to have endorsed the household codes as a means of self-discipline and to distinguish themselves from such libertine groups.

For all the differences belonging to the Christian 'brotherhood' (5: 9) brought about in the moral life of converts, provoking sometimes the charge, 'You don't party with us any more!' (4: 3–4), here was an opportunity to be part of the social structures of the day. Indeed, the key word 'Be subject' or 'submissive' (2: 13, 18; 3: 1; 5: 5) has been related, even etymologically, to the theme of 'order' in the cosmos and society. It has been claimed the accent is not on the prefix 'sub' in 'subordination' but on the verbal meaning, 'put yourself into the divine order of things'. This would fit with the references in 1 Peter that suggest God's arrangement of things in the divine household: namely, the *oikos* references in 2: 5 and 4: 17 (God's household, the church); Christians as 'good stewards' or household managers (4: 10); and possibly also the reference to 'servants' or members of the household (2: 18; the word here is not 'slaves', and 'masters' are not correspondingly addressed; the term means 'domestics'; the subject in 2: 18–25 may therefore be all Christians as 'household servants'; cf. Luke 12: 36–48; 16: 10–13).

Regardless of what Graeco-Roman concepts may lie behind these references, 1 Peter clearly addresses Christians about how to act toward such social structures as emperor, governor, marriage, and home, and in the work-place. Criteria for making judgements are even suggested. These include proper use of freedom (2: 16); conscience toward God (2: 19 AV; 3: 16, 21) or possibly 'consciousness of God'; and the legitimacy of 'human institutions' or creations (2: 13), although, ultimately, God is the faithful Creator (4: 19) who is over all. First Peter marks an important step toward a discerning participation by Christians in the structures of society—with the warning that obedience to their Christian principles may, none the less, mean suffering for believers.

✓ *Enigmatic Hebrews: A Rhetorical Appeal for Steadfast Faith in our Great High Priest and in the Better Covenant*

SOME scribes who in later centuries made copies of the Epistle called 'To [the] Hebrews' added, in a note at the conclusion of the text, that the letter had been written by Paul from Italy, specifically from Rome. These opinions became traditional. Yet every one of these points—Paul's authorship, the place of writing, the identity of those addressed, and even whether Hebrews is a letter—has been widely denied in subsequent study.

This most rhetorically elegant of all New Testament writings has for good reasons been termed, to paraphrase Winston Churchill, a riddle within a puzzle wrapped up in an enigma. Indeed, all three terms have been used by commentators to describe the book.

At the heart of Hebrews lies a series of earnest exhortations:

We must pay the closer attention to what we have heard. . . . How shall we escape if we neglect such a great salvation? (2: 1, 3)

Consider Jesus. . . . Take care, sisters and brothers, lest there be in any of you an evil, unbelieving heart, leading you to fall away from the living God. (3: 1, 12)

Let us hold fast our confidence . . . Let us then with confidence draw near to the throne of grace, that we may receive mercy and find grace to help in time of need. (4: 14, 16)

You ought to be teachers; you need some one to teach you again the first principles of God's word. . . . Yet in your case, beloved, we feel sure of better things that belong to salvation. (5: 12; 6: 9)

Let us draw near with a true heart in full assurance of faith. . . . Let us consider how to stir up one another to love and good works. . . .

Recall the former days when . . . you endured a hard struggle with sufferings. . . . You have need of endurance. (10: 22, 24, 32, 36)

Let us run with perseverance the race that is set before us, looking to Jesus. . . . Consider him. . . . See that you do not refuse him who is speaking. . . . Do not be led away by diverse and strange teachings. . . . Do not neglect to do good. (12: 1–2, 3, 25; 13: 9, 16)

Part of the riddle is the question, of to what Christian community, under what sort of circumstances, were such urgent admonitions were directed.

The admonitions are based upon and intertwined with a Christology that is both traditional and new. Accustomed titles appear like 'the Son' (1: 2, 5, 8; 3: 6; 5: 5, 8; 7: 28) and 'Son of God' (4: 14; 6: 6; 7: 3; 10: 29). Yet there are rare or new epithets like 'pioneer and perfecter of our faith' (12: 2; cf. 2: 10 and Acts 3: 15 (RSV 'Author of life') and 5: 31 (RSV 'Leader')). The Lord Jesus is depicted majestically in creation (1: 2) and as coming again (9: 28). Yet he is also presented in a gaunt humanity. The simple name 'Jesus' appears nine times (2: 9; 3: 1; 4: 14; 6: 20; 7: 22; 10: 19; 12: 24; 13: 12, 20), just as in the gospels, and he is presented as desolate and alone, presumably in the garden of Gethsemane (5: 7), perhaps even more in anguish than in the synoptics (cf. Mark 14: 32–42).

But the major emphasis in Hebrews' depiction of Jesus is in terms of priesthood (ch. 7) and indeed as 'high priest of our confession' (3: 1). No other New Testament writing develops so extensive a Christology along such lines. This *tour de force* is historically strained, for admittedly 'our Lord was descended from [the tribe of] Judah [*i.e. he was of the house and lineage of David*], and in connection with that tribe Moses [*and indeed the entire Old Testament*] said nothing about priests' (7: 14). Our author, therefore, presents Jesus as high priest 'after the order of Melchizedek' (5: 6; 7: 1–10). Part of the puzzle is how this extraordinary view of Jesus Christ arises in Hebrews, and to what end.

One could mention also how, for all this Christology, God and the Holy Spirit are not neglected. 'The living God' (3: 12; 9: 14) is a God who speaks (*deus loquens*, 1: 1–2; 4: 7; 10: 30) and acts in grace (2: 9; 12: 15), yet who remains judge (12: 23; cf. 10: 31). The Spirit likewise speaks (3: 7; 10: 15–17, cf. 29), above all in Scripture, which is almost personified. It is not a matter of citing what the Bible said, but of asserting what God or the Spirit is saying as Scripture speaks (cf. 1: 6, 7, 8; 4: 3; 8: 8, RSV 'he says'; 2: 12–13, Jesus says). And in Hebrews, the Scripture always speaks in the LXX Greek translation of the Hebrew text. There are other singularities in Hebrews, like the emphasis on covenant and the view of faith (see below), but the real enigma lies in the form of the document.

Traditionally labelled as an epistle, Hebrews lacks the salutation or address with which letters of the day, like Paul's, began. Yet it does have an epistolary ending in ch. 13. At least 13: 22–5 are like the closing of a Pauline letter—indeed, one where the writer takes pen in hand and gives personal news in the first person singular. This section includes the somewhat incongruous statement, 'I have written to you briefly' (13: 22b). One wonders how many chapters a long treatise would have involved? Or is the comment ironic, like the appeal just before it, to ' "bear with" my word of exhortation'? Other commentators take vv. 18–25 as the epistolary ending, and still others consider the entire chapter to be such an added ending. In any case, it is only the materials in ch. 13 that give Hebrews the trappings of a letter.

But there is great variety of topics in these verses of the last chapter. They skip from admonitions to keep 'the marriage bed undefiled' or 'your life free from love of money' (13: 4, 5) to biblical assertions ('We can confidently say [*as Ps. 118: 6 does*], "The Lord is my Helper" ', 13: 6) and confessional slogans like 'Jesus Christ the same yesterday and today and for ever' (13: 8). It has, therefore, been argued that some or all of Heb. 13 is a later addition to a treatise or sermon in disguise. All this is part of the enigma: what kind of document is this? How did it arise, with its great sophistication of contents, in the second half of the first Christian century?

These aspects of the riddle/puzzle/enigma have been part of the story of Hebrews through the centuries. The writing was known by the year 95 in Rome, for 1 Clement (which was written in Rome by 96) reflects Hebrews; in particular, 1 Clem. 36. 2–6 paraphrases the intricate Christology and some of the Old Testament quotations found in Heb. 1: 3–13. It was, however, Christianity in the eastern or Greek-speaking portion of the Roman Empire that earliest accepted Hebrews as canonical. This was in part based on the assumption that Paul wrote it. Clement of Alexandria (*c.* AD 200) claimed, for example, that Paul wrote it in Hebrew for the Hebrews, and that Luke translated it into Greek (see Eusebius, *Church History* 6. 14. 2–4). But such opinions were not unanimous. Another Alexandrian scholar, Origen (d. *c.*254), after noting differences in style from Paul, asserted, alongside the tradition about Luke, another that said Clement of Rome was the person involved. Then Origen made his famous remark, 'Who wrote the epistle, God, in truth, knows' (ibid. 6.25.11–14; cf. 3.38.1). Western Christianity was slower to accept Hebrews, placing it in the canon only in the fourth century. While one papyrus manuscript (P⁴⁶) locates Hebrews after Romans (probably on the grounds that it was sent to Rome), other manuscripts put it between 2 Thessalonians and 1 Timothy (i.e. in the Pauline collection, between letters to congregations and those to individuals), and still others place it after Philemon, at the end of the Pauline corpus, where we are accustomed to find it today.

Over the centuries, Hebrews has attracted attention for its priestly and cultic-sacrificial concepts. It has been read publicly in churches, especially in connection with the Christmas and Lenten seasons (see 1: 1–9; 2: 10–18 and 4: 14–5: 10; 10: 19–25, respectively). The sixteenth century began to question the traditional view that Paul wrote Hebrews (in comments by Erasmus and Melanchthon), but it was Luther who, in three penetrating observations, posed questions which are with us to this day. First, he suggested Apollos as author. Secondly, he seems to have brought about a new turn in the understanding of 'faith' at 11: 1 as 'conviction' rather than 'reality'. Thirdly, Luther was shocked at statements in Hebrews which imply that no second repentance or forgiveness is possible for a believer who sins and falls away (6: 4–6; 10: 26). For that reason Luther relegated

Hebrews to his lowest category within the canon—still part of the New Testament but on the periphery. To this day commentators must discuss this 'rigorist' stance in Hebrews on the impossibility of renewal for apostates, and ask whether it accords with the attitude of Jesus or of Catholic Christianity on God's forgiveness.

A literary masterpiece

One avenue for getting at the origins and meaning of Hebrews has been rhetorical analysis of its style and outline. Origen, in separating Hebrews somewhat from Paul himself, said 'the style (*phrasis*) and composition (*synthesis*) stem from someone who recalled the apostolic utterances and kept notes, as it were, of what the teacher said' (Eusebius, *Church History* 6. 25. 13). Luther was attracted to Apollos as author of Hebrews in part because Acts 18: 24 described this Jew from Alexandria as not only 'well versed in the scriptures' but also as 'an eloquent man', both features that fit Hebrews well. Early twentieth-century commentators likened the structure of Hebrews to ancient rhetorical arrangement; for example,

1. *Prooimion* (preface, introduction), to create good will (1: 1–4: 13), leading up to the thesis or statement of purpose (Greek *prothesis*) in 4: 14–16,

The great and heavenly high priest, Jesus Christ, the Son of God, who can sympathize with our weaknesses because he has been tempted as we are (yet without sinning on his part), is the ground for our confidence about access to the Throne of grace, to obtain help when we need it.

2. *Diēgēsis* (statement of the case), to persuade and to establish plausibility (5: 1–6: 20). A preliminary narrative assertion appears in these verses about the Son's High Priesthood.

3. *Apodeixis* (demonstration, proofs), to persuade more fully (7: 1–10: 18). Here, Christ's qualifications as priest after 'the order of Melchizedek' (6: 20) and as mediator of a 'better covenant' (7: 22) are argued in more detail.

4. *Epilogos* (epilogue, 10: 19–13: 21) containing exhortations,

above all to faith (ch. 11) such as is demanded by the doctrines presented, and a variety of practical admonitions, including the epistolary ending in ch. 13 (at least vv. 18–25).

More recent study of rhetoric in connection with the New Testament would classify the document as an 'epideictic oration', i.e. one that sets forth the praises of a person (in this case, Christ) and seeks to promulgate values which followers ought to live out. But it must be added that recent expositors, while agreed that Hebrews is highly skilled in the use of rhetorical devices, are by no means agreed on its exact structure and outline. Indeed, we may ask whether it was ever delivered orally. Was it meant to be read by people accustomed to such literary skills? And if so, by whom?

There is broad consensus that great blocks of exhortation or paraenesis appear in 2: 1–4; 3: 1–13; 4: 14–16; 5: 11–6: 20; 10: 19–39; and 12: 1–13: 17. Sample admonitions have been quoted above from each segment. There is less agreement on how to outline the remaining units and the overall document. Some are struck by the use of the term 'superior', the Greek for which (*kreitton*) occurs 13 times in the document (1: 4; 6: 9; 7: 7, 19, 22; 8: 6 (twice); 9: 23; 10: 34; 11: 16, 35, 40; 12: 24). This observation leads to a thematic outline of this sort:

1. The supremacy of Jesus, God's Son, in creation and salvation   (1: 1–4: 13)
   (a) Superior to angels, at creation and because of his flesh-and-blood suffering to expiate sin   (chs. 1–2)
   (b) Superior to Moses and to Joshua (Greek 'Jesus') in pioneering salvation and 'rest'   (chs. 3–4)
2. The supremacy of Jesus, the great High Priest and the mediator of the better covenant, in salvation now and in judgement to come   (4: 14–10: 39)
   (a) Superior to the earthly priests of the first covenant   (chs. 5–7)
   (b) Superior to the sanctuary and sacrifices of the first covenant   (chs. 8–10)

3. Faith, perseverance, and discipline for Jesus and the Zion of God (11–13: 17)
4. Personal exhortations and epistolary conclusion (13: 18–25).

Such an analysis takes seriously the parallelism between 4: 14–16 and 10: 19–39 ('Since we have a great high priest . . . let us draw near') as turning-points in the argument. A variation is to begin the 'great High Priest' section only at 7:1, taking the material in ch. 5 as anticipatory of the unit on priesthood and linking the Abrahamic references in 6: 13–18 with the Moses–Joshua history in chs. 3–4. All these outlines point up the crucial theological problem in Hebrews of two covenants, a first one legislated under Moses and a 'better' one mediated by Christ (7: 11; 8: 6). This 'superiority' of Christ is a theme some would prefer to sidestep in contemporary interreligious discussions ∩ between Christians and Jews (or with other world religions).

Still other outlines for Hebrews exist. One parallels what it calls units I and II, then III and IV in this way:

I. Christology (1: 1–2: 18), the leader of our salvation

II. Paraenesis (3: 1–4: 16), the 'wandering people of God'

III. Christology (5: 1–10: 18), Christ, our High Priest

IV. Paraenesis (10: 19–12: 29), the community's 'way of faith'

(ch. 13, further epistolary exhortations)

The long study of Hebrews by another scholar (Vanhoye, *Our Priest Is Christ*) has produced a 'concentric' outline for the architecture of the treatise. Three circles enwrap a central exposition (see Fig. 1). On this structured treatment, 13: 22–5 becomes 'A Word in Parting'. The analysis makes Christ's sacrifice central, and emphasizes aspects of eschatology and the church which might otherwise be overlooked.

A most recent commentary on Hebrews (Attridge, *Commentary*) after surveying all such efforts, remarks that the problem is not 'lack of structural indices' but 'their overabundance' (as is also true of Matthew's Gospel). No outline can hope to capture

————————— 1: 1–4   Exordium

— I. Eschatology (1: 5–2: 18)—a name so different from the
name of angels

— II Ecclesiology (3: 1–5: 10)—Jesus, 'whose house we are'
and in whom we share (3: 6, 14), was faithful (3: 1–4: 14)
and, even as high priest, is compassionate (4: 15–5: 10)

III. Central exposition (5: 11–10: 39) on Jesus' sacrifice

— Preamble (5: 11–6: 20), paraenesis exhorting on the basis
of God's promise and oath

> A. (7: 1–28) Jesus 'High Priest according
> to the order of Melchizedek'
>
> B. (8: 1–9: 28) In contrast to the old
> institutions of worship in Israel,
> Christ's sacrifice, once for all, is
> efficacious and definitive
>
> C. (10: 1–18) Christ, not the law, its
> priests, or sacrifices, suffices as
> cause of an eternal salvation

Exhortation (10: 19–39)—our confidence in contrast to the
frightening prospects for sinners

IV. Ecclesiological paraenesis (11: 1–12: 13)—the faith of
those of old and the endurance/discipline which is required
of us

V. Eschatology (12: 14–13: 19)—a warning from Esau's
case (12: 15–17) and admonitions about 'the peaceful fruit'
which justice/righteousness (12: 11) is to yield

————————— 13: 20–1   Peroration

FIG. 1.

all the 'web of interrelationships' (pp. 16–17). Attridge follows Vanhoye in seeing five movements, but labels 5: 11–10: 25 simply as 'the difficult discourse' (5: 11), a description based especially on the use of Ps. 110 in Hebrews 7 and the Melchizedek argument. The exhortations in part V are extended through 13: 19, and 13: 20–5 is integrated into the total structure.

The variations in outlines and rhetorical treatments of Hebrews stem in part from the decision made concerning the relationship of all or part of ch. 13 to the first 12 chapters. The case for Hebrews 13 as a later addition, in order to give the impression of a Pauline letter, was classically developed by Wrede in 1906. For many years this position has received wide support. 'Let brotherly love continue' (13: 1) is an abrupt shift after 'our God is a consuming fire' (12: 29). Two verses seem contradictory. At one point the writer says, 'Pray . . . that I may be released to you the sooner' (13: 19), but then, 'Timothy has been released, with whom I shall see you' (13: 23). The mystery is explained in a literary way if one assumes that v. 19 echoes Philemon 22 ('I am hoping through your prayers to be granted to you') and v. 23 imitates Philippians 2: 19, 23–4 ('I hope to send Timothy to you . . . just as soon as I see how it will go with me; and I trust . . . that shortly I myself shall come also'). Such 'parallels' can be argued elsewhere, as for Heb. 13: 24 ('those from Italy') with Phil. 4: 22 ('those from Caesar's household').

But the trend more recently has been to accept ch. 13 as part of the document, partly on the grounds that, for all the connections in Heb. 13 with the way other New Testament letters end (cf. esp. 13: 20–5 with 1 Peter 5: 10–14), the contents in Hebrews, even of verses most commonly assigned to an epistolary appendix, do fit thematically with the earlier chapters. In the benediction, for example, at 13: 20–1, three terms reflect prior emphases: peace (cf. 7: 2; 12: 14), covenant (chs. 8–9), and God's will (10: 7, 10, 26). If ch. 13 is accounted an original part of the document, it provides a few clues to origin of the writing, but makes the genre of this treatise with epistolary close more baffling. It is from 13: 22 that the phrase comes which most agree best characterizes the genre of Hebrews, as a 'word of exhortation' (*logos tēs paraklēseōs*).

Although rhetorical analysis of Hebrews as a whole can only to a certain extent help solve problems about the document, we are in a better position concerning individual literary devices and subsections. In the opening verses appear alliteration (5 Greek words beginning with 'p') and rhythm (the 'paean' pattern of three short syllables followed by a long, much recommended by Aristotle, though as a concluding prose rhythm), along with antithetical parallelism:

In many and various ways,	God spoke of old	to our fathers	by the prophets;
at the end of these days	(God) has spoken	to us	by a Son. (1: 1–2)

The decisive contrast of the singular revelation through Jesus Christ with previous word-events, or times when God spoke, in Israel's history is thus artfully announced. To paraphrase a manner of expression that Hebrews itself once employed (11: 32), a formulation common in ancient writers, 'time would fail (us) to tell' of examples of litotes (or the double negative, 4: 15 'not unable'), hendiadys (one thing expressed by two terms, 5: 2 'the ignorant and wayward'), or anaphora (constant repetition of a phrase, ch. 11 'by faith'). Chiastic structure was a favourite (reverse parallel order of phrases in the pattern ABB′A′). Examples are sometimes quite brief (e.g. Fig. 2). They may be more elaborate, as at 9: 11–12 (Fig. 3). Or chiasm may shape a longer argument, as at 5: 1–10 (Fig. 4).

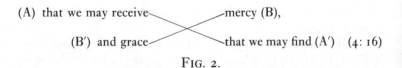

(A) that we may receive   mercy (B),

     (B′) and grace   that we may find (A′)   (4: 16)

FIG. 2.

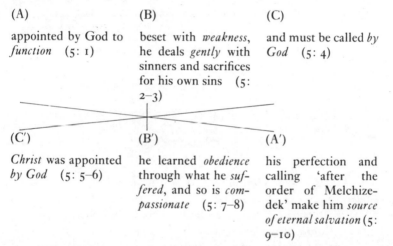

(A) through the greater and more perfect tent

(B) not made with hands, i.e. not of this creation,

(B') not through the blood of goats and calves

(A') but through his own blood.

FIG. 3.

Every (human) high priest is

(A)

appointed by God to *function*   (5: 1)

(B)

beset with *weakness*, he deals *gently* with sinners and sacrifices for his own sins   (5: 2–3)

(C)

and must be called *by God*   (5: 4)

(C')

Christ was appointed *by God*   (5: 5–6)

(B')

he learned *obedience* through what he *suffered*, and so is *compassionate*   (5: 7–8)

(A')

his perfection and calling 'after the order of Melchizedek' make him *source of eternal salvation* (5: 9–10)

FIG. 4.

Scriptural exposition

The rhetorical aspects of Hebrews show how much its author was at home in the Graeco-Roman world. But there is another side to the document in its use of the Old Testament. (Here it will not do to say 'the Hebrew Scriptures', for it is the Greek Septuagint that is employed; further, the writer has decided in favour of a 'better covenant' in Christ, in place of the first or old one at Sinai.) The treatise is full of expositions of God's

Scriptures, well wrought in accordance with Jewish and Greek expository principles. If one designates the argument employed at many points as *a minore ad maius*, by analogy from the lesser to the greater matter, it sounds Graeco-Roman. But if one calls it by the Hebrew phrase which the rabbis used, *qal we ḥomer* ('the light and the heavy'), we are in the Jewish realm. This type of argument is, at any rate, found several times, usually with phrases in Greek like 'by so much (better) . . . by how much (superior)'; see 1: 4; 7: 20–3; 10: 25; and cf. 2: 2–3; 3: 5–6; 9: 13–14 for this *a fortiori* argument which was also one of Hillel's seven rules for interpretation.

A good example of our author's skills is the interpretation of Ps. 8 in Heb. 2: 6–9. The Massoretic Hebrew of the psalm is a hymn about humankind's lofty domain over creation:

> What is man that thou are mindful of him,
>   and the son of man that thou dost care for him?
> Yet thou has made him little less than God
>   [literally, *elohim*, the creatures of Yahweh's court],
>   and dost crown him with glory and honour . . .
>   thou hast put all things under his feet.
>
>   (Ps. 8: 4–6 RSV)

The LXX quoted at Heb. 2: 6–8 differs primarily in taking *elohim* to refer not to God but to angels, and the adverb 'little' in a way that can be interpreted temporally rather than of degree; that is, 'thou dost make him less than the angels for a little while'. The author of Hebrews—aided by the parallelism between 'man' and 'Son of man' (seen as a title for Jesus) or between 'man' as Adam (Gen. 1–2) and Jesus as the new Adam (cf. 1 Cor. 15: 21–2, 27, a passage where Ps. 8 is also quoted)—applies the Psalm verses to Jesus' humiliation and exaltation: this person

> who was *made less than the angels for a little while*,
>   Jesus, we see,
> on account of the suffering of death, *crowned with*
>   *glory and honour*.   (2: 9, Psalm phrases italicized)

It suits the eschatology of Hebrews to add, 'As of now we do not yet see *all things subjected* to him' (2: 8), but it is to Jesus, not to angels, that God will subject the world to come (2: 6), because Jesus 'taste[d] death for every one' (2: 9).

It has rightly been claimed that Ps. 110, which Paul used and which is reflected elsewhere in the New Testament (Ziesler, *Pauline Christianity*, rev. edn., 38) runs through much of Hebrews. Thus 110: 1 is quoted at Hebrews 1: 13, 'To what angel has God ever said, "Sit at my right hand, till I make thy enemies a stool for thy feet"?' It appears there with the implication that God did say it to Jesus, who, 'after making purification for sins, sat down at the right hand of the Majesty [God] on high' (1: 3). Heb. 1: 13 and 2: 7–8 thus interrelate. This theme of Jesus' exaltation at God's right hand, employing Ps. 110, is repeated at Heb. 8: 1; 10: 12–13; and 12: 2; further, 110: 4 ('Thou art a priest for ever, after the order of Melchizedek') is used at 5: 6, 10; 6: 20; 7: 3, 11, 15, 17, 21, 24, 28).

Other passages that should be studied with the Old Testament in one hand and the Hebrews application in the other are Ps. 95: 7–11 at Heb. 3: 7–4: 13 about entering into God's 'rest' (Gen. 2: 2 is also woven in); Jer. 31: 31–4, about the new covenant, in ch. 8; or Ps. 40: 6–8 in 10: 5–10. In the last mentioned passage, the LXX rendering 'a body you prepared for me', instead of the Hebrew's awkward 'ears you dug for me', allowed the author of our treatise to see an incarnational reference to the body of Jesus Christ offered on the Cross (10: 5c, 10). A good annotated Bible or commentary will help in many of these passages.

The centrepiece of the entire epistle and its most complex example exegetically is the *tour de force* concerning Melchizedek in ch. 7. The reference to this priest figure in Ps. 110: 4 derives from an account in Gen. 14: 18–22, where Abraham paid tithes to a priest-king of (Jeru-)Salem. Our author follows, almost playfully, certain interpretative principles of the day, including use of etymology in 7: 2, which was meaningful to his audience, if not scientific (by our standards). As a result, the story (1) establishes a priesthood for Christ ('after Melchizedek', for ever) and (2) thereby shows Jesus' superiority to the Levitical priesthood. For Abraham had tithed to the superior figure Melchizedek, and Levi stemmed from Abraham (7: 9). Jesus, who 'by the power of an indestructible life' (like Melchizedek, vv. 16; cf. 3) thus lines up with Melchizedek, is therefore superior to Abraham's Levitical descendants.

Recent discoveries at Qumran have shed new light on speculations of the day about Melchizedek. A text from Cave 11 (11QMelch) deals with the Jubilee year (Lev. 25; Isa. 61) and tells how Melchizedek, a heavenly figure like the archangel Michael, releases captives from Belial, ruler of the forces of darkness. There is also a gnostic tractate from Nag Hammadi (NHC 9, 1; *Nag Hammadi Library*, ed. J. M. Robinson, 399–403); it tells of a vision Melchizedek has about his eschatological role. These new materials do not, however, solve our puzzles concerning the origin and meaning of the use in Hebrews of this enigmatic figure.

Such extra-biblical materials point to another avenue for exploration: the history-of-religions background. The contents and the traditional title 'To the Hebrews' have long caused students of the book to look to a Jewish background. But which one? From the mid-eighteenth century to the present, Philo, the Jewish philosopher of Alexandria, has been proposed as the sort of thinker who could parallel or even have influenced the letter to the Hebrews. Philo, too, in treating Melchizedek (*Legum allegoria* 3. 79–82), employed etymology and the argument from silence (cf. Heb. 7: 3; since Scripture never refers to his genealogy or death, Melchizedek must have been 'without father and mother', having 'neither beginning of days nor end of life'). The notion in Heb. 8: 5 of a 'heavenly sanctuary', of which the earthly one is but a copy (9: 23, 'true form' and 'shadow'), has been taken as Platonism, mediated through Philo. But Hebrews, for all its intricacies, is never so thoroughly allegorical as Philo, and differs sharply on eschatology. The affinities may be more with the Hellenistic synagogue and its homily style than with Alexandrian Judaism as we know it in Philo.

The tendency to back away from Philonic explanations for Hebrews was abetted by the discovery and applications of the Dead Sea scrolls (as in the case of Melchizedek). Here eschatology, priesthood, and covenant community have analogies. In early days of 'Qumran fever' in the 1950s, it was even argued that Hebrews was composed to combat Qumran beliefs. Some writers decided that Hebrews was addressed to Essenes or to ex-Qumranites, who were tempted to desert Christ now for their old faith. The view persists in claims that the addressees are Hebrew Christians, not necessarily from the Dead Sea group, but tempted to revert to some kind of Essenism. However, even the Qumran scrolls have proved no panacea for interpreting the document, in part because of the Greek rhetorical, LXX qualities of the treatise. What Jewish roots exist are varied.

At times gnostic categories have been invoked to expound Hebrews. Ernst Käsemann's efforts here, made long before the Nag Hammadi finds, have not met with much success in explaining the document's Christology, but they have left a permanent mark in the theme he stressed of 'the wandering people of God', i.e. Israel in the wilderness (3: 17) and now the church in pilgrimage (3: 7–4: 10). Others speak of 'apocalyptic gnosis' behind the book (Koester, *Introduction*, ii. 272–6). Attempts to see in Hebrews 'the beginnings of Christian philosophy', derived specifically from Middle Platonism, or connections with Jewish mysticism of the Merkabah type (deriving from the 'wheels' symbolism of Ezek. 1: 15–21) have their champions too. But by and large the materials from ancient religions have intensified rather than solved our problems with Hebrews. The current cautious rule is: 'Thou shalt not posit any one sole background'. The symbolic world of Hebrews is syncretistic. If 'Platonic', for example, it is not ahistoric (for Christ appeared and will come again), and is concerned about the existence of believers facing threats here and now.

Who, when, and where?

This richness of rhetorical contents and of religious backgrounds has led to a variety of views on the usual questions of New Testament introduction. The document is anonymous; its author remains unknown to us. We have noted above how Hebrews came, from the second century on, to be swept into the

Pauline corpus, but the theology is quite different from that in Paul's acknowledged or even pseudepigraphical letters. The statement in 2: 3–4 that the message of salvation came to 'us' in the second generation from 'those who heard the Lord' is itself sufficient to exclude Paul himself as author, for he claimed direct calling by Christ. Luke, Clement of Rome, and, more possibly, Apollos have been noted as possible writers. Barnabas, a Levite, called 'son of consolation' (Acts 4: 36), has also been proposed as writer of this 'word of consolation' (13: 22). Use of the pronoun 'we' at 5: 11 prompted Harnack to suggest Aquila and Priscilla (Acts 18: 2, 26), and women have urged Priscilla alone as authoress (the masculine participle at 11: 32 is against this proposal).

The identity of the place addressed and the location of the writer likewise remain guesswork. The phrase at 13: 24, 'those who come from Italy', has been invoked to support a Roman provenance. But it can mean, alas, either 'the Italians' around Rome or 'those away from Italy' who are sending greetings back home. In this vacuum of facts, scholars have suggested Ephesus, Corinth, the Lycus valley (because of supposed affinities with Colossians), Antioch, Caesarea, and elsewhere as the point of origin.

Ancients supposed the addressees to be in Palestine (priests, for example, of the Jerusalem temple), as have moderns (priests from Qumran or even discouraged Christians, addressed by the leader of a putative 'Christian monastery' in Jerusalem before AD 70 which practised celibacy—against whose views ch. 13 was added by a Church leader favouring marriage!). Others have located the recipients in or near Rome, Corinth, Colossae, etc. We simply do not know. A scenario that has achieved a certain amount of support holds that Hebrews was addressed by liberal Jewish Christians, like the circle around Stephen in Acts 7, to a quite conservative Jewish Christian enclave in Rome. The view that the treatise is addressed (in spite of the later title) to *Gentile* Christians faced by apathy has, however, also gained adherents over the last century and a half.

The date of Hebrews is one area where more agreed

conclusions are possible. If the writing is quoted by AD 96 and if it reflects a second-generation situation (2: 2–3) in a congregation that has had a more splendid Christian past (see below), a date between 70 and 95 is demanded. The fall of the Jerusalem temple in AD 70 does not enter into a decision here, since Hebrews is about the tent or tabernacle (9: 2) during Israel's sojourn in the wilderness, not the Solomonic or Herodian temple.

Only a partial social setting of the community addressed can be suggested. Its members were Christian long enough to have forgotten (5: 11–12) some of the basics in which they had been instructed (6: 1–2). They have a heritage of 'serving the saints' (6: 10–11). The admonitions in 10: 32–4 and 13: 1 ff. may suggest specific ways in which they had shown benevolence over the years, including hospitality for strangers and support for those in prison. In 'the former days' of their faith, they suffered persecution and even confiscation of property (10: 32–4, references which some have found attractive to relate to the persecution by Nero in AD 64). But there is no clear picture of persecution now or of false teachings imminently threatening at the moment. (The statement at 13: 9 is quite general, but see the discussion of Christology, below, for a further suggestion.)

What pressures—Jewish, Judaizing, Roman, or internal—had led to ennui with the confession of Christ remain a mystery. The situation is serious enough, however, to prompt some author to write a rhetorically exquisite 'hortatory word'. Indeed, so concerned is the author of Hebrews that 10: 26 insists that, for all that has been said about the death of Christ as an efficacious purification for sins, 'there no longer remains a sacrifice for sins, if we sin deliberately after receiving the knowledge of the truth'. Were those addressed really committing apostasy, crucifying the Son of God afresh and holding Jesus up to contempt (cf. 6: 4–6)? This stance of the author in not allowing a second repentance, a position which so shocked Luther and all Christians who stress forgiveness—that no repentance, even with tears, can restore those who knowingly sell their spiritual birthright (cf. 12: 17)— is not unparalleled in Jewish quarters, notably Qumran (cf. 1QS

7. 23–4; 8. 21–3). Philo said that blasphemy against God cannot be pardoned (*De Fuga* 84). Second-century Christianity vigorously debated whether 'second repentance' was possible. At Rome, a later writing called The Shepherd of Hermas could propose it only on the basis of a new revelation.

While Hebrews emphasizes clearly Christ's coming again, there is no suggestion that the parousia is so imminent that there will not be time to repent. We should not psychologize and say that 6: 4–6 mean simply that those who fall away cannot be renewed as long as they remain apostates, for the verses have been taken to mean that even God cannot renew them. That the author is trying shock treatment for their lethargy may also be regarded as a modern concept (though the *auctor ad Hebraeos*, to cover the author's identity with a Latin phrase, was certainly capable of rhetorical overkill). The judgement is therefore surely correct that the position is above all theological. The deep significance of the way Christians act stems from the decisiveness of Christ's sacrifice for them. He died 'once for all'. Those who once accept and then knowingly reject the Son of God and all that the Spirit and the word of God have brought to them are beyond God's forgiveness. For such persons, 'it is a terrible thing to fall into the hands of the living God' (10: 31, cf. 29–30).

Aspects of theology in Hebrews

The author and audience in Hebrews know the gospel as 'good news' about salvation that came to them just as it had come to ancient Israel in the wilderness, in the form of 'promise' about the 'rest' God offers (4: 2, 6). In each case, faith is demanded, and disobedience could keep one from the goal. In the case of the present addressees, their salvation was declared initially by the Lord Jesus and then 'attested to us by those who heard him', God witnessing also 'by signs and wonders and various miracles and by the gifts of the Holy Spirit' (2: 3–4). Legal terms like 'attestation' are employed here to describe the richly pneumatic, charismatic sort of Christianity to which Paul and Acts both refer.

For all the ties with Israel of old, 'kingdom terminology' is rare in Hebrews. Christians are to be 'grateful for receiving a kingdom that cannot be shaken' (12: 28). This reference is not simply to a realm that is to stand firm when 'the powers in the heavens will be shaken' (Mark 13: 25), but to God's reign now, which they already possess eschatologically, through access to God by the blood of Jesus (10: 19–21). The statement that 'you have come to Mount Zion and to the city of the living God, the heavenly Jerusalem' (12: 22) suggests the same eschatology, using Old Testament symbolic terms where 'the city' is equivalent to 'the kingdom'.

Much of the thought of Hebrews is couched in covenant categories. Yet even the translation of the Greek word involved, *diathēkē*, has been disputed. In the LXX, that term is used to render *bᵉrît*, referring to gracious arrangements God made with Israel or with individuals among the people, either with stipulations demanded of them (as at Sinai, Exod. 19, '*if* you will obey my voice', 19: 5) or unilaterally, depending solely on Yahweh's oath (with Abraham, Gen. 15: 7–21; with David, 2 Sam. 7: 8–16). In Greek usage *diathēkē* referred to a legal document, in particular a last will and testament. The RSV is right in generally translating as 'covenant', except at Heb. 9: 16–17, where the Greek sense of a will enters in (as it does also at Gal. 3: 15).

Out of some 33 occurrences of *diathēkē* in the New Testament, over half (17) are in Hebrews. In Hebrews, the reference is never to the Abrahamic or Davidic covenants. There is always a contrast between that with Moses at Sinai and the 'new covenant' (Jer. 31: 31–4, quoted at Heb. 8: 8–12) which has been effected in Jesus Christ. Our theologian regards Jesus' death on the Cross as inaugurating a new and better covenant, which delivers what the Mosaic arrangement and Levitical priests never could provide (9: 15): that is, it effects forgiveness of sins (8: 12; 1: 3; 9: 12, 14, 15, 25–6, 28; 10: 10, 12, 14) and within each believer interiorizes knowledge of the Lord (8: 11; 10: 15–18, 26, 34 'knowing that you yourselves have a better possession and an abiding one'). The great word in Hebrews for

Christ's death on the Cross is that it was 'once for all' ([*eph*]*hapax*) or unique (7: 27; 9: 12; 10: 11; 9: 26, 27, 28; 10: 2).

All the emphasis on Graeco-Roman rhetoric and the Old Testament and Jewish backgrounds in Hebrews must not, however, blind one to the extensive Christian materials in the book. Sometimes these take the forms of confessional statements and hymns. There is reference to 'our confession' (of faith) at 3: 1, 4: 14, and 10: 23. Among such common early Christian assertions are 1: 2b–3 (Christ in relation to God, the world, and salvation history); 2: 10 (God, 'for whom and by whom all things exist'; cf. 1 Cor. 8: 6); 3: 1 (Christ as 'apostle' as well as high priest); 4: 14; and 5: 7–10. At 6: 1–2 there is a list of six foundational and catechetical teachings: repentance, faith in God, washings (not necessarily just Christian baptism but possibly teaching against Jewish lustrations), laying on of hands (in healings, cf. 2: 4; confirming baptism?), the resurrection, and the judgement. One may be wary, however, of seeing in 5: 12–14 distinctions among (1) 'children' and 'milk', (2) 'solid food' for the 'mature', and (3) the author's own 'discourse which is hard to explain' (5: 11) for those really advanced, as if in a Philonic learning process. (Hebrews is not for those in an advanced seminar but for those reviving and building on basics.) The concluding emphasis in 5: 14 on 'distinguishing good from evil' fits well the book's concern for ethical paraenesis.

While Christology is not among the 'elementary doctrines' enumerated at 6: 1–2, it is the theme of the book as a whole. We have already discussed how titles new and old, and above all the theme of Jesus as '(great) High Priest of our confession' (3: 1), undergird all the ethical appeals (see above, p. 164). Outlines make the supremacy of Jesus or his sacrifice the dominant theme for Hebrews (see above, pp. 167–70). Rhetorical devices and Old Testament exposition employed in the service of the person and work of Jesus Christ have been illustrated (above, pp. 172–76; especially the Melchizedek tradition). Credal phrases or hymns (also noted above, p. 182) deal especially with Jesus, who remains 'the same, yesterday and today and for ever' (13: 8). That suggests his unchangeableness (6: 18–20) 'of old', 'in these last days', and as 'heir of all things' (1: 1–2); i.e. from creation through 'the days of his flesh' (5: 7), now as tested and perfected Son of God to 'help in time of need' (4: 16), and as unique priest who 'always lives to make intercession' for 'those who draw near to God through him' (7: 25). As such, he is guarantor or surety (7: 22) and mediator (8: 6; 9; 15; 12: 24) for the community's faith and life.

Christ, in Hebrews, is pre-existent. When he enters into the world (10: 5–7; cf. 1: 6), in a flesh-and-blood incarnation (2: 14), he speaks about how he comes to do God's will (in words from Ps. 40: 8). The purpose of that incarnation was, by dying, to destroy the devil (who has the power of death) and to deliver all who, through fear of death, were subject to lifelong bondage (2: 14–15). Thus, Jesus' sacrificial death is at the heart of the book, from the beginning (1: 3) to the end (13: 12), couched above all in priestly, Day-of-Atonement categories, such as Paul (or, more likely, earlier Jewish Christianity) employed at Rom. 3: 25 (cf. Heb. 9–10 and Ziesler, *Pauline Christianity*, rev. edn., 92–3). Oddly, 'resurrection' is not mentioned by Hebrews in connection with Jesus (cf. 6: 2; 11: 19, 35, however, for knowledge, even prior to Jesus' day, of the general resurrection); rather, the category of 'exaltation' is preferred (1: 3; 10: 12, with the influence of Ps. 110: 1). Jesus in Hebrews clearly comes from God to bring human beings salvation but is just as clearly presented as a human being (yet without sinning, 4: 15) who, first, before all others, as 'pioneer', achieves the God-willed goal of 'perfection' (2: 10; 5: 9; 7: 28, cf. 19; 10: 14; 11: 40; 12: 23).

Why Hebrews employs priestly categories to present Christ and his death is part of the problem of the treatise as a whole. Paul could occasionally employ sacerdotal terms (cf. Rom. 15: 16), and priests, temples, and animal sacrifice were well known in the Gentile world. But the imagery in Hebrews is so specifically tied to Israel's cult in the wilderness period and to a priesthood of Melchizedek that a background in Judaism is commonly assumed. Hence the conclusions that Hebrews is directed to Jewish Christians tempted to revert to Levitical religion, or to ex-Essenes who were returning to a Qumran type of religion. If, however, connections are made with the circle around Stephen—who, in his speech in Acts 7, was clearly anti-temple as well as opposed to the Mosaic law (cf. 7: 48–50, Solomon's great mistake was building a 'God-box', a structure where the deity is supposedly imprisoned, v. 47)—then it is attractive to see Hebrews as asserting a temple- and cult-free religion against those who insist that the essence of religion is to have priests offering sacrifices regularly in sanctuaries for their constituencies.

Christians must have appeared to contemporaries as eccentric 'atheists', since they had no cultic life of this sort. Hence Hebrews develops an elaborate argument about Jesus as *the* priest who offered *one* all-sufficient sacrifice, and who now intercedes for us in the real world of heaven, in order to support the claims that 'we do have a great High Priest' (4: 14; 3: 1; 7: 26; 8: 1; 10: 21), 'we have an altar' (13: 10), 'we do offer up a sacrifice to God—of praise, the fruit of the lips that acknowledge his name' in prayer and confession (13: 16; cf. Ps. 50: 14; Hos. 14: 2).

The eschatology of Hebrews includes, on the one hand, the future aspect of Christ's coming (9: 28) and the judgement day (10: 25, 30–1; 12: 26–9). Yet there is, on the other, an even greater emphasis on what has been accomplished for us in Christ, particularly in his atoning death, and on what believers already have through the work of Christ—e.g. forgiveness of sins (2: 17) and sanctification (10: 12–18), righteousness (see below), access to God (10: 19–22; 4: 16), and hope (3: 6; 6: 11, 18–19; 7: 19; 10: 23), along with other gifts from God (2: 4; 6: 4–5). The relation between these two poles of 'realized' and 'future' eschatology has sometimes been described as a spiralling, rather than a vertically ascending, line, moving cyclically upwards (so as to express the supposed Platonism of Hebrews); or as a progression of Christ and God's people through wilderness-testing to the final 'promised land' of the kingdom or heavenly Jerusalem.

One figure through which Hebrews expresses its eschatology in a multivalent way is the image of 'rest'. God had promised

Israel 'rest', meaning land (Deut. 12: 9–10) and eventually the temple (cf. 1 Kings 8: 5–6, 20, 56), and, in apocalyptic circles, hope of heavenly rest (cf. Isa. 66: 1 = Acts 7: 49, and extra-canonical texts like the Testament of Daniel 5: 12, 'Holy ones shall rest in Eden, righteous ones shall rejoice in the New Jerusalem'). Ancient Israel rebelled in the wilderness, however, and under its 'Jesus' (Joshua) never obtained God's promised rest (Heb. 3: 7–19). But 'we who have believed enter that rest' (4: 3). That is not only something to strive for (4: 11) but something to which believers already draw near (4: 16; 10: 22). 'You have come' not to the Sinai of old but 'to Mount Zion and to the city of the living God, the heavenly Jerusalem and to innumerable angels in festal gathering' (12: 18, 22; note the perfect tense), to God and to Jesus.

With regard to ecclesiology, the verse just cited goes on to include one of the two examples in Hebrews of the word that can be translated 'church': you have come 'to the assembly (*ekklēsia*) of the first-born who are enrolled in heaven' (12: 23). (The other one is 2: 12, where Ps. 22: 22 is quoted to depict Jesus in the midst of the congregation of brothers and sisters he has redeemed.) The 'first-born' are those who believe in the promised salvation effected by the great High Priest, God's 'First-Born' (1: 6). More commonly, though, the communal consciousness of Hebrews is expressed by covenant imagery and emphasis on the idea of the people of God. Our author sees the Christian community 'on the way', to a kingdom and salvation already granted, which can be lost, however, by unbelief (3: 12, 19) or disobedience (4: 6, 11).

Within the church community, 'leaders' are mentioned (13: 7, 17, 24) whose chief characteristic is that they 'spoke to you the word of God' (13: 7, cf. 2: 3). But nothing is ever said of apostles, bishops, elders, deacons, or—surprisingly when we recall the christological theme—priests in the community or the priest-hood of all believers. Later Christianity used Hebrews to develop the concept of 'clergy' as priests, but in the treatise itself such terminology is exclusively christological; when 1 Peter (and Revelation) use 'priesthood', it is of all the faithful.

The modest use in Hebrews of righteousness terminology (e.g. 5: 13; 12: 11) develops this emphasis on the basis of the death of Jesus once and for all and its implications for life. There is reference to 'the righteousness which comes by faith' (11: 7), and 12: 23 speaks enigmatically of 'spirits of just men made perfect' (RSV). (In 12: 23 the Old Testament righteous of ch. 11, along with justified Christians, may be meant, united with the parallel 'Church of the first-born who are enrolled in heaven', i.e. the 'perfected righteous' and those '*en route*'; cf. 11: 40). Paul's favourite verse from Habakkuk (2: 4; cf. Rom. 1: 17; Gal. 3: 11) is quoted more fully at Heb. 10: 37–9. The emphasis here is on the righteous living by faith and not 'shrinking back', in line with Hebrews' paraenetic concern.

Like Paul, Hebrews also emphasizes faith (indeed in connection with righteousness/justification, 11: 41), but the meaning is somewhat different. There is no question about the presence in Hebrews of the objective sense of 'believing' in God (it occurs at 6: 1; 11: 6) and more subjectively of faith as response to the gospel (4: 2–3; 6: 12), with the emphasis on having and living by faith (10: 38, 39). Such faith provides 'full assurance' (10: 22). The reference to Jesus as 'perfecter of our faith' (12: 2) points to what he has done for believers and to the faithfulness he exhibited toward God (3: 2, 6). While Christians, in running the race of life set before them, look to Jesus, who learned obedience by suffering (12: 2, 3; 5: 8), the only direct appeal in Hebrews to 'imitation' is to imitate the faith of the community's leaders (13: 7). Ch. 11 is the roll-call of heroes and heroines who experienced in their lives all sorts of hardships and glories 'by faith'. All of these are Old Testament or Jewish figures, from Abel (11: 4), through Abraham and Sarah (vv. 8–19) and even Moses (vv. 23–8), to the prophets and beyond into Maccabean times (vv. 35–8; cf. 2 Macc. 6: 18–31; 7: 1–10; 10: 6). The 'them'/'us' (Christians) combination in vv. 39–40 further indicates this, within God's overall plan. Similar catalogues exist in Sir. 44–50, Philo, and for salvation history in Acts 7. But this encomium centres on faith.

The famous definition of faith (*pistis*) at 11: 1 must be assessed in its own right and then in the fuller context of Hebrews. Faith is defined as

a *hypothesis* (reality or assurance) of things hoped for;
an *elenchos* (proof or conviction) of things not seen.

The meaning is orientated here to the future and a hoped-for invisible world, the 'true' realm of which Hebrews elsewhere (like Platonism) speaks (cf. Heb. 8: 2; 9: 24). The church fathers gave to the first term, *hypothesis*, the philosophical sense of 'reality' (Latin *substantia*). The second word is then to be taken in the sense of 'demonstration' or 'proof'. In the sixteenth century, Erasmus and Luther argued for the subjective sense of 'assurance' and 'conviction', and RSV and other translations so render the terms (TEV: 'To have faith is to be sure of the things we hope for, to be certain of the things we cannot see'). Cf. 10: 22, 'Draw near with a true heart in full assurance of faith.' Moderns object that the two Greek words did not appear in this subjective sense in contemporary use. But others appeal to LXX use of *hypothesis* for 'expectation' or the idea of 'standing firm with regard to what one hopes for', steadfastness, tenacity (cf. Isa. 28: 16e), not 'shrinking back' (*hypostolēs*, Heb. 10: 39). Still others suggest the legal sense of 'guarantee' or 'title deed' found in the papyri, 'surety' in classical sources.

The context sheds further light. At 11: 3 ('By faith we understand' about creation through the word) faith is cognitive (cf. also vv. 19, 26). At other points in ch. 11 it refers to what motivated Abraham (vv. 17–18) or Moses (vv. 24–5). In other examples, faith leads to actions (vv. 4, 7, 8, 27, 29) and endurance of suffering (36–8). Faith has to do at times with God's actions in history (vv. 10, 16, 28, 35a). The whole passage is bracketed by references to how faith is what attests or witnesses to such persons (11: 2, 39; the Greek verb is the same in both verses).

One must be careful, then, about making of 11: 1 a definition that covers all of the chapter, let alone expresses the full nuances of faith in Hebrews. If one wishes to bring into the picture the idea that faith includes the trust and obedience that Jesus showed (see the discussion on 3: 2, 6; 5: 8; 12: 2, above) and that

Jesus' followers are to exhibit (3: 6; 5: 9; 10: 39; 12: 7), then the subjective sense of personal conviction is involved. Although the object of faith in Hebrews is especially God (as in the Old Testament and Judaism), the Christology throughout the letter demands that the gaze of those 'who have believed' (4: 3) focus on Jesus (12: 2–3). 'Faith' also occurs in Hebrews together with 'hope' and 'love' (10: 22–4), a triad found in Paul and elsewhere (Ziesler, *Pauline Christianity*, rev. edn., 20).

Canonical criticism places considerable emphasis on the way Hebrews was moved into the Pauline orbit (via ch. 13 and the reference to Timothy, 13: 23). Thus the book is said to function 'canonically as distinct and yet complementary to the Pauline corpus', giving us, indeed, 'a canonical Paul, who extends far beyond the boundaries which historical criticism has set for the reconstruction of the historical Paul' (Childs, *The New Testament as Canon*, 418). That position gives the ambiguities of canonical development too weighted a vote. We do better to recognize in the 'Epistle' to the 'Hebrews' a distinct type of highly developed, later first-century Christianity. It is *sui generis*, although not unrelated to other New Testament witnesses, even if some of its background remains unclear to us.

√ The Wisdom of James: Practical Remarks on Faith, Life, and Other Topics

THE epistle by 'James, a servant of God and of the Lord Jesus Christ, to the twelve tribes in the Dispersion [Greek *diaspora*]' is a little over a third the length of Hebrews. It has stirred up even more controversy than the larger book.

In the last century of critical study, the Book of James has been left hovering between two opinions. Some have said, as was held traditionally from the third century or so, that James the brother of Jesus himself wrote it, at a quite early date, emphasizing the words of Jesus, in a Jewish(-Christian) setting. Others, for good reasons, have argued it is a much later writing, arising out of the Hellenistic-Jewish world, reflecting the evangelists' formulations of Jesus' teachings, especially in Matthew's Sermon on the Mount.

Fair-minded consideration of James's letter has often been complicated by disputes, particularly during and since the Reformation, over the relation of James 2: 14–26, asserting that a person 'is justified by works and not by faith alone', to the teachings of Paul. This 'doctrinal' problem—one of the few theological aspects to James—is best left for treatment later in connection with 'faith' and 'righteousness'.

By Jesus' own brother or a later hand?

The questions of author, and therefore of date, lay bare many of the issues. The opening verse provides a name, the rest of the letter little else about the writer. (3: 1–2 do suggest James was a teacher.) 'Servant of God and of . . . Jesus Christ' (1: 1) was a description that could fit any Christian, including Paul (Rom. 1: 1). 'James' (Greek *Iakōbos*, Jacob) was a common name. Four or five persons with this name appear in the New Testament.

The view came to dominate that the James involved here was the brother of Jesus. (By then patristic opinions varied as to whether there were literal brothers born of Mary, or children of Joseph by a previous marriage, or cousins.) According to other New Testament references, this James was not a disciple during Jesus' ministry (Mark 3: 31–5) but was converted by a post-resurrection appearance of the risen Lord (1 Cor. 15: 7; Acts 1: 14). The conflation of all possible scriptural references suggested that James the brother of the Lord became a leader in the Jerusalem church (Acts 12: 19; Gal. 1: 19), indeed, its head after Peter left the city (Acts 15: 13–21; 21: 18; Gal. 2: 9). Precisely what ominous position 'certain men from James' took in the dispute of Paul with Peter at Antioch (Gal. 2: 12) remains unclear.

Subsequent reports and legends describe James as a conservative figure, highly revered by the Jews in Jerusalem, called 'the Just', but martyred by the priestly rulers there before AD 70. A statement from Hegesippus (preserved in Eusebius, *Church History* 2. 23) suggests that a 'dynasty' of Jesus' kindred ruled the Jewish Christian church for a time. That would help account for the authority with which the Letter of James seems written.

The arguments for James, brother of Jesus, as author include the following. (1) He needed only to give his name to get a hearing, without using any title like 'apostle'. (Actually, Jesus' brother never was one of the twelve.) (2) James's position as head of the Jerusalem church would make him a natural choice to address 'the twelve tribes in the Dispersion'. In Judaism, the technical term *diaspora* meant Jews living outside Palestine. Jewish Christians might have adopted the same terminology, but the term could also refer to Christians dispersed throughout the world (Palestine included), away from their true homeland in heaven (cf. Phil. 3: 20; 1 Peter 1: 1, 'exiles of the dispersion'; Heb. 13: 14, 'the city which is to come', the heavenly Jerusalem,

12: 22). (3) The Palestinian colouring in the letter would thereby come naturally, as in references to 'the early and the late (rain)' (5: 7, cf. Deut. 11: 14; Jer. 5: 24) or to the cries of the poor labourers whose wages were being withheld, and who called out to 'the ears of the Lord of Sabaoth' (5: 4; cf. Isa. 5: 9 LXX). See further 2: 1–7, on discrimination in the assembly (literally, synagogue); and 4: 13–5: 6, on the misuse of wealth. (4) This James would have known the oral traditions from Jesus later recorded in our synoptic gospels.

Reflections of Jesus' teachings in the Letter of James have been a pivotal point in this case. Among the links to be noted are an emphasis on being 'perfect' (1: 4; cf. the logion of Jesus now recorded at Matt. 5: 48); asking God for good and perfect gifts (1: 5, 17; cf. Matt. 7: 7, 11); prayer in faith, without doubting (1: 6; Mark 11: 23 par. Matt. 21: 21–2); the contrast between those who are merely 'hearers' and those who are 'doers of the word' (1: 22–5; cf. Matt. 7: 24–7); obeying the whole law on every point (2: 10; cf. Matt. 5: 19); the admonition not to judge (4: 12; cf. Matt. 7: 1); and the statement that riches and possessions rot away and become moth-eaten, and that treasure oxidizes (5: 1–3; cf. Matt. 6: 19). Most impressive is 5: 12, 'Do not swear, either by heaven or earth, or with any other oath, but let your yes be yes and your no be no, that you may not fall under condemnation.' Some have felt this to be a more original form of Jesus' saying than what is preserved in expanded form at Matt. 5: 34, 'Do not swear at all, either by heaven, for it is the throne of God, or by the earth, for it is his footstool, or by Jerusalem, for it is the city of the Great King. . . . Let what you say be simply "Yes" or "No"; anything more than this comes from evil.'

A more elaborate argument is the claim that, of the eight beatitudes from Jesus recorded in Matthew 5, four are reflected in James and in the same order:

Matthew	*James*
Matt. 5: 3 the *poor*, theirs is the *kingdom* of heaven	2: 5 God has chosen the '*poor* in the world to be rich in faith and

5: 5 the meek shall *inherit* the earth	*heirs* of the *kingdom*' (2: 5)
5: 7 the merciful shall obtain *mercy*	2: 12, 13 '*mercy* triumphs over judgement'
5: 9 the *peacemakers*	3: 18 'those who *make peace*'
Cf. also 5: 12 *the prophets* were persecuted	and 5: 10–11 the *prophets*' suffering and patience as example

Not all these examples are equally convincing, but on this view James the teacher often used the teachings of Jesus, his brother.

The date of the book, on the theory that Jesus' brother wrote it, is early, but even here opinions vary. AD 60–5, just before James' death, has often been espoused. Others would put the writing about AD 40, thus making James the first New Testament book to be written. Such theories put the place of writing in Jerusalem.

Standing in the way of attribution of James to the Lord's brother as creator of so early a composition are some weighty arguments, however, in favour of an unknown Jewish-Christian writer toward the end of the first century. This person might actually have been named James or might have worked pseudonymously.

(1) Foremost among the facts are the language and style of the book. The polished Greek does not fit a countryman from Galilee, even if he settled in Jerusalem; it rather reflects the mannerisms of a Hellenistic Jew of the diaspora. The author echoes the wisdom tradition and its literature. Reflections of the Hebrew Scripture occur regularly in the LXX version (cf. 2: 8, 11, 23; 4: 6). Indeed, James cites as 'scripture' at 4: 5 a line about 'the spirit of the Lord' as a 'jealous lover', a line that we cannot locate in canonical (or other) literature. Origen suggested *The Secrets of Enoch* (in relation to 1 Kings 19: 10); moderns, the *Book of Eldad and Modad* (with regard to Num. 11: 29), or a Midrashic combination of biblical themes. Phrases in James like

'the cycle of nature' or 'wheel of birth' (3: 6, RSV text and note) and 'the implanted word' (1: 21) sound much more akin to Orphism or Stoic terminology respectively and thus to the Hellenistic religious world of the day. As we shall see in the discussion on genre below, the author reflects topics (*topoi*) from Graeco-Roman society (3: 13 ff., 'Who is wise and understanding among you?' 4: 1 ff., 'What causes wars, and what causes fightings among you?').

(2) A further factor militating against traditional authorship comes out of ecclesial tradition itself: the epistle was only slowly received into the canon—a fact which is strange if a brother of Jesus wrote it. Hegesippus, although a Palestinian who tells us much about James, never mentions a letter by James. Tertullian, Cyprian, and Irenaeus do not quote from it. There is no reference to James in the Muratorian Canon. Origen suggests its status was disputed in his day. Eusebius placed the document among the 'antilegomena', books spoken against, but in this case recognized by the majority, and mentions the Lord's brother as author. James, we can say, was accepted in the East by AD 360, in the West a bit later, but the Syrian church was uncertain about it into the fifth century. Jerome's doubts (*De Viris Illustribus* 2) echoed down into the Middle Ages.

(3) Other problems have to do with content. (*a*) Could a brother of Jesus, converted, as James supposedly was, after Easter, omit all reference to Jesus' death and resurrection? Probably no New Testament book says so little about Christ. One finds in James little of the 'personal spell' of Jesus or of his risen lordship. (*b*) A particular problem is the attitude in James toward the law. The position (see below) is not only far from that in Paul but reflects little of Jesus' critique of the sabbath and of legalism generally.

(4) The Letter of James seems to stem not from Jesus directly or to be immediately against Paul (2: 14–26), but to derive from the form of Jesus' teachings found in Matthew (see examples cited above) and to be against a post-Pauline situation (see below). Some have alleged that, for all the echoes of Jesus, the author, in disregard of what his brother taught, turns to the

Greek LXX, Jewish tradition (4: 5), and Greek Cynic-Stoic ethics at point after point. Even the prohibition against oaths in 5: 12 can be paralleled by statements in Epictetus and Pythagoras. The Jesus who teaches here is tailored to a world outside Galilee.

Those impressed by such arguments—and it has by now become the majority position as opposed to the traditional view—make James pseudonymous, to be dated in the second Christian generation or later (AD 75–150), most suggesting 80–100. Guessing at locale is difficult, but a case has been made for Syria, chiefly on the grounds of similarity at points to Matthew and to the Didache. (If this is correct, then the Syrian church's reluctance to canonize the work may reflect remembrance of its pseudonymous origins.)

Between these two positions there have been constructed, of course, numerous 'half-way houses'. The 'secretary theory' has been invoked: James had a good Greek stylist working with him. Or it has been suggested that James of Jerusalem, Jesus' brother, wrote it in Aramaic, for the Jews, or for a particular congregation; then a later hand expanded it into a general epistle to all twelve tribes. Ariston of Pella has been proposed as this reviser. More recently, a date in the 40s has been pressed, but with redaction between 55 and 80 in a more Hellenistic mode, so as to satisfy external tradition and internal evidence.

At times commentators, struck by the lack of specifically Christian features in James, have argued that it was originally a Jewish document, superficially adapted for Christianity by references to Jesus Christ added at 1: 1 and 2: 1. Ingenious is the suggestion that James (Greek *Iakōbos*) reflects Jacob and his twelve sons (tribes, Gen. 49), as in the pseudepigraphical writing, The Testaments of the Twelve Patriarchs, weaving in allusions to the twelve in the course of the letter. Thus, one could see Isaac in the theme of 'joy' (1: 2; cf. Gen. 21: 3, 6; 'Isaac' means 'he laughs') or Simeon (probably 'one who hears') in 1: 19 (be quick to hear (the word)). But such theories have fallen of their own weight, after being reflected in a commentary or two.

James as paraenetic wisdom literature

A most significant facet of James—long perceived but which has emerged more and more in recent study—is its polished rhetoric, especially apparent in the Greek. It is written in literary Koiné, not scruffy Jewish 'translation Greek'. The diction is good. Alliteration occurs (e.g. 1: 2, or 3: 2, each with three or four words beginning in Greek with the letter *pi*). For whatever is to be made of it (probably that a source is being quoted), the opening of 1: 17 scans as a Greek poetic hexameter line. When one reads James in Greek, one is impressed by the frequent word-play, vocabulary links (1: 15–18, use of the prefix (*ap(o)*)), and rhyming sounds (1: 14, *exelkomenos kai deleazomenos*, 'lured and enticed'; cf. 1: 6, *anemizomenōi kai rhipizomenōi*, 'driven and tossed by the wind'). The diatribe form is employed at 2: 1–3: 12, especially 2: 18, a device which involves quoting, then answering, a hypothetical opponent (as Paul does also at Rom. 2). Yet for all these literary features, James lacks much organization. Johnson (*The Writings of the New Testament*, 456) speaks of 'structureless structure' (Luther: 'one minute he talks about clothing, the next about wrath'). At best there is word-play or use of catchwords. 'Greeting' (1: 1, *chairein*) points to 'joy' (1: 2, *charan*). The statement, you will be 'lacking in nothing' (1: 4, *leipomenoi*), propels one on to the next theme, 'If any of you lacks (*leipetai*) wisdom, ask God' (1: 5).

Such observations are related to the establishment of the genre of James. In spite of the vague and minimal salutation (1: 1), it is not really a letter. Some have been impressed with affinities to the Hellenistic-Jewish synagogue homily, such as also can be sensed in Hebrews, Acts 7, and The Testaments of the Twelve Patriarchs, or 1 Clement. Use of '(beloved) brethren' is frequent as address (1: 2, 16, 19, etc.). But manifestly James is a wisdom writing, paraenetic in nature. It instructs and admonishes, in ethical matters, for a community, but eclectically—here a point, there a point, with little continuity. There is a certain repetitiveness, but no overarching aim. It is a treasure trove of aphorisms and short, vivid scenes. But no massive crisis, no persecution, no particular problem, and no central theme shapes the entire document. One recent devotional treatment has seen in the book a 'rogues' gallery' of those who wander from the truth (5: 19)—e.g. the doubter (1: 6), the rich (1: 9–11; 5: 1–6), the self-deceiver (1: 23–5), or 'the confident entrepreneurs' (4: 13–17); but interesting as such a list is, there is no indication that the author seeks to depict ten (or twelve) such groups.

Because of the dearth of internal references to any local situation, it has proved difficult to sketch any social setting for the community (or communities) addressed. One theory has been that James was composed to instil Christian patience in the face of social upheaval and the temptation toward political aggressiveness. Such a view, while possible for 1 Peter (see above), is scarcely popular today with Christian activists or liberation theologians. Could it in part fit James? Cf. 5: 7–11, on patience. In commentaries written in the last few years, one reads far more of James providing a base for developing issues of justice (see 2: 5–7 and the discussion of ethics below). But the fact of the matter is that the document does not speak of State authorities (as in the *Haustafeln*). It breathes far more the setting of the religious community and its assembly (2: 2), with only an occasional glance at 'the rich' who 'drag you into court' (2: 6). Others have preferred to see James as reflecting a Hellenistic–Jewish–Christian attempt to reach out to 'God-fearers', those Gentiles attracted to the synagogue by its moral stance. The document would thus be a Jewish bridge to Christianity for such people; those who are attracted to a type of Judaism are now invited to a kind of Christianity marked by certain features which the paraenesis in James brings out. Doctrine is not demandingly presented; the ethics are syncretistic, in terms attractive for the Hellenistic world of the diaspora.

Theology in James?

Our list of topical checkpoints for New Testament documents, therefore, turns out somewhat differently in James. Although it may not be unexpected that the term 'gospel' never occurs, either in its noun or verb form, it is surprising that Jesus' central theme of the kingdom of God occurs hardly at all. Only at 2: 5 is there reference to 'those who are poor in this world' being chosen to be 'heirs of the kingdom which God has promised to those who love him'. The 'royal law', which at 2: 8 includes the command, 'You shall love your neighbour as yourself', is literally 'the law with kingly or royal authority' or even 'the law set for kings', but there is no direct reflection of Jesus' theme. The nearest one comes in James to a sense of kerygma is the reference to 'the implanted word [*via baptism?*], which is able to save your souls' (1: 21).

The paucity of christological assertions has been noted. Jesus Christ is termed 'the Lord' at 1: 1 and 2: 1, but in each instance some have seen the words 'Jesus Christ' as a later addition to an original reference to God as Lord. At 2: 1 the awkward wording is especially open to such a view, but others take it as 'our glorious Lord Jesus Christ' (NIV) or as a further, separate title for Jesus, as 'the Glory'. Some patristic commentators took 5: 6 as a reference to Jesus: 'you have killed the righteous man', for 'the Righteous One' could be a christological title (1 John 2: 1). But context makes the reference here generic, to 'the righteous (sufferer)' of Old Testament, Jewish, and Christian literature. At 5: 7, 'Be patient . . . until the coming of the Lord', we could, of course, have a reference to Jesus' parousia, but it could also mean the Day of the Lord in an Old Testament sense. Similarly with 5: 11. When James appeals to examples, it is to figures of Israel's history, like Abraham (2: 21–3), Rahab (2: 25), Job (5: 11), or Elijah (5: 17). There is no 'imitation of Christ'.

One cannot detect much in the way of eschatology in James, but then that is true of wisdom literature generally. There is no 'gospel', kingdom, or promise said to be 'present' or 'fulfilled'. But life in community goes on, and occasionally there is a sense of judgement to come (2: 13; 3: 1; 4: 11–12; 5: 7, 9).

The community addressed meets in assembly (*synagogē*, 2: 2), attracting both the poor in shabby clothing and the well-dressed rich. One gets the impression from one passage (2: 1–7) of a basically poor, oppressed group, looking for justice, and from another (5: 1–6) of a well-to-do group concerned to admonish the rich, including tradespeople from the group (4: 13–16). Or are both 'set topics' in wisdom writings, from which no social profile of a community can be drawn? Once there is talk of the *ekklēsia*: 'the elders of the church' are to pray over the person who is sick and anoint him or her with oil (5: 14). This suggests some organization, but less than could be found in a typical Hellenistic synagogue.

Ethics are obviously the chief concern of the document, something that is true for much wisdom literature. Obviously social justice is an issue, at least within the society of the group. Hence the outcry about treatment of orphans and widows (1: 27), about the sick and other conditions of suffering or joy (5: 13–16). James has been read as exalting poverty or as seeking to bring poor and rich together in a single group, where all are urged to be patient (5: 7, 8, 10) and the rich to be compassionate as well (5: 11). But in James's practical advice, the practice of prayer (5: 16–18), submission to God (4: 7–8), wisdom (3: 13–18), and self-control (especially of one's tongue, 3: 1–12) all occupy a place.

A distinctive feature in James, and one not always tapped in grasping the document's thought, is its concept of law. There are some eight references, none of them in the famous passage in 2: 14–26 about faith and works. The initial one, at 1: 25, is striking: the person 'who looks into the perfect law, the law of liberty, and perseveres, no hearer that forgets but a doer that acts, shall be blessed. . . .' This beatitude occurs in the section (1: 22–5) on being hearers and doers of the implanted word 'which is able to save your soul' (1: 21). James's real interest is in 'doing'. The figure shifts at v. 23b from hearing 'the word' to looking into the mirror of 'the perfect law of liberty'. Our author seems to regard this 'law' as the side of the word which sets forth God's demands (Goppelt, *Variety and Unity*, 203–4; Johnson, *The Writings of the New Testament*, 459–60). To call it the 'law of liberty' has analogies in both Stoic and rabbinic thought.

This 'royal' law (2: 8) is to be fulfilled (1) in terms of love for the neighbour (2: 8), not by judging the neighbour (4: 11–12);

(2) as a totality, its individual commandments part of a total claim (2: 9–11); and (3) under the expectations of a final judgement (2: 12–13). These later verses refer to being 'judged under the law of liberty', with mercy for the person who has shown mercy (cf. Matt. 5: 7; 18: 33). But this law is never defined by reference to Moses, although some of the Ten Commandments and the love command of Lev. 19: 18 are cited, exactly as in the gospel tradition. The liberal sprinkling of sayings of Jesus throughout James, although never termed law, suggest that the 'perfect, royal law' is a Christian form of what Jesus and the Old Testament call for as God's will. This view of law differs from those in Judaism, Paul, or later Christianity, but could fit a community that stressed the imperatives of the word of truth, about which James so often speaks.

Faith emerges as a major subject in 2: 14–26, where 14 of the 19 examples from the root occur in James. Prior to that passage, 2: 1 enjoins, 'Show no partiality as you hold the faith of our Lord Jesus Christ, the Lord of glory' (RSV)—that is, you dare not show preference or deference to the rich over the poor as you exercise your faith in Jesus (objective genitive; a subjective genitive, denoting 'Jesus' faith', would exacerbate even more the odd word order, and there is no suggestion in James of any interest in 'how Jesus exercised faith'). Faith is something which James's readers are expected to possess. Indeed, they are to be 'rich in faith' (2: 5). It will be tested (1: 3), but is to be used in asking God for requests in prayer (1: 6; 5: 15).

Righteousness/justification is the other theme which abounds in 2: 14–26. It may be noted in addition, however, that James (1: 20), along with Paul and Matt. 6: 33, uses the technical Old Testament-Jewish phrase 'righteousness *of God*': 'human anger does not work the righteousness that God demands', i.e. the exercise of justice before God. 'The harvest of righteousness', mentioned in an isolated saying in 3: 18, refers most likely to the results of righteous conduct.

It is now appropriate to consider the celebrated diatribe at 2: 14–26 in favour of justification by works, not by mere faith in the sense of intellectual belief. The author follows a Jewish exegetical tradition, which combined Gen. 15: 6 with Gen. 22, in order to show that Abraham 'was justified by works', by offering up Isaac (2: 21); in this way Abraham's faith (Gen. 15: 6; James 2: 23) was completed by his works in Gen. 22 (2: 22–3—never mind that Isaac was not really sacrificed). A second example is then brought forward from the story of Rahab the harlot (Joshua 2: 1–21): she 'was justified by works when she received the messengers [*whom Joshua had sent to spy out the land*] and sent them out [*safely from Jericho*] another way' (2: 25). From these somewhat forced proofs, the conclusion is that 'faith apart from works is like a dead body, without spirit. James wants to move people to activity. But whom?

The passage is set in the context of some who claim to have faith but fail to give food or clothing to persons in need (2: 14–17). Such selfishness can occur in groups of all sorts. But 2: 18–20 sets up a further diatribe where our writer takes on those who separate faith and such works and believe simply in the oneness of God, a prime tenet of Judaism (Deut. 6: 4). It has often been maintained that Paul was the target here, but his distinctive phrase 'works *of the law*' is missing, and the Pauline belief system centred on salvation through Christ and not just on the tenet that 'God is one'. Most recent interpretation, therefore, sees no reference here to Paul but, at best, to later followers, who had terribly narrowed the concept of faith and sundered it from all response to those in need. James tries in a blunt and practical way to correct them, counterbalancing their false view by arguments for doing one's faith by carrying it out in practice.

It could also be that, in the style often found in wisdom literature, no specific group is historically the target; instead, we have a general admonition to involvement along with believing. In any case, one must note the implication of one phrase which our author has woven into the description of Abraham. Abraham is called 'the friend of God' (2: 23; cf. Isa. 41: 8; 2 Chron. 20: 7). Later in James, it is asserted that to be 'a friend of the world' is to be 'an enemy of God' (4: 4). Thus, for all the emphasis on activity, James does not embrace the world or 'worldly Christianity' here. Or is this another example of how difficult it is to fit together consistently the little units within James?

The one-sided stress in 2: 14–26 on works is also different from the picture in 1: 18–24 of Christians being begotten and brought forth by the word of truth through the implanted word. A total reading of the document leaves us with a kind of Christianity where the word makes Christians, that is, people who believe in Jesus as Lord (1: 18–2: 1). But hearers are to be persevering doers because they have taken a good hard look into the mirror of the liberating law (1: 22–5) and have heard the commands or imperatives of the word. And so they minister to the poor and needy (of the group), without getting caught up in the adulteries of the world (1: 27; 4: 4, 7–8). God's values are not those of current society.

This curious conglomeration of themes in James is typical of wisdom literture. Each paragraph is good for what it's good for, but readers must supply the situation in each instance, in which they work out the practical application (Blenkinsopp, *Wisdom*, 21–40). The document seems to intend neither a 'theology' of Jesus' teachings nor an alternative in any depth to Paul. Pithy, at times passionate, James at best offered warnings and directions in Christian wisdom that might have attracted people from the Hellenistic synagogue, and sought to help persons individually and in community to live out aspects of the word as commands for life.

Luther set the wisdom Christianity of James on the periphery of New Testament types of faith, not because of its paragraph on faith and works but ultimately because it said so little about Christ. That remains the complaint about James for any approach that looks on the New Testament as a 'Jesus book', or on 'Jesus the Jew now made Christ and Lord' as its unifying feature.

Relatively few treatments over the centuries, from the time of canonization on, have given James high priority within the New Testament canon; but many, like Søren Kierkegaard, have found its precepts useful to address the church of their day for its failings. Current 'canonical criticism' has sought to see in James a 'continuity between Israel and the obedient Christian life' and so a positive reminder of the values of Judaism; but this comes, admittedly, with the sayings of Jesus 'as the prism through which the Old Testament is now understood' (Childs, *The New Testament as Canon*, 433–4, 437).

At points, James invokes Israel's prophets (e.g. 1: 10–11 = Isa. 40: 6–7; 4: 8, cf. Isa. 1: 16; Zech. 1: 3). But to call James 'the Amos of the New Testament' makes the book too prophetic. It is as empirical wisdom that the Book of James speaks. Paul would have agreed that a faith which does not express itself in conduct is scarcely righteousness (1 Cor. 6: 9); he would have agreed that God stands as judge over all rites, sacraments, and conduct (1 Cor. 10: 5–13). But faith, righteousness, the word, and works he undertood in senses quite different from those allowed by James's blunt, practical concerns (cf. Ziesler, *Pauline Christianity*, rev. edn., 148). James cures misunderstandings, but is wisdom admonition, not foundational theology. It echoes Romans 12–13 without much of chs. 1–5, about salvation, although sin abounds. Compare James 1: 15; 5: 20; the last note struck by James is that sinners can be saved from death.

The Johannine Line of Development: Three Letters

THE unity and variety within the Johannine corpus has already been noted (pp. 63–4). Three epistles, two of them short, typical letters of the day, are contained in the New Testament canon, at some remove from the Fourth Gospel and separated by another little letter (Jude) from the Revelation to St John the Divine. We may consider these three Johannine letters together, for the longer one has doubtless helped preserve the other two and pull them into the canonical collection. But opinions vary on the origins of each, and over whether 1 John actually helped preserve the Fourth Gospel for orthodox Christianity or whether, on the other hand, the Gospel of John pulled the letters into the orbit of the canon by virtue of its own prestige.

First John is really not an epistle, since it lacks salutation and conclusion and contains no greetings or proper names. It commences as abruptly and majestically as Hebrews. The writing has been termed a tractate, homily, or manifesto. Second John is addressed by 'the elder' to a church ('the elect lady and her children'). It warns against receiving deceptive teachers who may come seeking hospitality. The equally brief 3 John is also by 'the elder', and here specific names abound. He writes to Gaius, who is commended for his hospitality. He writes against Diotrephes, 'who likes to put himself first' and 'does not acknowledge my authority' (v. 9). Another Christian named Demetrius is commended (v. 12). Thus, 3 John plunges us into an ecclesial politics of personalities and doctrines; 2 John reflects problems of the day in following 'the doctrine of Christ' (v. 9); 1 John gives the fullest detail about true and false teachings and ethics, in the face of the tragic fact that some members 'went out from us'—in schism—who thereby proved not really to have been 'of us' in faith and spirit (2: 19).

A generation or so ago it was vigorously debated—like the question of which came first, the chicken or the egg—whether 1 John was written in the wake of the Fourth Gospel or John's Gospel after the first epistle, to clarify it. Now it is pretty well accepted that the Gospel of John came first and that the epistle followed, in order to clarify John's meaning.

A further debate continues, however, over the sequence of the three letters. The usual treatment takes them up in their canonical order, so that 2 and 3 John represent later facets of the basic struggle depicted in 1 John and, behind it, the Fourth Gospel. An alternative is to argue that 3 John should be the starting-point, with its vivid dramatis personae. It can be taken as a letter of recommendation for Demetrius, who bears the other two documents, 2 John as a 'covering' letter to be read to the assembly, setting the stage for the exposition and exhortations in the treatise we call 1 John. Of course the matter is complicated if, as yet other commentators have proposed, 2 John is a fiction or 2 and 3 John are addressed to different communities.

Because of the relation to John's Gospel, the three letters are often dated to the last decade of the first Christian century, probably after AD 95. If they represent response and developments after the Fourth Gospel reached its basic form, the letters could spread out over a decade or so, from 96 to 105 or beyond. A locale in Asia Minor, Syria, or Palestine follows from whatever decision is made about the provenance of the Johannine Gospel.

Reconstructing a historical setting for 1 John

Recalling that Johannine Christianity was probably the result of a process of communal development (see above, pp. 64–6), we may picture a band of sisters and brothers gathered under the Paraclete around the Beloved Disciple as a group with a very high view of Christ—seeing him, indeed, as God (John 1: 1, 18;

5: 16–18; 20: 28)—but a relatively little-developed ecclesiology. This lack of organizational structure stemmed both from the basic pneumatic nature of the group, stressing the gift of the Spirit-Paraclete to each believer (14: 16–17, 26; 15: 26; 16: 13–15), and from the probable fact that it remained within the structures of a tolerant synagogue community longer than Christians did in most other places.

Both the experience of what Christ brings into life (1: 14, 16, 17) and the compensation the group experienced, once they were expelled from the synagogue (9: 22; 16: 2) but found themselves not orphaned (14: 18)—since Jesus in effect came to them as the Paraclete or 'another Comforter'—provided a richly 'realized' eschatology. This promise of 'the Counselor', as helper, Johannine Christians held aloft and held fast to in the face of persecution (16: 2–3) and even during a possible relocation of the group in the Dispersion (cf. 7: 35). They clung to their simple ethic of love for one another (13: 34). This was a community that saw itself in strong contrast to the world, out of which its members had been chosen (15: 18–19). It is this world, in which they live (17: 6, 9, 14–16), with which Johannine Christians are coming to terms in the three epistles. They have no illusions that they are 'of the world', any more than Jesus was (17: 16), but they feel 'sent into the world', with a mission to those who will believe that God sent Jesus, whom to know is eternal life (17: 18, 21, 23).

Any reading of 1 John must reckon with the point that there has been a split in the community. One group (and it may have been the majority) has broken fellowship and gone forth on its own, just the way the followers of the Beloved Disciple had gone forth from the synagogue, partly under pressure, partly to assert their true belief. First John refers to these separatists as the 'many antichrists', who 'went out from us, but were not of us', adding wistfully, 'If they had been of us, they would have continued with us', and concluding logically, as if to show God's will: 'they went out that it might be plain that they are not of us' (2: 18–19). The term 'antichrist' (note the use of the plural at some points) may have been coined by the author of 1 John to describe the heretical false prophets who oppose Jesus as messiah. There is nothing terribly mysterious about the term, certainly nothing apocalyptic, for our author defines an antichrist as one who 'denies that Jesus is the Christ', who denies that 'Jesus Christ has come in the flesh', who therefore 'denies the Father and the Son' (2: 22; 4: 1–3). Mixed into the picture are also accusations about the morality of 'those who have gone forth from us': in claiming to know Christ as intimately as they do (2: 4), they regard themselves as being beyond sin (1: 8, 10). The question of perfection in the Christian life thus enters in. Also at issue will be eschatology and the concept of the Spirit.

How can one account for the views held both by the author of 1 John and by those who have moved beyond to new positions? One way is to see the debate as having grown out of certain emphases or ambiguities in the Fourth Gospel. The dispute arose out of two ways of interpreting the basic, underlying document of the Johannine community, its written gospel and accompanying traditions. The community which thus put a premium on signs written up in order that people might believe and have life (20: 30–1; above, p. 66) was now forced in a subsequent document, 1 John, to clarify its faith.

Theological emphases: 1 John and the Fourth Gospel

The Fourth Gospel had presented Jesus Christ with great emphasis on his pre-existence (1: 1–4; 8: 58) and glory (1: 14; 17: 5, 24). Given the stress of the prologue on the Word's 'incarnation' (1: 14), it has always been very easy to overlook the theology in John that centres on the Cross. This emerges particularly in the way the crucifixion is presented as 'the hour' when Jesus is 'glorified' at his death (12: 23–4, 27–33). All in all, the Fourth Gospel, while speaking of how Jesus 'laid down his life for the sheep' (10: 11, 15, 17, 18), presents the crucifixion more as a triumph (so that Jesus may take his life up again at Easter), rather than as an atonement for sin. It also uses the self-sacrifice of Jesus for developing a disciples' ethic of response (13: 37–8; 15: 13–17).

In addition, the Johannine Jesus strides through Galilee, Samaria, and Judaea with a majesty that distinguishes him from the earthly world. To have him say, 'I am not of this world' (8: 23; 17: 14) could be misunderstood as disconnecting him from this world. If 'eternal life' is to know God and Jesus Christ, whom God sent (17: 3), the touchstone could be said to be 'the one true God' and a pre-existent, now glorified Christ. All the statements about Jesus becoming flesh (1: 14), becoming weary (4: 6) or thirsty (4: 7), or weeping (11: 35) could be taken as part of a relatively unimportant stage in the odyssey of Christ for our salvation. Thus one line of interpretation, christologically, could have been to see Christ as supreme—but not Jesus; to stress pre-existence and exaltation—but not life in the flesh. Precisely in the interests of a high Christology, developing further what is in the Fourth Gospel, one branch of the Johannine church could have taken up the positions sketched above.

The author of 1 John replies to this deviant position on Jesus by insisting that the message is that only those confessing 'Jesus Christ has come *in the flesh*' are of God (4: 2–3). To miss this is to miss both Christ the Son and God the Father (2: 22–3). Beginnings are important, but rather than pre-existence (as in John 1: 1), 1 John picks up with 'that which was from the beginning' in the earthly career of Jesus and the time when we first heard preached 'the word of life' or Christian message (1: 1–3). Our document, apparently deliberately, avoids the terms 'glory' or 'glorify'. The meaning of the Cross is specifically set forth: 'the blood of Jesus cleanses us from all sin' (1: 7); 'he is the expiation for our sins . . . and also for the sins of the whole world' (2: 2; cf. 5: 6, 'blood' referring to Jesus' death). The figure of 'laying down our lives for the brethren' (3: 16 RSV) is repeated, but grounded in the fact that 'Jesus laid down his life for us', thereby showing us what love is. And the ethic is more firmly tied to this world of 'goods' or possessions and of people in need (3: 17). First John several times called for a style of life where we walk 'just as Jesus walked' (2: 6; 3: 3, 7); 'as He is, so are we in the world' (4: 17).

Closely connected with the Christology of the opponents who

have left the group is their view of existence as sinlessness and perfection. The Fourth Gospel had taught that Jesus' followers possess 'the light of life' in Christ (8: 12) and so walk as children of light (12: 35–6); they know 'the truth' and so are freed from slavery to sin (8: 31–6). The result of encounter with Christ is no longer to 'have sin' or guilt (John 9, esp. 9: 41). Jesus was sinless (cf. John 8: 46). Those who receive him and believe become 'children of God', begotten of God (1: 12–13), clean 'all over' (by virtue of the word and baptism, 13: 10), having passed from death to life, beyond the judgement (5: 24). So it is that certain slogans in 1 John make sense if they are understood as emanating from a group which took this line of thinking: 'I know Christ' (2: 3) and am in the light (2: 9); 'we have fellowship with him' (1: 6), therefore 'we do not "have sin"' (1: 8), indeed, 'we have not sinned' (1: 10). Of course, such ideas could have been brought in from outside influences, for example, from converts who had been adherents of pagan mystery cults; but a good case can be made that the claims asserted in 1 John could have arisen from a one-sided appropriation of the Fourth Gospel.

In any case, 1 John responds with an emphasis on sin in the life of the believer that is more pronounced than that in John's Gospel. It is not denied that we know by revelation, for the verb *ginōskein* is used repeatedly (e.g. 2: 3, 5c (RSV 'we may be sure'), 13, 14, 18; 3: 6; 4: 2). But it is asserted that

if we say we have fellowship with God while we walk in darkness, we lie . . . (1: 6)

if we say we have no sin, we deceive ourselves . . . (1: 8)

if we say we have not sinned, we make Christ a liar . . . (1: 10).

The goal is that one should not fall into acts of sin (2: 1a). No one who abides in Christ can keep on sinning, and a person born of God cannot continue to practise sin (3: 6–9). Yet 'if anyone does sin, we have an advocate with the Father, Jesus Christ, the Righteous One' (2: 1b). Just as in the Gospel of John (20: 23) there is means for forgiving sins, through Christ, so here. But the overall position of 1 John is on the side of the committed, obedient life, even though there are occasional lapses. The document, while criticizing the perfectionism here and now which the opponents claim, holds to a relative perfection or maturity in the conduct of believers that characterized early Christianity generally.

Behind the Christology and ethics of 1 John and those whom it opposes lay a difference also in eschatology. The tilt in the Fourth Gospel on the question of 'future parousia' versus 'realization now' was definitely toward the latter (see above, pp. 67–8). Had this encouraged those who seceded from the Johannine community to lose all sense of future fulfilment? First John brings out the latter aspect while not going back on the 'already realized' aspects. If present eschatology is reiterated in 2: 12, 13, 14, or 20 (cf. also 3: 14), the futuristic side is presented not only by talk of 'the last hour' and 'antichrists' but also by verses like 3: 2, 'We know that when Christ appears, we shall be like him, for we shall see him as he is' or 2: 28 about 'when Christ appears'. The opening verses in 1 John 3 put together a balanced view. The first and chief point is the love which God has already exhibited through what we are (realized eschatology, 3: 1). But there is a future fulfilment, expressed in terms of Christ's expected appearance (3: 2). The two aspects together call for a moral response; purifying oneself, as Christ is pure (3: 3, cf. 3: 7).

Any profile of features in 1 John that reflect differences from the opponents, differences which in turn may have arisen out of traits in the Fourth Gospel, should also include the Spirit. John's Gospel articulated a very distinctive concept of the Paraclete in the sayings of chs. 14–16. Indeed, the Spirit/Counselor would make up for the presence of the absent Jesus as teacher of the Johannine community (16: 7–15). The opponents in 1 John took up this idea of themselves as Spirit-filled prophets and exploited it to the full. Perhaps the claim to an anointing or 'unction from the Holy One' (2: 20) was language of theirs. The author of 1 John does not retreat from the charismatic-pneumatic sort of Christianity to which the Fourth Gospel was committed; but the stern admonition is set forth: 'Do not believe every spirit, but test the spirits to see whether they are of God' (4: 1). A doctrinal criterion is provided at 4: 3. Much as Paul had to insist that 'Christ crucified' serve as norm for spirits and prophets claiming to speak in his name (1 Cor. 1: 23 is standard for what is said about spiritual gifts in that letter), so 1 John insists that valid prophet-spirits must confess that 'Jesus Christ has come in the flesh'.

The features sketched above for the theology in 1 John have been set forth on the assumption that, in Christology, understanding of the human situation ('Christian anthropology'), eschatology, and the Spirit, there were salient differences over how to interpret the Fourth Gospel that have their origin in a dispute between the author and opponents who were going off in their own direction. These points by no means exhaust the theological aspects of 1 John (see below). Nor does the distinctiveness of many of the aspects treated above depend on the historical reconstruction proposed. For it remains a fact that 1 John eschews language about 'glory', even though the Gospel of John revelled in it. Nevertheless, there are alternatives to seeing the roots of the heretical positions in over-realized eschatology and an extension of the Christology in the Fourth Gospel.

Traditionally, interpreters of 1 John have sought to relate the opponents with the Docetist branch of Gnosticism, with those who maintained Christ merely 'seemed' (Greek *dokein*) to be a human being but actually avoided all contact with the material world. In particular, it was popular to associate the heretics with a Docetist teacher named Cerinthus. Such connections came from a time when far less was known about gnostic movements than we know today and, on the basis of patristic reports, such groups were looked on as a Christian deviation caused by outside influences. However, what Cerinthus taught about Christ—that he was only temporarily united with the Jewish man Jesus—is not reflected in 1 John, and what 1 John scores as the menace in ethics is not substantiated in known accounts of the views of Cerinthus.

In reaction to these traditional attempts, others therefore stress our ignorance of the situation. While false teachers of a Docetic type are being opposed, 'I John is not to be understood as being in any way a writing intended for specific readers' (Kümmel, *Introduction*, 437). This position has the merit of rejecting, on good grounds, the somewhat fanciful proposals that have been made for a gnostic source or a Jewish sectarian document behind our text, but it leaves vague the nature of I John itself. The proposal has been reported above that 3 and 2 John are the keys to I John as an 'exhortation to a remnant community' (Johnson, *The Writings of the New Testament*, 507).

The sort of historical-social reconstruction presented above, into which the theological contents of I John are then placed for interpretation, has, it must be added, been vigorously attacked from the standpoint of canonical criticism (Childs, *The New Testament as Canon*, 482–5). The objections to the sort of history of 'the community of the Beloved Disciples' which Raymond E. Brown (with others) has articulated is that use of 'probably' or 'likely' too often marks the attempt 'to historicize the biblical text' (ibid. 483). Canonical criticism would prefer to let I John stand on its own, rather than be considered in such close conjunction with the Fourth Gospel. First John, it is pointed out, came to stand at a point in the New Testament canon removed from John (to which it is so closely related in content), the latter forming part of the collection of the four gospels. But are we to take I John as empty of authorial intent, isolated from the book to which it is closest in thought?

2 and 3 John

These two papyrus notes that have crept into the canon next to I John are so brief and devoid of theological content as not really to add much to thoughts of the New Testament. They serve chiefly to show the diversity that existed in early Christianity.

Historical circumstances behind the two documents are difficult to pin down. We do not know, for example, who 'the elder' was. If the Greek be rendered as 'the old man' and the writer identified, as traditionally, with the Beloved Disciple, the apostle John, then the letters say too little about identity, or at least far less than we might expect. Moreover, Papias, who lived closer to the period than we do, seems to have distinguished a shadowy 'John the Elder' from John, the son of Zebedee. If the title means 'the presbyter', it is a sign of emerging church office. But how the other persons in 3 John fit in remains disputed.

The usual presumption is that the elder is engaged in a contest with Diotrephes over the right of the elder's emissaries to preach their version of true Christianity in the local church which Diotrephes controls. When the latter is characterized as 'prating against me with evil words' (v. 10), Diotrephes emerges as a villain. Some have described him as a bishop who excommunicated the elder because his theology was too 'gnostic'. Others have identified Diotrephes as an ambitious secessionist, akin to the opponents in 1 John. Still others view him as an able local leader, determined to exclude from his region the conflicting voices of both sides, and willing to abandon the Johannine position of the Paraclete as teacher within an egalitarian community, in favour of a church where leaders like himself have authority. But the data are not sufficient to trace with exactness the drama which took place in the Johannine community.

Values in the Johannine letters

There is, of course, far more significance to the three letters than their role as a window on variety in New Testament thought, or on how Johannine theology emerged and was clarified, in the face of misunderstandings.

For all the christological debate, God is repeatedly the topic, or, as 1 John often puts it, the Father or the divine parent (5: 1 RSV), with whom, together with the Son, our fellowship is (1: 3). God is light (1: 5), God is love (4: 8, 16). Elsewhere, the New Testament says God loves (e.g. John 17: 26; Rom. 5: 8). In 1 John comes the quintessential assertion that God, as to innermost being, has been revealed as love. A great deal is made of 'birth' language, God begetting Christ or giving birth to him (the verb *gennaō* can be used of a male or female; cf. 5: 18, Christ is 'he who was born of God'), and God begetting or giving birth to believers (5: 18, 'any one born of God'; 3: 9; 4: 7; 5: 1, 4). Thus we by the new birth are constituted a family of God, rather than of the devil (3: 1–2, 10). It becomes a refrain: 'we are of God' (4: 4, 6; 5: 19).

To describe this momentous news, the term 'gospel' is never employed, any more than it was in the Fourth Gospel. But 'promise' is, in terms of eternal life (2: 25), and the air of 'announcement' hangs over the document from the outset (1: 2, 3, RSV 'proclaim'). 'Kingdom', which had virtually disappeared as a theme in John's Gospel, occurs nowhere in the Johannine epistles.

Christology and eschatology have been discussed above. There is greater emphasis on the meaning of Jesus' death as expiation for sins (2: 1–2) than in the Fourth Gospel, and on his work as 'saviour of the world' (4: 14; cf. John 4: 42). When 5: 6 describes Jesus as 'he who came by water and blood . . . not with the water only, but with the water and the blood', that too is probably an allusion to Jesus' death on the Cross, in its Johannine version, where with the spear-wound there came out blood and water (19: 34). (This is more likely than a reference to Jesus' baptism, which is at best a secondary meaning, for Jesus' baptism is not actually described in John 1, and far more so than a possible tertiary reference to the sacraments of baptism and the Lord's Supper, which are not emphasized in Johannine thought.) Eschatologically, there is now more realism added to the Camelot-like world of Johannine thought. Whereas 'the hour' once associated with 'the end of the world' had become a term in the Fourth Gospel suggesting that eternal life has broken into this age (John 5: 24–6), now in 1 John 'the last hour' brings with it antichrists as a plague for the paradise of the new life.

Ecclesiology is somewhat more overt in the Johannine letters than in the Fourth Gospel. The term 'church' appears only in 3 John, used to indicate the local assembly (vv. 6, 9, 10). By now, leaders like Diotrephes can 'put people out of the church', excommunication such as the Johannine community had experienced from the synagogue (John 9: 22; 16: 2). The community continues to be a band of brothers and sisters (1 John

3: 13, 14, 16; 3 John 3, 5). But the term *koinōnia*, fellowship, begins to have ecclesial dimensions (1 John 1: 3, 6, 7) for relations, not just individually with God and Christ, but increasingly with one another.

The ethics of the Johannine letters are rooted in the command to love one another (John 13: 34; 1 John 3: 11). This old theme, 'which we have heard from the beginning [*from Jesus and in the Johannine message*]', roots in turn in Jesus as paradigm of God's love, but it remains limited to the brothers and sisters within the community (3: 14; 4: 11). One may sense, perhaps in the face of the exclusiveness of 'those who have gone out from us', a new concern about sharing worldly goods with those in need (3: 17), above all through hospitality (3 John), but this is limited to Christians and, indeed, to those who hold the correct doctrine (2 John 9–10). While 'love' and 'fear' are incompatible (4: 17–18), the Johannine ethos puts a strong emphasis on the term 'command' (14 occurrences in 1 John; 4 more in 2 John). Keeping the divine commands matters (2: 3–4; 3: 22; 5: 2–3). But they boil down to the one old/new command, to 'love one another, just as he has commanded us' (3: 23). So one abides in God (or in the light or in the Son and the Father or in the teaching; 2: 6, 10, 24; 2 John 9).

Actually, the commandment is once taken to include not just loving one another but also the precept 'that we should believe in the name of God's Son, Jesus Christ' (3: 23). The concept of faith, which loomed so large in the Fourth Gospel (above, pp. 69–70), therefore stands out in 1 John. The only time the noun occurs in the Johannine epistles and gospel is in a sweeping statement at 1 John 5: 4, 'Whatever is born of God overcomes the world; and this is the victory that overcomes the world, our faith.' The context makes clear that Christian believers are conquering the world. ('Whatever is born of God . . .' (v. 4a) uses a neuter to denote all those begotten of God; v. 5 says, more specifically, that the person who believes that Jesus is the Son of God overcomes the world.) What can be meant in 4b by 'the victory that overcomes the world', especially since the participle is an aorist and could mean 'has overcome the world'? The latter subtlety is almost impossible to bring out in English, though J. B. Phillips tried with the rendering: 'In fact, this faith of ours is the only way in which the world has been conquered.'

The boldest answer may be that 'our faith' is a title for Jesus, for he had said at John 16: 33, 'I have conquered the world.' That would account for the past tense, as a reference to his triumphant death. But the thought is abrupt. The document is not in the habit of referring to Jesus as 'our Lord' or as 'our' anything else. Above all, it severs Jesus' victory from the overcoming of the world in which his children are now engaged. A second possible meaning is the coming to faith of Christians. 'Our faith' would be what they confessed, for example, at baptism, that 'Jesus is the Son of God' (5: 5). This would fit with 3: 23, the command to believe in the Son Jesus Christ. Such an interpretation allows room for both what was believed and the act of believing. It is to be preferred to a third possibility, that a victory over 'those who have gone out from us' is meant, although our document is capable of speaking about 'overcoming the evil one' (2: 14) and the antichrists (4: 4). Perhaps the author sees Christ's victory, that of our own personal confession, and triumph over adversaries as all being bound up together.

The two aspects of faith suggested above, content and personal commitment, are both apparent elsewhere in 1 John. Faith as *fides quae*, what one believes, is expressed in a series of slogans and creeds. 'Jesus is the Christ' (2: 22; 5: 1). 'Jesus is the Son of God' (4: 15; 5: 5; cf. 5: 23). 'Jesus Christ has come in the flesh' (4: 2). 'We have an advocate with the Father, Jesus Christ the righteous' (2: 1). Perhaps also 'God is light' (1: 5) and 'God is love' (4: 8, 16). 1 John can also go part of the way with some of the apparent slogans of the opponents, such as 'We have fellowship with him' (1: 6) or 'I know him' (2: 4). It is implied that one believes the Spirit and the spirit-prophets sent by God, but not every one of them, not at least without testing in accord with the criterion of Christ having come in the flesh (4: 1).

The other aspect of faith, as the trust and obedience with which one believes (*fides qua*), is apparent in 1 John in two ways. First, there is insistence throughout on a deep sincerity of commitment, in contrast to those who never were 'of us' in belief; second, one meets with the concepts of profession and witnessing. The person who 'confesses the Son has the Father also' (2: 23). Spirits (prophets) must profess that Jesus Christ has come in the flesh (4: 2–3); that is the acid test. It is the deceivers in the world who do not confess that Jesus Christ has come in the flesh (2 John 7). 'Whoever confesses that Jesus is the Son of God', God abides in such persons and they in God (4: 15).

The testimony which Johannine believers are expected to transmit concerns the Son, and the experience that 'God gave us eternal life . . . in his Son' (5: 9–11). This is the burden of 1 John, to announce such life (1: 2), for it is the witness of the Father (4: 14), the Spirit, and Christ (5: 7–8). For Christians to be able to testify that the message has been received and bears fruit is grounds for joy (3 John 3, 6). Then the message and faith have done their work.

The Johannine Line of Development: Revelation

THE other book in the New Testament traditionally attributed to John is like nothing else in the canon. (Daniel in the Old Testament comes closest.) 'The Revelation of Jesus Christ, which . . . he made known by sending his angel to his servant John', as the book announces at 1:1, in introducing its 'words of prophecy' (1:3), is an amalgam of visions, letters, and sequences of catastrophic judgements which devastate the sinful world, particularly the oppressor 'Babylon'; all interspersed with precious glimpses of hope, including a thousand-year reign by Christ and then the consummation in the new Jerusalem. Sounds and silence, vivid colours, exquisite song and fateful dirge, mysterious numbers, beast figures, mythic symbols, hints of persecution, gore, famine, death, and tangible details about the promised city of God combine to overwhelm the reader/hearer privileged to share this extravaganza for God's faithful servant-saints. Yet for all its massive uniqueness, this Apocalypse to John has tantalizing affinities with the Fourth Gospel (connections emphasized by tradition) but also with Paul's letters, early Christian prophecy, the Hebrew Scriptures, Judaism, the Roman world, and perhaps gnosticism and ancient Near Eastern, even Babylonian, mythology. A grand and puzzling book!

Not surprisingly, Revelation has had its ups and downs as Christian Scripture. It was clearly alluded to by second-century writers. Papias seems to have been positive about it, but then this bishop of Hierapolis was himself a 'chiliast' or 'millennialist', one who, like Rev. 20, hoped for a literal thousand-year (Greek *chilioi*, Latin *mille + annus*) reign of Christ on earth. Melito of Sardis wrote a commentary on Revelation, unfortunately lost.

The general opinion arose that the 'John' mentioned at 1: 1, 4, 9 and 22: 8, who spoke at times in the first person (1: 9–20; 4: 1–2; 5: 1–5; 6: 1–2; 7: 1–2, 9, 13–14, etc.), was none other than John the son of Zebedee, the Beloved Disciple (so Justin Martyr, before AD 160).

But patristic opinion was far from unanimous. Marcion rejected the book as too Jewish. Dionysius of Alexandria, in opposing the chiliasts, denied that the apostle John could have written it. Adoption of the book by gnostics or groups like the Montanists (who were declared heretical) caused others to shun the writing. The sometimes lively debate, which in the case of Dionysius included arguments to show how the style differs from that of John's Gospel and how Revelation could not, therefore, be by the same author, eventually led to acceptance of Revelation and a fateful place at the end of the New Testament, as if, for some, it were the climax of the whole Bible. On the other hand, Revelation was copied in a smaller number of manuscripts than most New Testament books, and its text is less certainly attested than many of them.

Over the centuries, Revelation has often attracted those apocalyptically inclined and repelled others. About AD 1200, Joachim of Flora (Fiori in southern Italy) wrote on the book and made it the linchpin of his theology of 'three ages', those of the Father, the Son, and the Spirit. In this scheme, the new age of the Spirit was identified with the rise of Joachim's own, new monastic movement. The beast in Rev. 13 was said to involve the Muslims, partly wounded in the crusades. For later followers of Joachim, the beast became the pope. (See Umberto Eco's novel, *The Name of the Rose*, translated in 1983, for reflections of this fascination with apocalyptic schemes in this period.) In the times of the Renaissance and Reformation, Erasmus listed reasons why John the evangelist could not have written Revelation, Luther relegated it to the lowest category in the canon, and Calvin, the prolific interpreter, never wrote a commentary on it. Yet the Radical Reformation often embraced the book. The Anabaptists embodied its millennial ideas in trying to bring the kingdom into earthly form at Münster, 'the New Jerusalem', in 1534.

Although later John Solomon Semler, at the very outset of modern rational criticism, raised the author question anew, most clung to the theory of apostolic origins. Again and again, Bible students became enamoured of the book; as a nineteenth-century observer put it, however, all too often study of the book 'either found a man cracked or left him so!'

The record of influences from Revelation is well known. Sects have often taken it up as a kind of 'New Testament Nostradamus', to predict events of the day. The code number '666' (Rev. 13: 18) has been applied to Napoleon, Hitler, US presidents, and any unpopular world leader, if the right combination of numerical values for each letter can be worked out in some alphabet. The climactic battle described at 16: 16 as taking place at 'Armageddon' (Hebrew *Har* or Mount Megiddo, a strategic site for battles at Judg. 5: 19–20 and 2 Kings 23: 29; cf. Zech. 12: 10–11, more correctly 'the plain of Megiddo') has become stock-in-trade for television evangelists and modern 'prophets' claiming to know how all history will end in a Russian invasion of Israel. The reference at 14: 1–3 to 144,000 who are redeemed with the Lamb (chaste male virgins, 14: 4) has been taken by Jehovah's Witnesses to apply to an élite who will go to heaven in contrast to the 'other sheep' (John 10: 16), for whom an earthly paradise must suffice. The coding system used for electronic checkout scanners has been called by others the fulfilment of 'the mark of the beast' mentioned at Rev. 13: 17. A pervasively influential book Revelation still is!

Orthodox Christianity, Catholic or Protestant, has lived with the Book of Revelation and found positive values in it in a number of ways over the centuries. At times its contents were allegorized, as by Origen (e.g. the seven heads of the beast, 17: 3, are the seven deadly sins) or by Ticonius, a Donatist (the seven heads are the sum of all the kings of the earth; the 'two witnesses' of 11: 3 are the church preaching Christ in the Old Testament and the New Testament). But generally the book was taken literally, as history. Then at least three options were open.

One line of interpretation was the 'futurist' understanding, where events in the book are taken not to have happened yet, but to be in store at the last days to come. Revelation is, then, about history that is still future for us (although eager interpreters often sought the clue to just how soon the end events would begin). This view is sometimes called in German *endgeschicht-lich* — concerning the history of 'the End'. On such a view, 4: 1 becomes the key: 'I will show you what must take place after this'. Pietism favoured this approach. A second method was to interpret Revelation in a 'continuous-historical' way, i.e. as a picture of what was happening from the time of the author, John, until the coming end of the world. The book, then, becomes either *kirchengeschichtlich*, about church history, or *weltge-schichtlich*, about the history of the world. Daniel 7 provided parallel and precedent about a series of world kingdoms. The two beasts of Rev. 13 were identified in the Middle Ages and Reformation as the Holy Roman Empire and the papacy.

The third possibility that at times occurred to interpreters was that Revelation addressed its own day, in the first century. It was *zeitgeschichtlich*, or contemporary with its own times historically. Sometimes in English the term 'preterist' interpretation has been used, denoting that which happened in past times. It is this approach which application of the historical-critical method has made dominant in scholarly circles over the past century. But once the first-century meaning is worked out, then we are left with the question of what Revelation means, if anything, for our day. But so widespread has the historical-critical approach become that one finds it hard to believe that E. B. Elliott's *Horae Apocalypticae* was standard stuff long after it appeared in nineteenth-century England, with its application of the chapters in Revelation to the age of Constantine, the rise of Islam, and the period of the Reformation (the angels announcing the eternal gospel and judgement on Babylon (Rome), 14: 6, 8, was a natural here).

Results from historical-critical study

One point in ancient tradition that modern investigators have generally accepted is the opinion of Irenaeus (quoted in

Eusebius, *Church History* 3. 18. 3), that Revelation was written 'at the end of the reign of Domitian', i.e. in AD 95 or 96. That provided not only a date but also an occasion in history for such a writing. The new wave of persecution, as this emperor sought to claim divine prerogatives, touched off the resistance John proclaims: only Jesus Christ, not the Roman emperor, is Lord. Revelation was thus directed to an immediate and dire threat about 'what must *soon* take place' (1: 1), 'for the time is *near*' (1: 3).

Commentators even related details mentioned in Revelation to events of the day. For example, the saying at 6: 6, 'A quart of wheat for a denarius, and three-quarters of barley for a denarius; but do not harm the oil and wine', may reflect imperial decrees. This statement, presumably about a famine (cf. the black horse, v. 5, following upon war, vv. 3–4), where grain for a day would take a whole day's wages but luxury items like olive oil and wine would abound, was thought to have something to do with Domitian's decree in AD 92 forbidding the growing of vineyards in the provinces and instead encouraging production of grain. (The emperor may have been trying to help vintners in Italy and thus create monopolies for rich friends.) In any case, destruction of the vineyards in Asia Minor, to allow for planting more wheat and barley, provoked such an outcry that the decree was reversed in AD 93. Some commentators thought the words in Revelation 6: 6 protest at the removal of the earlier decree because the prophet's asceticism opposed wine (cf. 18: 3, 13). In similar fashion, many other details were related to social and historical phenomena in Rome's eastern provinces and the oft-embattled frontier with Parthia.

Having given the book a specific setting in history, critical study also helped demystify Revelation by identifying the genre that this puzzling book embodies. It is an apocalypse, an 'unveiling' of what has been heretofore hidden. While, in older analyses, Daniel in the Old Testament and Revelation in the New have long stood out like sore thumbs, singular and awkward, attention to an increasing number of apocalyptic writings that came to light in the eighteenth and nineteenth centuries made the contours clearer. As one analogy put it, if we had the fragmentary foundations of just one medieval monastery, we could scarcely grasp how chapel, cloister, chapter house, herb garden, grazing lands, cemetery, and library all fitted together; but once the plans of 20 or 30 monasteries are known, how the totality functioned becomes apparent. So with apocalypses. There are a few instances in the Old Testament, besides Daniel; cf. Isa. 24–7 or Zech. 9–14. Further examples came from Judaism, often preserved only in Christian circles, sometimes in far-off areas like Ethiopia. From comparison of examples like Enoch, The Testaments of the Twelve Patriarchs, 2 Esdras (4 Ezra), the Assumption of Moses, 2 Baruch, and the Qumran finds, especially the War Scroll, and then from Christian examples, in the New Testament (1 Thess. 4: 15–17; 2 Thess. 2: 1–12; 1 Cor. 15: 20–8; 2 Cor. 5: 1–10; Mark 13 and parallels, the 'Little Apocalypse') and in Christian writings outside the New Testament (like the Apocalypse of Peter or The Shepherd of Hermas), a series of characteristics emerged.

Apocalyptic literature was said to have arisen after the decline of prophets and prophecy in Israel, and to have developed in part under Persian influence (e.g. the idea of a final conflict between light and darkness, in Zoroastrian terms Mazda vesus Ahriman). Its obvious features included (1) an attempt to predict the (immediate) future; (2) despair of the present world, a pessimism that held only supernatural intervention could change things; (3) the fact that it was written, not spoken, by a chosen individual whom God commands to seal away these secrets for the chosen few, not a public figure addressing heads of State about the whole nation; (4) the writing was often pseudonymous, frequently borrowing the name of some worthy of the past (e.g. 'Daniel' may derive from the figure mentioned with Noah and Job at Ezek. 14: 14, 20; Ugaritic 'Danel'); (5) the writing is full of symbolism; (6) it promises life after death and so reflects a line of doctrine that emerged in Israel only late and among some Jews, notably the Pharisees. One can add other phrases like universalism, otherworldliness, occultism, or mechanistic determinism, in an attempt to catalogue aspects of the genre.

Of course, it was observed that the Book of Revelation did not always fit completely with this characterization of apocalyptic literature as written prediction of the immediate future, telling of God's intervention through the Messiah and granting of life to those faithful during persecution, all encoded in a symbolism that members of the community would presumably understand but which their harassers and persecutors would not. Revelation as (1) prediction was better understood to be forthtelling of the lordship of Jesus, in contrast to Caesar's claims, rather than as foretelling of sequential events, step by step. Its promise of (6) life after death was modified by the Christian assertion that Jesus was already 'the first-born of the dead' (1: 5), and that we are already freed 'from our sins by his blood' and are made 'a kingdom, priests to his God and Father' (1: 6). Christians slain for the word of God may 'wait' under the altar of God (6: 9), but there is a sense in which they have already overcome and are conquerors (5: 5; 12: 11). With regard to (3), it was emphasized that the New Testament apocalypse was, while written, not to be sealed away (22: 10; contrast Dan. 12: 4) but to be read aloud (1: 3) to a wide circle in the seven churches (chs. 2–3) and even beyond (22: 16–19).

It was in connection with authorship that historical criticism probably made the biggest adjustment in its analysis of Revelation as apocalyptic literature. It was often concluded by critics that 'John' was not a pen-name adopted by the author to borrow the fame of the son of Zebedee, but the actual name of an early Christian seer of some prominence in the region around Ephesus. This was not to accept the view, voiced often from Justin Martyr's time onwards, that the apostle whom tradition identified with the Beloved Disciple wrote Revelation as well as the Fourth Gospel. Nor was it even the view occasionally heard that John the Elder (cf. 2 and 3 John; so Papias, bishop of Hierapolis, early second century) wrote Revelation. Rather, it meant an agreement with the arguments amassed by Dionysius of Alexandria, Erasmus, Semler, and numerous moderns that the style and content of Revelation are so different as to demand an author other than John the apostle or John the Elder. Rather than leave the author nameless, there has been a tendency to accept the document at its word as the work of an otherwise unknown John. Unlike the Fourth Gospel or 1, 2, and 3 John, Revelation gives the writer's name. He is of enough standing with those whom he addresses as a brother (1:9) to need no titles or credentials. Not an apostle (21:14), he was a witness in exile for his faith, a confessor but not (at least not yet) a martyr (1:9).

A great deal of historical–critical effort went into characterizing the language and style of, and Old Testament influences on, the Book of Revelation. Notions that the book was originally written in Aramaic or Hebrew have generally been rejected, but it is clear that the author thought in Hebrew, even though he wrote in Greek. The Greek is, therefore, often rough, as in the phrase for God (1:4, 8; 4:8; cf. 11:17; 16:5), which in English disguises its awkwardness, 'from him who is and who was and who is to come'. The preposition 'from' is followed here by the nominative case, not the genitive which it should take. Participles are used for the first and last expressions, but the middle one consists of the article 'the', followed by the finite verb form 'he was'. This style would be the despair of any Greek grammarian, although, in John's defence, it should be noted that the verb has no past participle form in either of the pertinent tenses (the imperfect or the aorist). The grammatical irregularities should not disguise the fact that 1:4 gives a picture of God as something more than one who exists in past, present, and future (for the sequence is present, past, future), not simply as 'I am who I am' or 'I will be what I will be' (cf. Exod. 3:14), but rather as 'the one . . . who is going to come', appropriate for the imminent futurity of the book. It is also agreed that the author's mind was saturated with phrases from the Old Testament, which, however, he never quotes (least of all with a formula like 'It is written' or 'This is that which was spoken by the prophet'). Rather, John internalizes Scripture and weaves it into his own inimitable expressions. And it is the Hebrew, not LXX, that is usually reflected.

One result of such analysis was a search for sources. Sometimes it was assumed that the book takes over a Jewish apocalypse or apocalypses, to which a Christian framework, in chs. 1–3 and at the end, was added. It has more recently been argued by J. M. Ford that chs. 4–11 stem from the circle of John the Baptist, while 12–22 (also by Baptist disciples, possibly become Christian) come from the 60s, pre-dating the fall of Jerusalem (chs. 1–3 and 22: 16a, 20b, and 21 would then be by a Jewish Christian disciple of John the Baptist); on this view, the book is not 'Christian apocalyptic' but originally from the Baptizer's movement. Others have argued for a Christian first edition stemming from the time of Nero in the 60s, and a reworking in the time of Domitian. An example of the Preterist approach is an outline that in 1–11 presents, in terms of history already transpired, symbolic depiction of God's judgement on Israel, in order to establish confidence in what the author wants to emphasize as soon to come (chs. 12–20), namely, God's judgement on 'Babylon', i.e. Rome; therefore, the pattern emerges of past triumph over Judaism and of predicted survival for the church against Rome's onslaught.

There are often, literarily speaking, doublets or triplets in Revelation (e.g. seven seals, seven trumpets, seven bowls). There are inconsistencies (so much is destroyed in early chapters that one wonders what more can remain to face the destruction wrought at each trumpet call, or with the pouring of bowl after bowl of wrath on the earth). One can ask how the 'interludes' fit in (chs. 7; 10: 1–11:13; 12; 14). How are the three woes announced at 8: 13 superimposed on the seven trumpets (presumably as trumpets 5, 6, and 7; see 9: 12 and 11: 14)? Or is the third woe to be found in ch. 13 (cf. 12: 12)? Or do the seven bowl-judgements in chs. 15–16 make up the third woe? All such cases prompt a search for literary solutions—in sources, in inconsistent redaction, or as the result of a none-too-bright pupil of the seer botching the task of putting the whole together. For all the theorizing, however, no one view on source and redaction has carried the day, and most have been consigned to footnotes in the history of scholarship.

On sounder ground is the observation that Revelation contains liturgical materials. There are hymns, such as the *trisagion* ('Holy, holy, holy . . .', 4; 8; cf. Isa. 6: 2); the song of the Lamb (5: 9–10, 12, 13); the song of Moses and of the Lamb (15: 3–4); and a triumphant liturgy at the fall of Rome (19: 1–8). As perverse contrasts, there are dirges about the vanquished (e.g. 18: 2–3, 4–8, 9, 16–17, 19–20, 21–4). Some passages are formulaic, like 12: 10–12. There is a prayer at 11: 17, 'We give thanks to thee, Lord God Almighty, . . . that hast taken thy great power and begun to reign', but it goes on more vindictively about 'rewarding thy servants, the prophets and saints, . . . and . . . destroying the destroyers of the earth' (11: 18). There are also the woes (8: 13), paralleling perhaps the threefold 'Holy' or the beatitudes (7 examples, at 1: 3; 14: 13; 16: 15; 19: 9; 20: 6; 22: 7 and 14), much as 19: 17–18 is a grim parody of the invitation to the Lord's Supper: 'Come gather for the great supper of God', addressed to the birds, to gather like vultures, in order to 'eat the flesh of kings, captains, mighty men' slain in battle! It is possible that some of these materials reflect early Christian worship on earth, but the ones most likely to do so, like 4: 8; 5: 9–13; 15: 3–4, are all set in heaven, sung by the four living creatures, 24 elders, and those by the sea of glass. Caution is in order when seeking to reconstruct Asia Minor liturgies from such materials. Most schemes that seek the book as a whole to be modelled on worship in the Jerusalem temple or on a Jewish calendar—or on a eucharistic or paschal liturgy as *the* pattern—seem more imposed on the text of Revelation than arising from it.

The historical-critical method did, however, bring immense gain in understanding Revelation as a meaningful tract for its own day, even if some points remained obscure. Such an assessment, attained by scholars of all sorts, was spread by popular commentaries, at least from the 1950s on (e.g. Preston and Hanson, *Revelation*). World War II had brought a new interest in the book. Historical study helped make sense of it for many readers.

One ally of the historical-critical approach was often history-of-religion comparisons. Although not all regarded the *Religionsgeschichtliche Schule* as welcome, or as disciplined enough, it had the effect, especially in Germany, of turning attention away from what was often a wild-goose chase after sources, in the direction of mythical influences from age-old oriental themes. Ch. 12 in Revelation proved a particularly fertile area. It is the story of the woman, the child, and the dragon, the birth of a deliverer, and war in heaven. Hermann Gunkel and Wilhelm Bousset in the nineteenth century called attention to Babylonian accounts of chaos and creation through a battle victory, and suggested how ancient oral traditions could underlie the account in Revelation. Reflections of a chaos monster do appear in the Old Testament (e.g. Isa. 27: 1; 51: 9; Job 7: 12). For all the allusions to Israel in Revelation, or reflection of current, first-century AD events—like the Roman emperor as the beast from the sea and his fawning priesthood in Asia Minor as the other beast 'which rose out of the earth' (13: 1 and 11) some details may pick up age-old themes These include the colour of the dragon (12: 3), red as the Babylonian snake; or the many heads of Leviathan (Ps. 74: 13–14 and in ancient Near Eastern myth), repeated in the beast of Rev. 13: 1. What strikes one is how these old tales of a conflict between God the creator and a rebellious chaos monster are being re-used—again—to mediate a message about a new conflict, this time between Rome and those who follow the Lamb, Jesus (14: 4). Appreciation of the history-of-religions background, complicated as it often is, must have increased the impact on a first-century audience, and helps one today to grasp the multi-level meanings of the book.

Literary, social, and other approaches to Revelation

Although Revelation has been widely read in recent years along the lines indicated above, there were also dissenting voices within the historical-critical school itself. For example, the supposition of a severe Domitianic persecution in Asia Minor has been questioned, partly on internal grounds. Only one martyr is mentioned by name in the entire Book of Revelation, Antipas of Pergamum (2: 13). The external evidence about the days of Domitian comes in Roman sources chiefly from the time of Trajan, who ruled AD 98–117, and who may have encouraged a picture of his predecessor's cruel nature in order to enhance his own image. Perhaps, therefore, one should think, not of all-out persecution, certainly not empire-wide, but merely of local harassment, with informers ready to cause trouble for Christians with the authorities, as in the time of Trajan and his governor in Asia Minor, Pliny the Younger. One problem for the significance of the Book of Revelation is, then, the fact that the major crisis which the author expected never broke upon the church with the fury and devastation the seer had expected. History did not end.

The date of AD 95–6 under Domitian could therefore plausibly be criticized and an earlier one proposed in the time of Nero, toward the close of his rule, between 64 and 70 (cf. Robinson, *Redating the New Testament*). In its favour is the claim that ch. 11 suggests the Jerusalem temple is still standing; 17 and 18 could reflect events in Rome during the tumultuous period of Nero's suicide, rumours that he would return alive leading an army from Parthia, and the 'year of the three emperors', AD 69, when Galba, Otho, and Vitellius, one after another, claimed the throne in Rome. The number 666 in 13:18 fits 'Neron Kaisar' in Hebrew. Rome could appropriately be called 'Babylon' because its armies, under Titus and Vespasian, were to destroy Jerusalem and the Herodian temple in AD 70, just as the Babylonians had destroyed both city and Solomonic temple in 586 BC.

The classification of Revelation as apocalyptic literature has been challenged too. Even supporters of this position had to admit that certain features were modified, as noted above, especially on account of the Christian impact. Others have seen influence in Revelation from Jewish mysticism of the 'Merkabah' variety, stemming from Ezekiel and embodied in the 'Hekhaloth' literature, i.e. descriptions of the halls of heaven. A more serious debate has been over whether Revelation really belongs to prophetic (see below), not apocalyptic, literature. Still others have stressed the seven letters in chs. 2 and 3 as utterly non-apocalyptic. Each letter reiterates the same pattern of (1) a command to write to the 'angel' (guardian in heaven or prophet-pastor) of the local congregation; (2) a description of Jesus appropriate for the message which follows; (3) the body of the letter: what the Lord knows of the trials, glories, or failings of that church, and so praise (for Smyrna and Philadelphia), severe rebuke (Sardis), utter condemnation (Laodicea), or approval mixed with criticism (Ephesus, Pergamum, Thyatira); completed by (4) a concluding exhortation and promise. Some have seen in the common theme of the seven letters—'Hold fast!'— the basic concern of the entire book. When these are called 'prophetic letters' and the apocalypse is nudged closer to prophecy, then the whole tractate can no longer be distinguished sharply into categories of 'apocalypse' or 'letter'. Even the emphasis on the words as *written* (1: 3; 2: 1, 8, etc.; 22: 7, 9), said to be a feature of apocalyptic literature, can also be related to the emphasis previously pointed out for the Fourth Gospel—to write in order to produce faith (see above, p. 66); here, written to encourage average Christians to keep the faith.

As suggested above, literary attention has at times been given to sub-units within the book. Besides the seven letters or liturgical elements noted earlier, one could also study the beatitudes we have listed, or the 'heavenly ascent' or journey of the seer depicted in the book. But fruitful as such study has often been—and analysis of this sort may allow one to see a certain unity with ascents, beatitudes, or hymns elsewhere in the New Testament—the trend away from supposed sources has led more and more to concentration on the book as a whole. One time-honoured approach of this kind was to conceive of Revelation as a drama. Thus, a widely quoted analysis claimed to find seven acts, each with seven scenes, in the Book of Revelation. Others spoke of an earthly drama (the conflict with the state in Asia Minor) and a heavenly drama (Christ or Michael in 12: 7–12 fighting Satan, the old dragon, who continues the fight on earth).

The entirety of Revelation can be outlined to show a linear movement through history ('what is' or 'revelation for the present', chs. 2–3; what will be or 'revelation for the future', chs. 4–21). Or the plot line can be conceived as a conic spiral or cyclic repetition in the sense of seals opened, trumpets sounded, and bowls or vials poured upon earth. Or it can be structured to show the heart of the book to be the 'little scroll' of 10: 1–15: 4, with its prophetic contents, embedded in a framework of the scroll with the seven seals (4: 1 ff.), visions, and letters (1: 9–3: 22; 19: 11–22: 9). Thus it is argued that the interpreter must grasp the artistry of Revelation as a whole and not get lost in its details. One can relate to this also the contention that the power of the book is in the evocative nature of its language, not our precision in identifying its components.

As far as social setting is concerned, one has seven distinct Christian communities to reckon with, each one briefly described, and about which we sometimes know from other early Christian writings; the island of Patmos, where the writer is in solitude (by choice or political banishment is not clear); and western Asia Minor. The clash with the Roman Empire is obvious, and so there is a political edge to the book. But the most challenging work for understanding Revelation involves recent attempts to relate this document, and the Christianity for which it stands, with types of Christianity we know, from other sources, to have existed in Asia Minor in the last quarter of the first century AD. Traditionally, Revelation has been associated with Johannine Christianity. But we have also seen how the Pauline School developed in this geographical area with writings to Colossae and the 'Ephesians' (see above, Ch. 8), not to mention 2 Thessalonians and the pastoral epistles (see above, Chs. 8 and 9). There are also affinities with the synoptic gospels. And if Revelation is prophetic, one may also have to reckon with a prophetic movement, indeed perhaps with rival ones. In looking at Revelation and such types of Christianity with which it may have overlapped, aspects of agreement and of difference will be seen.

Considerable attention has been paid above to the debate, going on since the second century, over whether, or to what extent, Revelation is a part of the Johannine corpus of the New Testament. The traditional view that the Beloved Disciple wrote the fourth Gospel, Revelation, and 1 John has given way in many critical circles to the position that the apostle John wrote none of these documents. Some examples of the arguments from vocabulary and style have been noted. How people react to these delicately balanced statistics may depend on their predilection for, or aversion to, a particular theory of authorship. For example, Revelation and the Fourth Gospel share eight words that are found nowhere else in the New Testament ('lamb', *arnion*, is significant, until one notes that it occurs only once in John's Gospel, where the regular word for lamb is *amnos*; that 'palm tree' occurs once in each book is probably a coincidence). But this figure pales in significance when it is added that Revelation and Paul share 53 words found nowhere else in the New Testament, and Revelation and Luke almost as many. The *differences* between John's Gospel and the Revelation to John are more striking: Revelation never uses favourite Johannine concepts like 'truth', 'joy', or the Paraclete; John lacks such words found in Revelation as 'Almighty', 'first-born', or 'church'/'assembly'.

All sorts of proposals have, none the less, suggested some connections between Revelation and the Fourth Gospel. They include the following. John's ideas changed as he grew older and situations differed. Or the son of Zebedee composed an apocalypse in Ephesus, and one pupil developed it into the Book of Revelation, another wrote the letters, still another John 1–20, which was then re-edited into our gospel. Or John the Elder wrote an apocalypse before AD 70, then letters, and finally a gospel overcoming all his earlier apocalyptic ideas, but a pupil about AD 95 revised the apocalypse so as to speak in opposition to Domitian. There have often been 'secretary hypotheses': John's ideas came out differently, depending on who the scribe was. Currently the view is popular of a Johannine 'circle' or 'school'. This approach may not assign authorship of each work so precisely, but allows for interplay among various members in producing the several Johannine documents in our New Testament. The school can be called both apocalyptic and prophetic in outlook. Through the 'school hypothesis', some recent critics have veered closer to the traditional position, allowing this explanation for affinities between Revelation and the Gospel of John, without endorsing single authorship, let alone by the son of Zebedee.

That there are connections between Revelation and Paul or the Pauline corpus may be more surprising. Links are forged in a number of ways. Paul was, it has increasingly been acknowledged, very much an apocalyptist; Revelation is an apocalypse. Both are determined in their outlook by the Christ who died and is risen. Paul's term was 'Christ crucified' (1 Cor. 1: 23); Revelation speaks of 'the Lamb that was slain' (5: 6, 9, 12, etc.). For all their common emphasis on Christ's victory and their use of apocalyptic categories, Paul and Revelation agree that suffering Christians in this world do not yet possess the fulness of what God promises. In Paul, this has been called his 'eschatological reservation', the insistence that there is a future aspect still ahead for Christians (cf. 1 Cor. 15; 22, 51). That this is the view of Revelation will be suggested below.

It can also be argued that John in Revelation and Paul claim authority on the basis of a similar revelatory experience. For Revelation, see 1: 10–20 and the book title used, 'The *Apokalypsis* of Jesus Christ . . . to John' (1: 1). For Paul, see Gal. 1: 12, 16 (his gospel 'came through a revelation [*apokalypsis*] of Jesus Christ') and 1 Cor. 1: 7, the *apokalypsis* of our Lord Jesus Christ. Further, a case can be made for similarities between Paul's opponents and those in Revelation. This similarity is seen by some in terms of the Judaizers in Galatians and the Nicolaitans of Rev. 2. 6, 16, or the Nicolaitans and the gnosticizing enthusiasts in 1 Corinthians. Note 'those who say they are Jews but are not, but are a synagogue of Satan' (Rev. 2: 9, cf. 3: 9, a harsher judgement than any on Jews in Paul) and teaching about the 'deep things—of Satan' (2: 24, possibly a gnostic theme). Finally, there is the suggestion that the structure of seven letters in Rev. 2–3 influenced, or was influenced by, a collection of seven letters of Paul in the early 90s (Rom., 1, 2 Cor., Gal., Phil., 1 Thess., and Philemon).

It is also worth reminding ourselves that Revelation has certain affinities with the synoptic tradition. Jesus, after all, impressed people as a prophet, and there was an apocalyptic cast to some of his sayings. His self-designation 'Son of man' appears in Rev. 1: 13 and 14: 14 (admittedly without the article, simply *huios anthrōpou*, as in Dan. 7), the only place it is found, apart from Acts 7: 56, outside the synoptics in the whole New Testament. 'Q' sayings like Matt. 10: 32 par. Luke 12: 8, about acknowledging or denying someone before the Father, seem reflected in Rev. 3: 5, 8. The tag-line in the seven letters, 'S/he who has an ear, let him/her hear' (2: 7, 11, 17, etc.), echoes Jesus' injunction at Mark 4: 23 and elsewhere, 'If anyone has ears to hear, let him/her hear'. The 'thief in the night' crops up at Rev. 3: 2–3; 16: 5, much as it occurred in Matt. 24: 42 par. Luke 12: 39–40 (cf. also Paul's use at 1 Thess. 5: 2–3). Indeed, efforts have been made to parallel Revelation with the synoptic apocalypse in Mark 13: the 'beginning of woes' in Rev. 5–6 is like 13: 7 13; the great tribulation in 12: 1–14: 10, reminiscent of Mark 13: 14–23; and Rev. 19: 11–21 reminds one of the parousia in Mark 13: 24–7.

Can it be, however, that the web of Christian assemblies in which the Book of Revelation first circulated was—for all these connections in thought and style with Johannine, Pauline, and synoptic Christianity—basically a prophetic community in its own right? There is considerable evidence for thinking so, even though the sharp dichotomy sometimes inherited from Old Testament studies between 'prophetic' and 'apocalyptic', and the tendency to concentrate on 'Jewish' aspects of Revelation and so miss the widespread presence of prophets in early Christianity, have sometimes blinded investigators to the point.

The obvious fact is that Revelation claims to be prophecy. At the outset, John calls what he writes 'words of prophecy' (1: 3). The phrase is repeated as an *inclusio* at 22: 7, 10 and with variations at 22: 18, 19, thus framing the whole book. The 'little scroll' of 10: 2, which some identify as the heart of the 22 chapters, is plainly prophetic: eaten, in its honeyed bitterness, it leads to prophecy (10: 8–11; cf. 11: 3, 10, 18 and 10: 7). Lest we forget, 16: 6; 18: 20 and 24 remind us of martyred and victorious prophets.

John is himself a prophetic figure, recounting what he saw and heard 'in the Spirit' (1: 10–20, etc.). Hence the old Israelite term 'seer' (1 Sam. 9: 9) is sometimes applied to the author, since he never uses 'prophet' to designate himself alone but only in the plural, of a group or for the whole community (see 22: 9). This corporate self-understanding as prophets/saints/servants of God (the three terms are often closely related, as at 11: 18) is coupled with a strong emphasis on witness (*martyria*), testifying or becoming a witness, even to the point of martyrdom (1: 2; 22: 16). Jesus was a 'faithful witness' (1: 5; 3: 14). Followers are to give testimony to Jesus in response to the witness by Jesus for them, for the phrase (RSV) 'testimony of Jesus (Christ)' (1: 2, 9; 12: 17; 20: 4) implies both aspects of the genitive 'of Jesus'. Prophets are people who speak out!

When one reckons with the fact that the ecclesiology of Revelation knows nothing of bishops, elders on earth, or other community leaders (see below), the picture is suggested of a group that regarded itself as basically prophetic. It stands in succession to Jesus here. Some have attempted to align the prophets of Revelation more directly with classical Old Testament prophecy, chiefly on the grounds that they are engaged in a 'rereading' of the Hebrew Scriptures and in presenting a programme of salvation history. But we have seen that John reflects rather than quotes or interprets the Old Testament. As for *Heilsgeschichte*, it is true that all notions of two or three 'ages' or 'aeons' root in an apocalyptic way of thinking. We have noted outlines for Revelation where the sequence is 'what has happened' (to Israel) and what, in the light of Jesus Christ and imminent crises, will happen to his servants, the prophets and saints who hold fast to Christ in the world. But if it is 'salvation history', Revelation is even more a history of judgement, preaching the need for endurance in the short time that remains.

Others have credited Revelation with reflecting Christian prophetic circles, but in opposition to rival prophet movements in Christianity. There was, of course, a widespread problem in the first and second centuries in distinguishing true from false prophets. Recall the practical tests proposed in the Didache:

itinerants are false if they stay too long (more than three days) and milk the local church for gifts (Did. 13. 1–7). Evidence for competing prophets is vivid in the letters to the seven churches. Whatever 'the Nicolaitans' (Rev. 2: 6) stood for, they must have been, or claimed to be, prophets too. If the name goes back to Nicolaus, a proselyte from Damascus (Acts 6: 5), several of his Hellenistic colleagues can be considered prophets, specifically Stephen and Philip the evangelist. John's reference to the Nicolaitans as holding 'the teaching of Balaam' harks back to a famous non-Israelite prophet (cf. the legend at Num. 22–4 with the negative judgement provided at Num. 31: 8, 16; Deut. 23: 3–4; Mic. 6: 5). 'Jezebel' of Thyatira (Rev. 2: 20) is called a prophetess, and the fact that she has 'children' (2: 23) suggests a prophetic school or assembly where she was the guiding figure.

Is it possible to designate an issue over which John differed violently from these other prophetic circles in the (seven) cities of western Asia Minor? If there was a gnostic tinge to their teaching (as in the 'deep things' of Rev. 2: 24), and if the issue in the 90s was whether or not to conform with public rites in honour of the emperor, it is possible that the split in opinion came over whether a Christian could take part in such activities. A gnostic, claiming to be already fully saved and with disdain for things of this age, could regard a pinch of incense for Domitian as a harmless thing. Not so for John. Either Jesus Christ or Caesar is lord, and one's worldly testimony, even in a doomed society, matters eternally. How much freedom, based on what kind of eschatology, do believers have in their coexistence with imperial society?

Overall theories about the situation within the Christian communities mentioned in Revelation differ considerably. One is that the seven churches of Rev. 2–3 were Jewish-Christian conventicles which combined the sort of prophets found in Jewish apocalyptic circles, who interpret the Hebrew Scriptures, with the Christian emphasis on Jesus' resurrection. They existed, however, in territory that was basically Pauline, and they possessed structured leadership far beyond that of mere prophets. In contrast to this view that Jewish Christians after

AD 70 created a prophetic church order in Asia Minor, another reading of the evidence is that 'John' and his prophetic circle stem from primitive Palestinian Christianity. On this view, the seer is an itinerant, much like the prophets in the Didache, but keenly reflective of imminent expectation of the end. Such a figure would stand in opposition, not only to emerging Church orders such as will appear later in Ignatius of Antioch, his concept of one bishop in each city, and all ideas of episcopacy, but also to the 'realized eschatology' found in 'gnostics' as well as in Colossians and Ephesians, for example. Thus Revelation relates to church order as well as to civil or societal demands.

Theology in the Revelation to John

One need not pin down precisely (or to the satisfaction of all critics) the historical, literary, and social aspects of Revelation in order to be able to describe the theological emphases that emerge. But some of these emphases are peculiar to the Apocalypse, and other themes that we have traced through most of the New Testament or found prominent in other Johannine writings are lacking. Is this due to the changed circumstances? Christology and, of course, eschatology are particularly important. If it is assumed that much of Revelation comes from sources, and Jewish ones at that, then the amount of original, Christian theology will be somewhat limited. But the attitude has been adopted above that, whatever the origin of portions of the book, the author means it to be taken as a whole, all of its parts contributing to the total picture.

Revelation is not a book of 'good news'. The term 'gospel' occurs just once as a reminder of this New Testament theme when, at the heart of the book (in some analyses), an angel flies 'in midheaven, with an eternal gospel to proclaim' to all those on earth (14: 6), but no specific content is here announced except 'Fear God . . . for the hour of his judgement has come' (14: 7), and two other angels fly by, announcing Babylon's fall and a warning against worshipping the beast (14: 8–11). The only two instances of the verb 'to preach gospel' do not alter that impression. See 14: 6, RSV 'proclaim', and 10: 7, RSV 'announced' (God's purpose of triumph). The book is just as much (or more) about judgement (14: 7; 16: 5, 7; 18: 10; cf. 6: 10; 19: 2; 20: 12–13) and God the judge (18: 8, 20) as it is about salvation, which also belongs to God (7: 10; 19: 1). Judgement of those who oppose God's will is the reverse side, so to speak, of deliverance for those who hear God's word.

The connections of Revelation with the synoptic tradition might lead one to expect some reflection of Jesus' theme of the kingdom. Examples do occur. John shares with other Christians three things 'in Jesus': tribulation, the kingdom, and patient endurance (1: 9). 'The kingdom of God', paired with salvation, power, and 'the authority of his Christ', is said to have come (to earth) (12: 10). Jesus has 'made us a kingdom' (1: 6; 5: 10, echoing Exod. 19: 6), and his followers will reign as kings (5: 10; 20: 4, 6 of the millennium; 22: 5), when Christ takes his power and reigns (11: 17) and 'the kingdom of the world has become the kingdom of our Lord and of his Christ' (11: 15). For the present, the abyss of chaos has its destructive king (9: 11), the beast has a kingdom (16: 10), personified in Rome's kings (17: 12, 17, 18). But faith declares Jesus to be 'the ruler of kings on earth' (1: 5; 19: 16) and God is declared 'King of the ages' (or, variant reading, of the nations, 15: 3). The kingship imagery reaches its climax in references to the throne of God (4: 2–10; 5: 6–7), which becomes 'the throne of God and of the Lamb', i.e. Christ (22: 1; cf. 5: 13; 7: 10). This kingship motif stems from Jesus and the Old Testament, but doubtless came into prominence in Revelation because of the conflict with the Roman emperor and his claims.

A great deal is said about God in the Revelation to John. The Lord, the Almighty (*Pantokratōr*, 1: 8; 4: 8, etc.; nine of the ten New Testament occurrences are in this book), the living God (7: 2) appears as creator (4: 11; 14: 7) and as judge (noted above). Unlike the Fourth Gospel or 1 John, Revelation never said 'God is love' or loving (although Christ is described as the one 'who loves us and has freed us from our sins by his blood', 1: 5b). But it would be a mistake to conclude that God, in Revelation so much like Yahweh in the Hebrew Scriptures and different from any other New Testament portrayal of the deity, is but a figure of wrath or retribution (11: 18, 'destroying the destroyers of the earth'); actually, wrath is more commonly attached to the Lamb (6: 16). This is not simply because God attends to his suffering 'servants, the prophets and saints' (11: 18), but above all because God holds in his hand the scroll that is the plan for the world, to save as well as to judge (5: 1). Granted, it is the Lamb who opens the scroll by breaking its seven seals, but this is to carry out the will of the Holy God (4: 8), whose deeds are great and wonderful (15: 3). What 'must take place' (4: 1) is what this God wills. The very power of God in the Apocalypse is the trait with which some theologians have trouble. Has God become a power symbol, along the lines of a Roman emperor? Are the few passages in Revelation about divine compassion, like 7: 16–17 or 21: 3–4 (God wiping away tears from every eye), enough to balance the picture of the Pantocrator?

The Spirit in the Book of Revelation never takes on the roles of the Paraclete in the Fourth Gospel or the charismatic functions noted in Paul's letters. While ranked with God 'who is and was and is to come' and with Jesus Christ (1: 4–5) and referred to (as in Paul) variously as spirit 'of God' (3: 1; 4: 5; 5: 6) and by implication 'of Christ', the term often employed is one out of the Old Testament, 'the seven spirits' (1: 4; 3: 1; 4: 5; 5: 6). The phrase seems to combine the sevenfold spirit of the messiah in Isa. 11: 2 and the seven lamps in Zech. 4 which are 'the eyes of the Lord' (4: 10) and the spirit of Yahweh that empowers Zerubbabel (4: 6). Elsewhere 'the Spirit' is spoken of in the singular (e.g. 14: 13; 22: 17) and functions especially in prophecy. John was 'in the Spirit' for his initial (1: 10) and later visions (4: 2; 17: 3; 21: 10). The Spirit it is who speaks to each of the seven churches in chs. 2–3 (2: 7, 11, etc.). The Spirit invites to the living water (22: 17). The statement at 19: 10, although open to several interpretations, ties together many themes in the book, 'The testimony of Jesus is the spirit of prophecy' (RSV). It implies that both what Jesus himself witnessed to and the witness of Christians about Jesus since Easter is what the Spirit brings alive in the community's key activity of prophecy—of which this book is 'Exhibit A'. Hence the importance and integrity of its text: no one is to add to or take away from it (22: 18–19).

Against this depiction of God and the (seven) spirit(s), Christology takes on all the more meaning. Revelation is a 'Jesus book', using at times just his name, without titles, as in the opening scene (1: 9) and the closing one (22: 16), and in 'testimony of Jesus' passages like 19: 10 (cf. also 14: 12; 17: 6; 20: 4). For all this, Revelation reports nothing of the earthly life and little of the teachings of Jesus, save his death, and that in terms of a now risen Lamb bearing the marks of slaughter (5: 6). It is the enthroned Christ of glory, who will come to reward fidelity and wreak vengeance on infidelity, that is the focus of the book. Traditional titles are employed: 'son of God' (2: 18), Christ (1: 1), and Lord (22: 20). Attention has already been called to the titles 'Word of God' (19: 13) and 'Lamb' (28 occurrences), which Revelation shares with the Fourth Gospel. But they are used with variations in vocabulary (*arnion*, not *amnos*) and emphasis—not meek or even merely atoning, a 'lamb who takes away the sin of the world' (John 1: 29), but a warrior-Word, 'treading the wine press of the fury of the wrath of God' (19: 15), triumphant and conquering. That he is 'like a son of man' in Daniel (1: 13; 14: 14; cf. Dan. 7: 13) suggests exaltation, dominion, and a corporate (or communal) nature to Jesus, in the midst of his community (see the discussion of ecclesiology, below).

The Book of Revelation also uses other phrases for Jesus Christ, drawn often from the Old Testament. He is, for example, 'the first and the last' (1: 17), the alpha and omega (22: 12), the one 'who has the key of David, who opens and no one shuts, who shuts and no one opens' (3: 7), 'the Lion of the tribe of Judah, the root of David' (5: 5). These unusual epithets may fly past our ears, as 'poetry', without evoking what the author is seeking to convey, or may, as a melange of the bizarre or psychedelic, turn us off completely or produce a garish image such as artists like William Blake delighted in (or like the lurid covers for popular books on Revelation): a golden girdle, 'eyes like flame of fire', feet of burnished bronze, seven eyes, a head with many diadems, a bloodied robe, etc. (1: 13–16; 5: 6; 19: 12–16).

For all the scenes in heaven and 'unveilings' of God and Christ, the Apocalypse, however, never departs from the Bible's general reticence about seeing or presenting God 'face to face'. The book proceeds with images and metaphors, drawn from Scripture, especially for the vision of God in Rev. 4 from Ezekiel 1, Daniel 7, and Genesis 9 (the rainbow). Likewise with the exalted Christ in ch. 5. But the significant fact is that what the Old Testament had said of Yahweh is now ascribed to Jesus Christ. Thus 'first and last' (1: 17) was 'God language' in Isa. 44: 6; 48: 12. 'Alpha and Omega' is the equivalent (from the first and last letters in the alphabet) in Greek of what the rabbis said of God; at Rev. 1: 8 it is used of the Almighty, before being transferred to Christ at 22: 12. The 'key of David' image stems from Isa. 22: 22, and is used in Revelation to speak of the risen Christ's control of death and Hades (1: 18). For most phrases about Jesus there is Old Testament background, and what was once predicated of God the Father is now used to make, in colourful terms, the fundamental confession of Revelation: 'Jesus Christ is Lord', Lord together with his God and Father.

Jesus is the one who carries out God's plan (5: 8–10); he alone is 'worthy' so to do. But in the amazing blend of ideas that make up the Christology of Revelation, we cannot always decide which was dominant in the author's mind. If we read with many scribes at 19: 13 that Christ wore 'a robe sprinkled with blood', the allusion may be to Isa. 52: 15 (in the Hebrew, cf. AV, NIV: the servant will 'sprinkle many nations'). But the more likely wording at 19: 13, 'dipped in blood', may pick up on Isa. 63: 1–3, where Yahweh comes from Edom, announcing vindication, garments stained with the blood of his slaughtered enemies (cf. Rev. 14: 14–20; 19: 17–21)—unless it be Jesus' own blood from the Cross, where he was slain for the host of saints, prophets, martyrs, and servants who call on his name.

If the Christology of Revelation features a triumphant Christ, slain but alive, exalted and coming, so that one can say the crucial battle has already been fought and won (12: 1–6, 7–12), even if struggle still goes on upon the earth (12: 13–13: 18), what kind of eschatology does this book present?

The popular impression has long been that Revelation is oriented entirely to the future. For those regarding it as an account of the 'endtimes', it was thought to provide a blueprint either for the divine plan for the centuries or for coming events of the subsequent interpreter's immediate future (the dates 1844, 1917, 1984, 2000, 2007 have, for example, been favourites for expecting Armageddon or 'the End'). From the historical-critical viewpoint, it presents what John thought was soon to come to pass (e.g. in the few years or months after AD 95). The feature that again and again caught the popular eye in futurist eschatology was the 'millennium', or hope for a chiliastic reign of the resurrected martyrs with Christ for a thousand years. According to 19: 11–21, the warrior Logos-Christ will appear and defeat the beast, his false prophet, and kingly allies, and then chain Satan in a pit for a thousand years. For that millennium, those who had been beheaded because of their testimony to Jesus, and who had not worshipped the beast, are given life in 'the first resurrection'; they reign with Christ (20: 1–6). After the thousand years Satan will be loosed and will gather Gog and Magog (cf. Ezek. 38), and their hosts will surround 'the camp of the saints and the beloved city'. But fire will come down from heaven, and the devil, beast, false prophet, and their minions will be thrown into a lake of fire and brimstone for eternal torment (20: 7–10). A general judgement will then follow, with 'the second death' for those not in the Book of Life (20: 11–15). Such a graphic depiction of a kingdom for the martyrs which lasts for a thousand years appears nowhere else in the Bible, unless one reads it in between the lines at 1 Cor. 15: 24.

These verses in Rev. 19–20 about the millennium were often, in orthodox circles, taken to refer to the spiritual renewal of Christians ('the first resurrection'), and the thousand years related to church history. In modern Fundamentalism there has been fierce debate among 'pre-millennialist', 'post-millennialist', and 'amillennialist' positions. Will Christ appear before or after the thousand years, or should we be reserved or negative on all such views? It has been remarked that the arguments by proponents of each position 'seem to them convincing' but 'do not persuade those outside their circle' (Morris, *New Testament Theology*, 297). Liberals have often blended millennial expectations into their ideas of a utopian kingdom to be brought about by human progress.

Historical criticism has been bold to suggest the following. (1) In Revelation, John was ultimately concerned to tie together two Old Testament themes: a glorious kingdom on earth (cf. Isa. 11, 65) and the apocalyptic emphasis that earth is so corrupt that 'a new heavens and a new earth' (Isa. 65: 17) must be prepared by God. In Rev. 20, the 'first heaven and earth' pass away and the new Jerusalem comes down out of heaven from God. The millennium enables our author to keep some notion of a renovated present world as the scene for (part of) the coming kingdom. (2) It is, of course, possible that the material came from an earlier source; 2 Esdras 7: 29 refers to a reign by the messiah for 400 years. (3) More important was the practical concern to encourage Christians to stand fast, even unto death. The millennium unabashedly offers special incentive for martyrs. It makes tangible what may have been otherwise too vague in the concept 'eternal life'. (4) A more speculative answer is that this millennium is a necessary 'day of rest' after the six days of creation in Gen. 1. That is an argument from biblical theology, assuming that 'a day' with the Lord is 'as a thousand year' (Ps. 90: 4; 2 Peter 3: 8), but it is not asserted by the Book of Revelation itself.

The general tenor of Revelation and features like the millennium have caused many readers to dismiss the book as hopelessly futurist. Somewhat to our surprise, there is a strong case, however, for '*realized* eschatology' in the book. Its basis has been hinted at under Christology: the Lord Jesus has already won the decisive battle, and everything is henceforth to be seen from the standpoint of heaven. There Satan is already defeated and cast out (12: 7–12). But that is nothing more than a mythic way of describing the victory that Christ has already won by his death and resurrection. As a result, Christians can say that Jesus 'has freed us from our sins by his blood and has made us [*past tense*] a kingdom' (1: 5). The old apocalyptic scenarios, inherited from Daniel and elsewhere, are interpreted as already past action. Hence voices can say, 'Babylon is fallen' (14: 8; 18: 2). Those who emphasize this view see the victory as past fact, calling to the duty now, in the present, to hold fast to 'the testimony of Jesus'. The saints are 'in Jesus' (1: 9) and die 'in the Lord' (14: 13), even if the Pauline phrase 'in Christ' is not found. A great deal of the apocalyptic eschatology in Revelation can then be claimed to express the author's certainty that God was at work in history, without claiming a programme of key events to come. For the decisive is past history.

However, even those who press for realized eschatology must allow for a future hope of some sort in the book. At the least, this includes the winning of other individuals to the testimony that Jesus' servants give, their martyrdom sometimes a means of conquest first achieved by the Lamb (12: 11). More fully, this hope must embrace the corporate life of all humanity, and so may be opened again to visions of 'renewal' and 'progress'. The argument for realized eschatology is sometimes sustained by taking the words 'Come, Lord Jesus', at 22: 20, not as a prayer for the parousia or for Christ's presence in life generally, but solely as a eucharistic epiclesis or invocation, calling down the divine presence upon a celebration of the Lord's Supper. But such an interpretation of the *Marana tha!* (1 Cor. 16: 22) misses the future side of the Lord's Supper itself, and too easily 'eucharisticizes' the eschatological reference at Rev. 3: 20 to hearing and eating with Jesus. It requires an exegetical *tour de force* to dispense with all the future emphases in Revelation. Moreover, there is some evidence that Revelation, like 1 John, may be reacting against the stress on realized eschatology in the Fourth Gospel. The formulation at 1: 5–6, possibly a baptismal hymn, about Christ who 'made us a kingdom' is seemingly corrected or at least amplified at 5: 10, when the 'new song', after repeating the phrase about the kingdom, insists, 'They shall reign on earth' (future tense; cf. also 22: 5). We spoke above of an 'eschatological reservation' in Revelation, akin to Paul's. Satan is too active in the pages of the Apocalypse to make it an entirely realized eschatology.

All in all, it is best to see both present and future aspects to the eschatology of the book.

The ecclesiology of Revelation has in part been noted above (pp. 228–9, 233–6), in discussing the prophetic community which some see as involved. Unlike the Fourth Gospel and 1 John, the book does use the term *ekklēsia* (1: 4, 11; 2: 1, 7, etc.), chiefly for local congregations, but with a sense of totality (22: 16). Apostles are known, twelve (21: 14) and holy (18: 20), but in heaven; at least at Ephesus there were false apostles (2: 2). No bishops appear. The 24 elders are in heaven (4: 4). Christians all have been made to be priests to God the Father (1: 6; 5: 10), a phrase deriving, as at 1 Peter 2: 5, 9, from Exod. 19: 6, for the entire community. But whereas older commentators sought to depict communal worship in the churches on earth by reference to the heavenly liturgy in Rev. 4–5, more recent writers have become wary of reading too much from such passages into the life of these prophetic conventicles. There are no references to priestly liturgical service on earth in the book; doxology at God's throne will come later for us. The servant concept is, instead, strong (literally, *doulos*, slave, 1: 1; 2: 20; 7: 3, etc.), as is that of 'saint(s)' (5: 8; 8: 3, 4; 13: 7, etc.). Their task of bearing witness has been commented on above. They are 'sealed' by God to mark them as belonging to Christ in the face of tribulation (7: 1–8). The community is meant to include people of all tribes, tongues, and nations (7: 9).

Certain ethical characteristics mark their life. 'Patient endurance', derived from obedient faith (1: 9; 14: 12, among other references), is a hallmark. Witness, prayer (5: 8), and worship of God alone, not angels (19: 10; 22: 8–9) or the dragon (13: 4), characterize them. There are no *Haustafeln*, certainly not sections on obedience to the State; just the reverse! But there is no call to violence or armed resistance. This is worth noting, given the (to many) distressing cries for vengeance in the book. 'How long, O sovereign Lord . . . until you judge and avenge our blood . . . ?' is the outcry of those slain for the word of God (6: 10). They want more than a white robe and the admonition to rest a little longer (6: 11). When God does act, they respond with hallelujahs because smoke rises from Rome's destruction (19: 1–3).

'Sub-Christian' is often used to describe this 'vengeance' aspect of the book. There is, however, a continuity here with some of Israel's prophets, and even with Jesus at times. Revelation is not a treatment of justification but a cry for justice, doing right (22: 11), a cry for a God who judges rightly (15: 3; 16: 5, 7; 19: 2) and for a Christ who 'judges and makes war in righteousness' (19: 11). One will probably not understand the thirst for divine punishment of the oppressors unless one is a powerless, oppressed person. Hence Revelation strikes a certain chord with peoples today who are exploited or facing grim death from tyrants. But the question remains of whether Revelation's presentation of God as power does not itself fall into the 'power game'. Or is the book a New Testament version of Israel's 'holy war', or a continuation of Jesus' battle as exorcist with the demonic powers under Beelzebul?

Faith emerges as a salient theme in Revelation, indeed, as the backdrop to the call for endurance on the part of the saints (13: 10, in the sense of fidelity). Jesus showed faith (14: 12, taking 'the faith of Jesus' to include his faithful witness as a martyr, 1: 5). He is the object of faith (taking 14: 12 to include belief in Jesus on the part of the saints; cf. 2: 13). The saints are to exhibit both aspects, trust in Jesus and fidelity under persecution (14: 12; cf. 2: 19). This is to be faithful (2: 10, 13; 17: 14), as Jesus was (1: 5; 3: 14; 19: 11), in witnessing. John does not worry that *pistis*, along with *agapē*, *diakonia* or service, and patient endurance, thereby becomes one of a series of 'works' (2: 19), for he means the deeds and conduct of life (2: 2–3) which must be exhibited in order to get through the present crisis. No reflection of supposed debate between Paul and James is to be assumed here. The aside at 19: 8, 'the fine linen [*of the Bride*] is the righteous deeds of the saints'—which may be a scribal gloss, for the dress has been given to her (v. 8), like the white robe of the saints (6: 11)—

suggests the same moral earnestness. It is the faithless who get punished (21: 8).

Canonical aspects

The values of the Book of Revelation within the totality of the New Testament have been assessed in widely different ways. Some have made it the centre for interpreting not only the New Testament but also the whole Bible. It has become the tail that wags the dog in crisis times and among sectarian groups. Others have demoted the book in influence, as 'sub-Christian', as degenerate prophecy, or as weakly Christianized Judaism. People reflecting many different theologies have insisted it must be measured theologically, and that has usually meant 'on the basis of a gospel of love'. The attempt above has been to try to hear Revelation in its own right, as the only canonical voice of book length for a prophetic-apocalyptic Christianity desperately trying to ensure survival in the face of Caesar's onslaught. It is not 'world-affirming', but then neither was the Fourth Gospel. Almost everyone would also agree that Revelation preserves a necessary other side to Jesus and Christianity: in contrast to 'sweetness and light' or a 'gentle Jesus, meek and mild', Revelation shows us stern justice and judgement, even if these seem at times overdone.

Canonical criticism (Childs, *The New Testament as Canon*, 514–17) sees in Revelation, besides hermeneutical guidelines on Christian apocalyptic literature and how symbols function kerygmatically, two particular contributions. The 'canonization formula' at 22: 18, warning of dire consequences for anyone adding or subtracting words in this book (cf. Deut. 4: 2), is viewed as reinforcing the authority of Revelation for generations to come. Secondly, its title, admittedly secondary but taken as a genitive of authorship, 'The Revelation *of John*' (the apostle), causes Revelation 'to be read in conjunction with the Johannine corpus' (517; cf. Johnson, *The Writings of the New Testament*, 518–20).

Actually, both points are more complicated. Because of

Revelation's eventual position at the end of the New Testament and of the total biblical canon, the words about 'purity of text' for this book of prophecy came in the popular mind to apply to all 27 books and, indeed, to all of Scripture. But the location of Revelation, apart from the Gospel of John and separated from 1, 2, and 3 John by Jude in most New Testaments, cannot be said to have promoted a Johannine corpus by canonical arrangement. That is, rather, based on decisions about authorship and perceptions of how different or similar the contents are. Furthermore, it leaves undecided the crucial question of whether Revelation should be read in light of the Fourth Gospel, or John's Gospel in light of 'John's' Apocalypse. Which controls?

A superlative advantage of including Revelation in the biblical canon and positioning it at the end has been the resulting ability of biblical theology to fix its gaze from creation in Gen. 1–2 to 'the end' in Revelation. The fact that the Apocalypse sometimes drew on age-old materials from world religions about a chaos battle, re-enacted in Jesus' crucifixion and now in the struggle with Domitian, abetted such linkage. But the danger was that protology (the study of 'first things') or apocalyptic eschatology (about 'last things') might obscure the centre, God's redemptive acts, above all in Jesus' cross and resurrection.

Two Blunt Apologists for Early Christianity:
Jude and 2 Peter

THE Second Epistle General of St Peter, as a letter of three chapters has sometimes been known that claims to be by 'the prince of the apostles' and refers (at 2 Peter 3: 1) to 1 Peter, and the little note said simply to be by Jude form a sub-corpus within the catholic epistles and the New Testament canon. They have certain features in common.

Each letter has been attributed to a prominent early Christian figure, one to the leader of the twelve apostles, Peter, the other to the 'brother of James' (v. 1) and (on the tradition that this is James the brother of Jesus who also wrote a New Testament letter) a brother of the Lord. Thus we would have writings by the Galilean fisherman whom Jesus chose to be first among his disciples and by his own brother who, while not a follower during Jesus' lifetime (cf. Mark 6: 3), must have come to faith after Easter and was active in the Christian movement (cf. 1 Cor. 9: 5).

The two letters have been recognized over the centuries as sharing certain similarities of content. Put most simply, much of Jude vv. 3–23, the bulk of that little book, appears in 2 Peter, especially in ch. 2. Compare these references, here outlined:

Jude	*2 Peter*
v. 3 purpose, concerning *faith*	cf. 1: 5 *faith* basic in life
v. 4 *opponents* who have, with their licentiousness, gained admission to our midst and deny our	2: 1–3 *false prophets* and *teachers*, bringing in destructive heresies, denying the Master in

Master and Lord, Jesus
  Christ

vv. 5–7 Old Testament
  examples as reminders of
  those who did not believe

vv. 8–10 a further example
  (Moses) about 'reviling'

v. 11 Cain, *Balaam*, Korah
  as examples

vv. 12–13 the opponents as
  'blemishes on your love
  feasts (*agapais*) . . .
  waterless clouds carried
  along by winds . . . for
  whom the nether gloom of
  darkness has been reserved
  for ever'

vv. 14–15 a reference to
  Enoch

v. 16 malcontents, following
  their own passions,
  boasters

vv. 17–19 *remember* the
  predictions of the apostles
  of our Lord Jesus Christ
  about *scoffers*, following
  their own ungodly
  passions

vv. 20–3 build yourselves
  up on your . . . faith, pray
  . . . wait . . . .

licentiousness

1: 12 I 'remind you' of Old
  Testament *examples*, 2:
  4–10a

2: 10b–12 'reviling'

2: 15–16 *Balaam*, son of
  Beor, and a dumb ass that
  talked

2: 13 'blots and blemishes,
  reveling in their
  dissipation' (*apatais*;
  variant, *agapais*); 2:
  17 'waterless springs . . .
  driven by a storm; for
  them the nether gloom of
  darkness has been
  reserved'
(*not* found in 2 Peter)

2: 10 'those who indulge in
  . . . defiling passions'; 2:
  18 'licentious passions',
  loud boasts

3: 2 *remember* the
  predictions of the holy
  prophets and the
  commandment of the Lord
  and Saviour through our
  apostles

3: 3 *scoffers* will come,
  following their own
  passions

1: 5 supplement your faith
  with virtue, knowledge,
  etc.

3: 14 be zealous. . . .

Of course, there are differences in the way the key words and phrases in these 'parallels' are used. There are verses unique to Jude, like the closing benediction (vv. 24–5; but cf. 2 Peter 3: 18b). Second Peter adds much more in chs. 1 and 3. But in the aggregate and sequence, the echo of one letter in the other calls for some explanation.

There is also the fact that neither letter, whatever its fortunes as to canonicity, was included in the standard Syriac translation of the New Testament, the Peshitta, in the fifth century. Each met with resistance in the Syrian Church on the issue of acceptance as Scripture.

For many centuries the standard view was that 2 Peter must be by an apostle, and so it was preferred over little Jude, authorship of which was less certain. Thus Luther listed Jude among those books which 'need not be counted among the chief books which are supposed to lay the foundations of the faith', but ranked 2 Peter higher. However, most modern critics have reversed that judgement, regarding Jude as the older and basic writing; 2 Peter is treated as an expansion and rewriting of Jude.

Among the reasons for deeming Jude earlier than 2 Peter are the precise ways in which the latter handles some of the contents in Jude. One instance has to do with the three Old Testament examples cited in Jude 5–7 and the sequence of the parallel examples in 2 Peter 2. Jude takes them up in the order (1) Israel in the wilderness (v. 5; the exodus and destruction of those not believing, Num. 14: 1–35; this example is also cited at 1 Cor. 10: 1–11 and Heb. 3: 7–4: 11); (2) in v. 6, the evil angels of Gen. 6: 1–4 and subsequent Jewish tradition; and (3) Sodom and Gomorrah in v. 7 (Gen. 19). The somewhat strange chronological order here is straightened out in 2 Peter. Here the sequence runs (1) fallen angels, 2: 4; (2) the flood and Noah, 2: 5, a substitute for the wilderness story; and (3) Sodom and Gomorrah, 2: 6–7, expanded with a reference to Lot. All these examples deal with non-Israelites. Jude has here been characterized as 'spontaneous', 2 Peter as 'more reflective'.

It has also been observed that 2 Peter generally omits allusions or quotations made in Jude to non-canonical books. For example, Jude 8, in its example about the archangel Michael disputing with the devil over the body of Moses, reflects a pseudepigraphical writing, the Assumption of Moses. Jude 14–15 actually quotes from the book of Enoch (specifically 1: 9 and 60: 8 of this volume in the Pseudepigrapha). In avoiding such references to literature outside the canon, 2 Peter may reflect the views about canon developed at a slightly later period.

There is also the general argument that it is more probable that a short note, Jude, was expanded than that 2 Peter was truncated to produce Jude. Further, one discovers, Jude often seems fresh and original, 2 Peter's adaptation contrived and inept. It is one thing in Jude 12 to call the ungodly persons who have secretly gained admission to the Christian community 'blemishes on *your* love feasts, as *they* boldly carouse together', but another thing in 2 Peter 2: 13 to speak of these 'blots and blemishes, reveling in *their* dissipations' as 'carousing *with you*'; that makes the addressees carousers too! The phrase 'nether gloom of darkness' makes more sense in Jude 13, where the referent is 'wandering stars', than in 2 Peter 2: 17, where the line is applied to 'waterless springs and mists'. For such reasons, Jude seems earlier, and a source for 2 Peter.

The possibility remains that Jude and 2 Peter each draw on a common source; but most scholars prefer to avoid positing such putative sources unless a compelling case can be made. Still others have argued that when 2 Peter 3: 1 says, 'This is now the second letter that I have written to you, beloved, and in both of them I have aroused your sincere mind by way of reminder (*hypomnēsis*)', the most obvious reference for that first letter, among all the New Testament and other early Christian writings, is Jude. That little note by 'Jude' explains that its author planned to write a larger treatise, 'Concerning Our Common Salvation', but was compelled by the immediate threat from 'ungodly persons who pervert the grace of our God' to dash off a note of urgent warning (vv. 3–4). Since Jude also uses the theme of 'reminding' (v. 5) and 'remembering' (v. 17), it is attractive to suggest that the same author first penned Jude, then, in more detail, 2 Peter. That one document claims to be by 'the brother of James' and the other by 'Simeon Peter' (2 Peter 1: 1), with considerable emphasis on how he had been with Jesus at the transfiguration (1: 16–18), is no barrier, since many critics regard *both* as pseudonymous. But the fact that whoever wrote 2 Peter wishes the author to be considered the apostle Peter would require an elaborate series of hypotheses to sustain the notion that one person wrote both Jude and 2 Peter. For example, one would have to suppose that the second treatise by 'Jude' was 'Petrinized'. Such difficulties have dissuaded all but a few scholars from pursuing such theorizing.

A more compelling link between the documents is the fact that the opponents are similar. Many of the phrases in Jude 4–19 also appear in 2 Peter, as noted above. Most commonly these 'ungodly' persons (Jude 4, 15, 18: 2 Peter 2: 5, 6; 3: 7) are called by modern critics 'gnostics' of some sort, such as increasingly troubled the church in the second century. In each letter their licentiousness is singled out, although 2 Peter adds more about the doctrinal or philosophical underpinnings for their positions. In Jude they are plainly within the Christian fellowship (vv. 4, 22–3). In 2 Peter they are more specifically denounced as false prophets and teachers (2: 1) and the attitude is one of polemic against them. Yet the all too easy 'gnostics' theory has been attacked because the profiles do not fit any specific gnostic sect of which we know. Instead, we may have a generic picture of heretics, using stock phrases, the aim being to let readers know that the enemies of the last days have arrived (Jude 18, 'In the last time there will be scoffers'; 2 Peter 3: 3, 'scoffers will come in the last days'; cf. Paul's 'Farewell Address' to the Ephesians, Acts 20: 29–30; or 1 John 2: 18). This eschatological situation leads in both letters to more stringent ethical appeals.

Finally, there is the claim of a number of modern critics that both Jude and 2 Peter reflect inroads of 'early catholicism' into Christianity. The term, which is also applied by some to the viewpoint in Colossians, Ephesians, and the pastorals, reflects the German word *Frühkatholizismus*, and denotes the beginning of the 'catholicizing' of the Jesus tradition that was later to come to dominate in the institutional church after Constantine made

Christianity the official religion of the Roman Empire. It involved especially a shift in eschatology and therefore in ethics. This meant a shift from the imminent expectation of the parousia and from life lived 'on tiptoes', with great vigour and stringency, in favour of a settling down for continuing existence in bourgeois society. An ecclesiastical, doctrinal system results where the church seems to act in the stead of its absent Lord. This leads, in turn, to more church structures and formalization of leadership. The Jewish elements in Christianity may recede, and the influence of the Hellenistic outlook expand.

Definitions of such incipient or early catholicism vary, but among the additional characteristics of this 'blight' on 'genuine discipleship and belief' are the following: the concept of faith as what must be believed (*fides quae creditur*), rather than as the commitment of personal trust in and obedience to Jesus (*fides qua creditur*); eschatology as simply concentration on the future parousia of Christ; Scripture as an authoritative collection, a canon; and an emerging emphasis on 'church' and ministerial office as instruments of salvation. These points will be discussed below for Jude and 2 Peter. But it must be said that certain other key ingredients in 'early catholicism' and the patristic church that emerged are missing in these two documents. Chief among them are the lack in Jude and 2 Peter of any references to bishops, presbyters, deacons, or other forms of ministry. Likewise, one does not find the sacraments emphasized in either letter. Therefore the term 'early catholicism' should be used only with great caution here, and must be carefully defined if it is to be a common denominator for Jude and 2 Peter.

Jude: an emergency alert about the salvation we share

Reasons have been cited above for regarding Jude, in accord with the opinion of most modern critics, as a pseudonymous tract from around AD 100–25, on which 2 Peter later drew. The document warns against an immediate threat to 'the faith which was once for all delivered to the saints', a threat posed by 'godless' persons who have 'slipped into' the church, perverting grace and denying Christ (v. 4).

More traditional alternatives, assuming a date between 50 and 80, depend on identifying the author with one of the persons named Jude whom we know from elsewhere in the New Testament. But the tradition is here by no means unanimous. The claim that this Jude was the 'brother of James' (v. 1), the brother of Jesus, has been mentioned above. According to Hegesippus (as preserved in Eusebius, *Church History* 3. 20. 1–6), this Jude (third in the list of Jesus' siblings at Mark 6:3; fourth in Matt. 13: 55) was probably dead by AD 70, but had descendants said to have 'led the churches' on into the second century.

Another view is that Jude the letter-writer was the apostle 'Judas son of James' (Luke 6: 16; Acts 1: 13; AV wrongfully supplied the noun '*brother* of James', to accommodate itself to Jude v. 1; cf. John 14: 22, 'Judas (not Iscariot)'). This 'apostle Judas' or 'Jude' does not appear in the lists of Mark or Matthew for the twelve, but must be there equated with 'Thaddaeus' (Mark 3: 18; Matt. 10: 3, variant reading 'Lebbaeus'). Other guesses include a Jude described as the third bishop of Jerusalem (according to a list in the *Apostolic Constitutions* 7. 46) or 'Judas called Barsabbas' (Acts 15: 22), a prophet (Acts 15: 32) from Jerusalem, possibly the brother of Joseph Barsabbas (Acts 1 : 23). The latter view has recently been revived, with a dating between 55 and 65 for the document and a theory about Jude as a Midrash. None of these specific answers as to author and, therefore, date commands as much support currently as the view favouring pseudonymity, with a dating about AD 100–25. That the writer is a Jewish Christian is agreed.

The genre of Jude is, on the surface, that of 'letter', in length like a typical papyrus note of the day. But the earnest and authoritative tone has caused some to describe Jude as a general tract, a pamphlet, or even an 'encyclical'. Yet there is no hint of an episcopal office speaking. Because of the conventional methods employed from Jewish exegesis of the day (e.g. v. 9, the struggle of good and bad angels, in v. 9 Michael and the devil, over the body of Moses, which the devil claimed because Moses had been a murderer—on the basis of Exod. 2: 11–15), Jude has been termed a Midrash on the judgement theme in Old Testament texts. These passages include Gen. 19 (Jude v. 7, 'punishment'); Gen. 4, Num. 22–4, and Deut. 23:4; Num. 16 (v. 11, Cain, Balaam, Korah); or Enoch (v. 14); cf. the term 'judgement' in vv. 6, 9, and 15. But others have also detected Hellenistic elements in the document, including in v. 13, in the words, 'wild waves of the sea, casting up the foam of their own shame', a possible allusion to the story of the birth of the goddess Aphrodite, 'foam-born' from the sea. And since Jude, with its use of pseudepigraphical writings, does not reflect the notion of a closed canon characteristic of Jewish Midrash, this term is best avoided.

In any analysis it is Jude's approach to heresy as a theological phenomenon, involving Christology, grace, and ethics, that stands out. Paul, of course, and 1 John, to mention just two examples among New Testament voices, had insisted that Christian teaching and the morality of Christians go together. Jude's passion for the totality of salvation that Christians share makes his attack the more comprehensive. By employing so many examples from the Hebrew Scriptures of false teaching and immoral living, from the time of Moses (vv. 5, 9, 11) and previously, in the days of Abraham and Lot (v. 7) and even of the fallen angels (v. 6; Gen. 6: 1–4), and Enoch's prophecy about the judgement of the ungodly (v. 14), the author implies that heresy was always there, from at least Cain onwards (v. 11). There is thus a 'heretical succession' against right faith and truth.

But for the letter's positive side the term 'gospel' is never employed, nor is 'kingdom'. In so short a piece of writing, such statistical facts may be less significant than in a longer work and ought not to be pressed. But the theme signalled as central, 'our common salvation' (v. 3), is, along with 'God our saviour' (v. 25), one that became increasingly common in later Christian use. Although occasionally found in Paul (cf. Phil. 1: 28; 3: 20), such terminology is much more common in Luke's writings (e.g. Luke 2: 11; Acts 4: 12), Hebrews (e.g. 2: 3, 10), or 1 Peter (1: 9, 10).

The more immediate theme is contending for 'the faith that has once and for all been handed on (*as tradition*) to the saints' (v. 3). By 'the saints' are meant the sanctified members of the community who are to build themselves up in, on, and by their 'most holy faith' (v. 20). This faith has definitively been entrusted to them, as indicated by a favourite word in Hebrews, *hapax*, 'once for all times'. It is commonly agreed that 'the faith' here involves doctrinal and ethical content, not subjective apprehension of Christ. At issue is whether this sole sense in Jude is a sign of later developments or even 'early catholicism' (see above) or whether it can sufficiently be explained by pointing to prior examples like Gal. 1: 23 or Rom. 10: 8. Is it equivalent to ' the gospel'? Jude never mentions 'believers', but is concerned about 'those who did *not* believe' among the Israelites and who died in the wilderness (v. 5). Perhaps that suggests a concern that 'the saints' keep on believing and so achieve final salvation, 'through the mercy of our Lord Jesus Christ, to eternal life' (v. 21). But the emphasis is more on faith as a body of truth, to be believed for salvation.

Christology in Jude is assumed, rather than developed. Jesus Christ, for or by whom those called are 'kept' or preserved (v. 1), is 'our only Lord and Master' (v. 4). 'Christ alone' is spoken of as 'master', by which is meant not only 'earthly teacher' but also 'sovereign' (NIV), a term of power normally used for God, as at Acts 4: 24 or Rev. 6: 10. Presumably Jude's longer treatise would say more about Christ, but his little note preserved in the New Testament is content with stressing Jesus as Lord (vv. 17, 21, 25).

The eschatology focuses apocalyptically on judgement to come. Compare v. 2, 'kept for Jesus Christ'; the prophecies of vv. 14–16, 17–19; 21, wait for Jesus Christ; 23, snatch some from the fire (of judgement; cf. Amos 4: 1; Zech. 3: 2–5); and the picture of standing 'without blemish before the presence' of God 'with rejoicing' in v. 24. Now is 'the last time' (v. 18). The term 'parousia' is, however, never used. Moreover, 'our salvation' already includes 'the faith' we believe, grace (v. 4), mercy (v. 21), the Holy Spirit (v. 20), and above all 'the love of God' (vv. 2, 21). And so there is a kind of 'realized eschatology', in that God's judgement has been taking place in Israel's history (v. 5), in the time of Sodom and Gomorrah (v. 7), and currently in the condemnation of opponents (v. 4).

An ecclesiology is suggested in Jude by reference to 'the saints' (v. 3), into whose midst false teachers have wormed their way (v. 4). The author looks back to 'apostles of our Lord Jesus Christ' and their predictions about such scoffers. But nothing is said about communal leadership or officials.

To contest for the faith against such opponents is only part of the ethical message in Jude. Holiness, not licentiousness, is a major emphasis, as Christians deal with doubters and those tainted by false teachings; see v. 23, although the wording is textually uncertain and the exact sense difficult to arrive at, beyond the general idea of showing mercy mixed with fear toward such people, 'hating even their very clothes, stained with their sinful lusts' (TEV).

It has been hard for many readers over the years to work up much enthusiasm for the Book of Jude. Textbooks are often content to salute its beautiful doxology (vv. 24–5). There is in these verses a solid appeal to God through Christ, the God who loves and preserves us, to whom belong 'glory, majesty, dominion, and authority'. But Jude, although brief, is a forthright testimony against corruption of the faith within the church via bad doctrine and/or dissolute living. It calls for Christians, in a fivefold programme, to remain in God's love, wait for mercy and life, build up community upon sound faith, pray, and hate sin. With regard to erring companions, they are to convince doubters, saving some and showing mercy—but with proper fear (vv. 20–3).

2 Peter: defending Christ's parousia and power against heresies

Second Peter is Jude writ large. What Jude says briefly in warning about false teachers, 2 Peter amplifies in ch. 2, and surrounds with further material on the virtues that lead one into the kingdom (1 : 3–11); the aim and personal authority of Peter in writing (1: 12–21); the certainty of Christ's parousia (3: 1–13); and admonitions to wait for God's promises, as Paul had taught (3: 14–18).

That 2 Peter is a pseudonymous writing, based on Jude, to be dated, therefore, well into the second century (some think as late as AD 150), has been argued above, as the prevailing opinion in modern criticism. The document would thus be the last work to be written that found its way into the New Testament canon, surely later than some of the so-called apostolic fathers (writings like 1 Clement and the Didache) and even some of the second-century apologists (like Diognetus). The author 'doth protest too much' that he is Peter, using 'I' and 'we' to show that he was with Jesus at the time of the transfiguration (1: 17–18) and so is an eyewitness (1: 16). The reference, however, to 'scoffers' coming 'in the last days', who doubt that Christ will come again, because, 'since the fathers fell alseep, all things have continued as they were from the beginning of creation' (3: 4), suggests that the first Christians have long since died. So also the allusion to 'all Paul's letters' as 'Scripture' (3: 15–17). That suggests not only a collection of, but also an authoritative status for, Paul's epistles.

This view is borne out by the weak attestation for 2 Peter in early Christian writers on into the fourth century. Irenaeus seems to refer only to one letter by Peter. Origen knew of a second one that was questioned. Eusebius listed 2 Peter among books 'spoken against'. Tertullian, Cyprian, and the Muratorian Canon were silent about it. To this lack of external support and the internal features noted above, others would add reflections of Hellenistic concepts (like 'partakers of the divine nature' in 1: 4) and gnostic ideas ('cleverly devised myths', 1: 16), so as to see early catholicism here with a vengeance. The letter then becomes an apology or defence of the second coming, against heresy, in Peter's name, with Paul's blessing claimed!

Where Peter's traditional authorship is still defended, it is usually with the latest date possible before his martyrdom in or about AD 68, with appeal to the hypothesis of a secretary. Since Silvanus, who was the scribe for 1 Peter (5: 12), is not mentioned in 2 Peter, some other amanuensis is assumed, thus explaining the different style. It must be claimed, in sustaining an early date, that 'the fathers' in 3: 4 are the Old Testament patriarchs, and 3: 15–16 is scaled down to imply mere acquaintance with some of Paul's writings. But why the document was not then referred to as Peter's until the time of Origen is harder to explain, as is the Hellenistic contrast of 'corruption' and 'divine nature' in 1: 4. Even if the latter term is taken over from opponents, it is difficult to envisage such usage in Peter's day. A more recent position is to claim that author and audience knew the Petrine pose to be a fiction in the form of a 'farewell address', but that later Gentile Christians missed the writer's intention and took the work to be by the real St Peter. Such a stance accepts pseudonymity, but stresses authorial intent on the part of some leader in Rome to write thus with authority.

What is the aim of 2 Peter? (1) Clearly, it is to warn against false teachers (ch. 2), with a sharper profile of their gnostic-like deviations than in Jude (see above, pp. 249–50, 253); they bring in 'destructive heresies' (2: 1). (2) Another purpose is to (re-)establish faith in the Second Coming, in the face of the scoffers' denial of this promise (esp. 3: 1–10). But this eschatology about a day of judgement by fire (3: 7, 10) serves to support another aim, (3) ethical admonition (3: 11–14). The fact should not be underestimated that 2 Peter, from its beginning in 1: 3–11 to its end (3: 18), stresses 'growth in grace and knowledge of the Lord'. Finally, there is (4) a concern to show that Peter and Paul are in substantial agreement (3: 15–16) on issues of salvation, eschatology, and ethics. Is this because of misuse of Paul's letters by (gnostic) opponents who 'twist' them (3: 16)?

It has been maintained that 2 Peter reflects a 'Petrine line of development' that was outdistancing the Pauline course of development in the second century, at least in Rome, if that is where 2 Peter originated. But others have regarded the pastoral epistles, especially 2 Timothy, as the post-apostolic 'testament' of Paul, just as 2 Peter is such a testament for Peter. Still others find 1 Peter, 2 Peter, and the documents (found in the New Testament apocrypha) such as the Apocalypse of Peter and the Gospel of Peter so different as not to suggest a 'school' or a single line of development. One must also be cautious about any Petrine 'trajectory' outpacing a Pauline one, since there are also later writings attributed to Paul outside the New Testament, such as the Acts of Paul.

In terms of genre, 2 Peter possesses minimal features of a letter. But the audience addressed is vague: 'to those who have obtained a faith of equal standing with ours'. Is that an address to Gentile Christians in contrast to 'us Jewish Christians', or to 'laity' in contrast to apostles like Peter (1: 1)? But if a letter, 2 Peter lacks all semblance of closing greetings or ties with recipients. Therefore, others characterize the writing as a 'farewell address', a form well known in the Old Testament (e.g. Gen. 47: 29–49: 33; 1 Sam. 12), Jewish literature, and the New Testament (cf. John 13–17; 2 Tim.). A figure of authority, about to die (2 Peter 1: 14), declares what will happen (1: 15; 2: 1; 3: 2–4) after his death and charts a course to be followed. In this sense it is Peter's last will and testament for future days, but in reality concerns present problems: what will happen shades into present description (cf. 2: 2–3 with 10b–22, or 3: 3 and 5).

It is only in general terms that one can speak of social setting in 2 Peter. Clearly, the writer warns about what he (as Peter) thought to be the real dangers. But it is difficult to identify any specific gnostic sect, geographical locality, or precise crisis, let alone a particular Christian community. The plural, 'destructive heresies' (2: 1), describes the many faces that menace those who live 'lives of holiness and godliness' (3: 11). But there is growing agreement nowadays on the Hellenistic overtones to the opponents' views and our author's replies. Some see connections with Epicureanism, in that the opponents reject divine providence and have a deterministic view of the universe, denying Christ's power (1: 16), all authority (2: 10a), and 'the Lord who bought them' (2: 1). They claim that the world goes aimlessly on, continuing from creation, with God's promises never fulfilled (3: 4, 9). Scoffing at judgement, these opponents feel free to live as they wish, reveling in licentiousness and greed (2: 2 and 3; details in 2: 12–22). They promise freedom but become enslaved in corruption. Better never to have heard 'the way of righteousness' than to end up thus, where their last state is worse than the first! Our author mounts an argument, not merely for the Second Coming and a judgement to come, but also for the created world as the work of the word of God (3: 5) and for the power of God's word to use the stuff of creation—water or fire—to judge and create (3: 6–7, 10). Hence the hope for 'a new heavens and a new earth in which righteousness dwells' (3: 13). Ultimately, 2 Peter is a defence of God and a 'theodicy' for Christ.

'Gospel' is not a term used in 2 Peter. The kingdom is viewed as eternal, belonging to 'our Lord and Saviour Jesus Christ' (1: 11). Christians confirm their call and election by holding to a course of virtues—faith, moral excellence, knowledge, self-control, steadfastness, godliness, brotherly affection, and love (1: 5–7)—so that entrance into the kingdom will be richly provided (by God, v. 11). The sense of this single use of the term 'kingdom' has previously in 2 Peter been expressed in terms of the idea of becoming 'partakers of the divine nature' (v. 4), a concept familiar in Greek thought. From this reference was to grow the patristic theme of *theosis* or 'deification' for Christians.

The word salvation, which we might expect from the reference at Jude 3 to 'our common salvation', occurs but once in 2 Peter, and that in passing at 3: 15: 'Count the forbearance of our Lord as salvation.' That fact makes less likely the notion that 2 Peter is the longer treatise which the author of Jude intended to write, for in that case more should have been said about 'our salvation . . . yours no less than ours' (NEB).

The Johannine theme of life is mentioned just once, at 2 Peter 1: 3. It occurs in connection with a favourite topic in 2 Peter, godliness (*eusebeia*; cf. 1: 6, 7; 3: 11; 2: 9 'the godly'): 'divine power has granted us all things that pertain to life and godliness, through knowledge (*epignōsis*) of him who called us to [*or* by, *RSV note*] his own glory and excellence.'

This verse at 1: 3, with its connections to so many New Testament themes like 'life', 'calling', and God's glory, yet with strong accents from the Hellenistic world in terms like 'divine power' and 'divine nature' (v. 4), 'excellence' (*aretē*), and God as divine benefactor, is a good starting-point for taking up

Christology in 2 Peter. Who is meant by 'him who called us' and 'his divine power'? Presumably God. The reference is back to 1: 2, 'knowledge of God and of Jesus Christ our Lord'. But the compressed Greek also harks back to 1: 1 and its reference to 'the righteousness of our God and Saviour Jesus Christ'.

Whereas Jude employed 'saviour' only for God (v. 25), 2 Peter consistently uses the title for Jesus Christ (see also 1: 11; 2: 20; 3: 20, and thus also 3: 2). Is it possible that 2 Peter also calls Jesus 'God' at 1: 1? The term 'righteousness of God' has been taken as a technical expression, especially in Jewish apocalyptic thought, deriving from Deut. 33: 21 ('just decrees of the Lord'), and is found in Paul (Rom. 1: 17; 3: 25–6), Matthew (6: 33), and James (1: 20). But here this phrase has become, in the preferred manuscript reading, literally, 'the righteousness of the God of us and saviour Jesus Christ'; hence, in the RSV and NIV, deity is ascribed here to Christ, as God. (The RSV note recognizes the later reading followed in the AV, 'the righteousness of our God and the Saviour Jesus Christ'.) This high Christology about the righteousness of Jesus Christ, our God and Saviour, is the reference point in light of which 'divine power' (v. 3) and 'divine nature' (v. 4) are to be understood.

Jesus Christ is, then, Lord, Saviour, and God in 2 Peter, as well as 'the Master who bought' even those who now deny him (2: 1). Of this Christ, those who have obtained faith have knowledge (1: 1, 3, 8), especially about his 'power and coming' (*parousia*, 1: 16). Yet for all this emphasis on the divine Christ, 2 Peter is perhaps the only book in the New Testament outside the gospels to offer 'eyewitness' testimony to an event in Jesus' life, the transfiguration (1: 16–18). Of course, the sermons in Acts allude briefly to Jesus' life of doing good (10: 38). Paul's letters and Hebrews, among other books, draw on many images to show the meaning of Jesus' death. Jesus' resurrection is frequently asserted and, in Eph. 4: 8–11, his ascension. Second Peter takes up his 'coming' at the mount of transfiguration.

The parousia of Jesus, in the sense of a second coming, is an issue in 2 Peter (see 3: 3–10). Our author fights those who scoff at it as myth (1: 16) by stressing the personal experience Peter (and

James and John) had, according to the synoptics (Mark 9: 2–8; Matt. 17: 1–8; Luke 9: 28–36), in being on 'the holy mountain' (a phrase of reverence for a sacred place *not* found in the gospel narratives) and hearing God, the 'Majestic Glory', declare, 'This is my beloved Son, with whom I am well pleased'. The passage adds two more titles for Jesus, Son (of God) and 'my [*or the*] Beloved One'. The vision provides credentials for apostolic witness (though Scripture is a testimony even 'more sure', 1: 19–21). It has also provided the traditional epistle reading at the Festival of the Transfiguration. Gospel criticism has long debated whether the transfiguration of Jesus was merely a foretaste of his future glory or a post-Easter resurrection appearance story that has been retrojected into our gospels. Second Peter employs the account in a way that lends support to the resurrection emphasis, in that it describes the occasion as one when Jesus 'received honour and glory from the Father', and cites it in the way that Paul appealed to resurrection appearances (cf. 1 Cor. 15: 3–11), as the grounds for apostolic authority.

The eschatology of 2 Peter seems at first glance almost entirely futurist. Entrance into the kingdom will come if Christians are zealous and do not fall (1: 10–11). 'We wait for new heavens and a new earth' (3: 13). A major preoccupation is the promise of Jesus' future coming and defence of it, even though the years have dragged by and people doubt. The writer pulls out many stops for his argument that adventism personifies orthodoxy, that the hallmark of proper Christianity is holding fast to the second coming of Christ: (1) The very presence of scoffers is a sign that we are in the last times (3: 3). (2) Apostolic witness asserts Christ's power and parousia (1: 16–18), and Paul agrees (3: 15). (3) Scripture—the 'word of the prophets', rightly understood—supports this position 'until the Day dawns and the morning star rises in your hearts' (1: 19; cf. Num. 24: 17; Mal. 4: 2; Luke 1: 78; Rev. 22: 16 for the type of thinking involved). (4) The delay is also explained scripturally: God is patiently giving people time to repent (3: 9, 15, forbearance). 'A thousand years' in God's sight is like a day or 'a watch in the night' (Ps. 90: 4); conversely, one of God's 'days' may last a thousand years (2 Peter 3: 8). (Hence all the 'alarms and excursions' in some varieties of Christianity concerning AD 1000 or 2000.)

For all this future emphasis there is, however, some sense of present eschatology in the document. 'God has given us everything we need for life and godliness' (1: 3). The divine calling and promise suffice (1: 3, 4; 3: 9, 13). There is a sense of God preserving and judging throughout Israel's history (ch. 2) and of divine forbearance as salvation (3: 15).

The ethics of 2 Peter are rooted in the position that bad doctrine (about divine power, etc.) and a wrong eschatology (rejecting a coming judgement) lead to false teaching, heresies, *and* greedy, licentious lives. Some of the admonitions are in continuity with most other New Testament writings, for example, holy conduct (3: 11; but there are no tables of duties spelled out, and there is a tendency to gild the past with the adjective 'holy', applied to a mountain (1: 18), commandment (2: 21), prophets (3: 2), and interpreters (1: 21), or zeal for peace (3: 14)). Yet Hellenistic emphases are introduced through the stress on godly piety (1: 3, 6–7; 3: 11), as in 1 Timothy. Above all, this is to be seen in what sounds like a 'ladder of virtues'. Most of these, sandwiched in between the New Testament emphases of faith and *agapē* (1: 5, 7), sound typically Greek—virtue, knowledge, self-control, steadfastness, godliness (piety), and 'brotherly affection' (*philadelphia*), 1: 5–7. There is a hint of baptism when it is said that the person who lacks these things 'has forgotten that s/he was cleansed from his/her old sins' (1: 10).

Faith plays proportionally less a role in 2 Peter than in Jude. It is the starting-point in 1: 5, to be supplemented with the virtues that follow. It is something 'obtained' by all Christians with 'equal standing' (1: 1); this probably refers to 'right confession', the faith which all are to believe, although other commentators wish to find a capacity for trusting in Christ or commitment to Christian responsibility here. The fact that it is 'equally privileged' (TEV, NIV 'as precious as ours') suggests a gift equally given.

Righteousness plays an interesting part in 2 Peter, beginning with the phrase at 1: 1, 'a faith of equal standing with ours in the righteousness of our God and Saviour Jesus Christ'. It is common today to interpret this reference in a Greek, 'early catholic' sense of equity and fairness, such as benefactors dispensed in an even-handed way in the Graeco-Roman world: people 'enjoy equal privilege' (NEB). But our author knows and defends 'our beloved brother Paul' (3: 15). Therefore, 2 Peter may carry over a Pauline sense from Romans, either of the justice of God (Rom. 3: 5) or even of 'God's righteousness through faith in Jesus Christ' (Rom. 3: 22). In ch. 2, both Noah (2: 5) and Lot (2: 7) are presented as righteous, in contrast to the unrighteous (2: 9). At 2: 21, the phrase 'way of righteousness' (cf. Matt. 21: 32) probably means Christianity itself (cf. 2: 2, 'the way of truth'; 'the right way' of orthodoxy and orthopraxis, versus 'the way of Balaam' and all false prophet-teachers). The most intriguing reference is doubtless 3: 13 about 'new heavens and a new earth [*cf. Isa. 65: 17; 66: 22*] in which righteousness dwells'. It would be appealing to see here a hope for justice, when God will recompense all the poor and disenfranchised peoples of this earth. But 2 Peter has paid little attention to social issues of the day. Clearly, the righteousness here is future and eschatological, the promised age when the righteous dwell with their Lord in peace and justice as envisioned by the prophets (cf. Isa. 11: 4–5; 32: 1, 16–17; 45: 8), not forensic justification or compensating justice.

Ecclesiologically, 2 Peter never mentions 'church'. It addresses no local congregation and says little about leadership. There were apostles and holy prophets (in the past, 3: 2). The author is presented as the apostle Peter (1: 1, 12–18), but no chain of command through bishops or other successors is mentioned. The Holy Spirit continues to work through holy persons interpreting Scripture (1: 21). From the fact that there are 'false prophets and teachers' (2: 1) one may infer that true ones exist, but little is made of the church community 'in the last days'. See also below on 'inspiration'.

Second Peter's polemic, with its reminders of truth (1: 12, 13;

3: 1–2, an emphasis also in Jude), many examples from Israel's history (2: 4 ff.), and mixture of apocalyptic with Hellenistic concepts, has in modern times seldom been appreciated in the way Luther praised it for showing, in ch. 1, 'what Christendom was to be like in the time of the pure gospel'. The document poses, for canonical criticism especially, the problem of pseudepigraphy. The eschatology of the future parousia helped push Christian creeds in the direction of saying only that Christ 'will come again to judge'. It heightened emphasis on orthodoxy and its corollary of right living. Peter is made the vehicle for endorsing and passing on the way of truth and righteousness, but this by recalling past teaching and experiences and directing one to Scripture (prophets, commandments, apostles, Paul).

One final, often overwhelming influence from 2 Peter has been its understanding of Scripture as inspired. Two verses at 1: 20–1, along with 2 Tim. 3: 16, have provided the biblical foundation for all later theories of verbal inspiration. Verse 20 has widely been taken to mean that no prophecy is of 'private interpretation'; instead, a community (with corporate checks and balances) is needed for authoritative interpretation. Even more emphatic in vv. 20–1 is, however, the point that the origin of what becomes Scripture lies in 'men and women moved by the Holy Spirit' who 'spoke from God' (NRSV), i.e. witnesses directed by the impulse of God at the outset, just as God's same Spirit is active in interpretation in later days. Thus 2 Peter places an emphasis on Paul's letters (3: 15–16) and in these verses on the Spirit at beginning and end of the interpretative process for Scripture, that is, in connection with the Bible's origins and our understanding. In this way, 2 Peter was influential in developing subsequent views of Old and New Testament writings as *holy* Scripture, created and read under the Spirit.

✓ Another Look at Luke's 'Acts of the Apostles': History? Theology? Narrative? Canonical Connective?

THE second volume in the canon attributed to Luke traces the advance of the Christian faith from Jerusalem to Rome in a series of stages. At Acts 1: 8 a possible outline for these stages is provided: Jerusalem; Judea and Samaria; and the ends of the earth. The Book of Acts has often been alluded to above, especially in discussing Luke's Gospel (Ch. 5) and at times with regard to Paul (Ch. 6). Here we shall look at Acts again, briefly, in its own right.

Sometimes Luke–Acts has been treated by scholars as the unity its author intended (e.g. Johnson, *The Writings of the New Testament*, 197–240; Morris, *New Testament Theology*, 144–221). Sometimes each book is taken up separately, the way the canonical arrangement presents them (e.g. Ladd, *A Theology of the New Testament*, 311–14; Kümmel, *Introduction to the New Testament*). But this is often done with a proper awareness that 'Acts sees itself in direct continuity with the Gospel of Luke' — New (Childs, *The New Testament as Canon*, 220).

In The Oxford Bible Series, Acts has been referred to in fixing Luke's Gospel as to place (in Rome, Asia Minor, or Caesarea) and time (perhaps between AD 80 and 85, or a decade later; cf. Stanton, *The Gospels and Jesus*, 99–101). The Acts of the Apostles has also been characterized (by Ziesler, *Pauline Christianity*, rev. edn., 133–6) as a book that 'misses the heart of Pauline Christianity', providing 'only a superficial grasp of Paul's thought'. And it has been hailed as 'an attempt to "solve" the problem' of 'the witness of the spirit to the individual' versus 'the decisions of apostolic authority', by restricting 'charismatic endowments' to the apostolic age (Brown, *The Origins of Christianity*, 146).

For centuries Acts has been seen, like the gospels, as history. Illuminating comparisons continue to be made between Luke's techniques and those of Hellenistic historiographers or, in some instances, the style and approach of Jewish historians like the authors of 1–4 Maccabees or Josephus. But in the 1950s there was a shift toward viewing Luke as a theologian and his book as a creative theology of 'salvation history' (cf. Stanton, *The Gospels and Jesus*, 97–9). The tripartite structure of Luke's view of salvation in history has been sketched above (pp. 58–60). The theological programme of Luke was increasingly emphasized, to the detriment of his historical accuracy (cf. Haenchen, *The Acts of the Apostles*).

More recently, the narrative nature of the Book of Acts has been stressed, just as for Luke's Gospel (see above, pp. 56–7). The genre of Acts has thus at times been termed 'biography' (in particular of Peter and Paul, as in Plutarch's *Parallel Lives* of Greeks and Romans); 'romance' or novel (like those by Xenophon of Ephesus, from which readers could 'profit with delight', as Horace said); or even 'aretalogy', an account where divine power is exhibited in the lives of followers and the acts of God praised (Koester, *An Introduction to the New Testament*, i. 132–40, ii. 316). Such approaches have brought Acts scholarship into a period of seeking *The Narrative Unity of Luke–Acts* (the title of Tannehill's book) by literary interpretation.

Debate, of course, continues over what sources Luke employed, and with what aims the total account was constructed. But Acts is rightly said to reflect Christianity coming to terms with the Graeco-Roman world in a positive way. This involves above all an affirmative view in the narratives of Roman governors, centurions, and other officials (see Acts 16: 37–9; 18: 12–16; 19: 31, 35–40; 21: 31–5; 23: 10, 18–22; 25: 9–12; 27: 42–3), a point to be remembered in assessing Luke's idea of 'liberation' (Luke 4: 18; 1: 51b–53); it turns out to be liberation from Satan and sin (Luke 13: 12, 16; Acts 13: 38–9).

A great many of the theological themes in Acts have already been enumerated in discussing Luke's Gospel (see above, pp. 59–63), where representative citations from Acts were given. Emphatic in the second volume are Luke's emphasis on the kerygma, an 'order of salvation', and the church. The apostolic preaching is lavishly illustrated through major sermons in Acts 2, 10, and 13, and by briefer speeches (usually by Peter or Paul) throughout the book. A pattern for salvation emerges whereby— in light of the proclamation about how God has been at work in Jesus of Nazareth and has raised him from the dead to be Lord and Christ—hearers are called upon to repent, believe, and be baptized, receiving forgiveness and the gift of the Spirit. The coming of the Spirit is usually made apparent by physical signs like speaking with tongues (*glossolalia*, 10: 44–6; 19: 6; in Acts 2 this phenomenon is interpreted as a miracle of speaking or understanding foreign languages). Believers are brought into a new community life which is marked by disciplined use of possessions, devotion to the apostolic teaching, fellowship (especially at meals), prayer, and concern for the poor (2: 42, 44–7; 4: 32–5). Churches composed of those who give heed to Christ arose wherever missionaries shared the story of Jesus, in synagogues, homes, and the 'house churches' (e.g. 8: 4, 40; 9: 31; 11: 19–26; 13: 43, 49; 16: 13–15).

A great deal has been written about further aspects of Lucan thought in Acts and the situation(s) which gave rise to this particular theology, as current scholarship proposes and disputes them (cf. Talbert in *NTMI*, p. 430). Among such aspects are God, salvation, and a world-wide outlook (cf. Acts 3: 21, 'universal restoration', NEB), an expanded horizon which includes women, children, and both poor and rich (cf. Morris, *New Testament Theology*, 144–56, 196–212). Balancing a preoccupation in the Gospel of Luke with the poor and those 'down-and-out', Acts particularly reaches out to the 'up and outers', government officials (13: 7–12, among other references), philosophers (17: 18–34), and at Philippi (16: 13–34) what has been called a microcosm of the Pauline ideal, namely, Jew or Gentile, slave or free, male and female, as expressed in Gal. 3: 28.

For the narratives about Philippi portray three persons who are confronted with the gospel of Jesus Christ by Paul during his stay in that city: a businesswoman from a pagan city attracted to the God of Israel, a slave-girl ventriloquist in bondage to the god Apollo the Python-Slayer, and a Roman jailer who owed allegiance to Caesar. But we shall concentrate here on the links between Acts and Luke's Gospel, the various ways of reading Acts as a whole, and the contribution of the book to New Testament unity and variety.

The continuity between the Gospel of Luke and Acts can be seen as one where events in Jesus' ministry foreshadow themes in Acts. For example, the scene in the synagogue at Nazareth (Luke 4: 16–30) serves as a dramatic frontispiece, pointing to the ongoing empowerment of individuals by the Spirit, offering a narrative demonstration of how Scripture is fulfilled, and portraying rejection (of Jesus) by some (Jews), to be followed with acceptance by many more (Gentiles), in the advance of God's plan (cf. Stanton, *The Gospels and Jesus*, 82, 90–5; for examples of these points in Acts, see 2: 2–4; 9: 17–18; 4: 25–8; 28: 24–9). But it is also possible (although less often done) to read Luke's Gospel through the prism of Acts. Acts 7, for example, recounts the story of Moses, as 'mighty in his words and deeds', sent to visit and deliver the people of Israel (7: 22–5). But they reject him (7: 26–9). Moses comes a second time, with signs and wonders, liberating them (7: 35–6). An analogy is drawn through use of the promise in Deut. 18: 15–19: 'God will raise up for you a prophet from among your brethren', just as God raised Moses up (Acts 7: 37; 3: 22–3, 26; cf. 2: 22–3). This God did, in the prophet Jesus (Luke 7: 16; 24: 19), who came, was rejected, killed, and raised up to lordship (Acts 2: 34–6). The command, 'Listen to him' (Deut. 18: 19 = Luke 9: 35) still applies; everyone who does not, will be cut off, just as Deuteronomy warned (Acts 3: 23). And Jesus will come again. To an extent, Acts thus tells us, from a post-Easter viewpoint, what Jesus in Luke's Gospel was about (cf. Johnson, *The Writings of the New Testament*, 207–11; see above, pp. 92, 93–4).

There are also, of course, connections between Acts and Paul (born Saul; Acts 7: 59; 8: 1; ch. 9; 11: 25–6; 12: 25; chs. 13–28; see above, pp. 71–2), Acts and Peter (who appears in Acts 1–5, 8, 10–12, 15; see above, pp. 151–2), and Acts and Timothy (see above, pp. 131–2; scattered references in Acts 16–21). By its contents and location in the canon, the Book of Acts links the gospels with the epistles, Jesus with the church, a time when Jesus 'went about doing good and healing' (Acts 10: 38) with a time when Christians are also to do good and heal (4: 8–10), all in light of God's benefactions (14: 17).

But how is Acts in its entire, epic sweep to be construed? Traditionally, Luke's Gospel has been said to present Jesus' earthly ministry and Acts the work of the Spirit poured out by the exalted Christ. But interpreters over the centuries have gone along several different lines of emphasis with the evidence in Acts. One avenue was to stress the twelve apostles (as the traditional title to the book does, although it is a misnomer in the face of the concentration on the apostle Peter and the 'thirteenth apostle', Paul); this line of interpretation often further emphasized the successors whom the apostles appointed, like the seven in Jerusalem (Acts 6: 2–6) or the presbyter overseers Paul speaks of at Miletus (20: 17–18, 28), as well as Jerusalem as the centre whence proceeds all legitimating authority (1: 8; 8: 4; 15: 1–35). Acts thus fed the idea of a hierarchical, centrally organized church. But Reformation theology could point to the strong emphasis in Acts on proclamation of the word of God and its dynamic results (2: 41; 4: 4; 6: 7; 12: 24; 19: 20; 28: 30–1). Pietism and Evangelicalism found the account of Saul's conversion and Paul's two recountings of it to be a model for becoming a true Christian (9: 1–22; 22: 1–11; 26: 12–18). The Pentecostal movement derives its very name and paradigm from Acts 2 and the continuing references to the Spirit in Acts. Charismatics draw on the references in Acts to miracles and speaking in tongues to support their profile of Christianity. Thus Acts, read with such different emphases, has spawned major but very different denominational families.

Given this kaleidoscope of scenes and streams of influences from Acts, what in the book unifies it and contributes to the unity of the New Testament? Luke himself has constantly depicted the Christian community as united 'with one accord' or 'in one place'; the word thus translated, *homothymadon*, is a frequent refrain (1: 14; 2: 1; 5: 12; 15: 25). His focus on the twelve apostles and specifically on Peter, then on Paul is a way of showing united leadership for Christ's church. The Lucan arrangement of the two volumes makes Acts the open-ended climax of the ongoing story of a church established, by the end of the narrative, in the capital itself of Rome's empire. Luke's artistry thus provides the bridge from Jesus in Palestine to Christians in public places of the great cities of the Mediterranean world; the transition from Jews to Gentiles (even if one thinks that Luke keeps the door open at the end of Acts for a mission to the Jews); a shift from itinerants in the Upper Room to house churches; a movement from waiting at 'home base' in Luke 24–Acts 1 to mission in action over a widespread area.

But Acts certainly employs variety of all sorts in providing this picture of the churches growing mightily, the churches which the word produces (9: 31; 16: 5). Recall the geographical spread, huge cast of characters, and *mélange* of experiences that bring Simon of Samaria, Saul of Tarsus, and the centurion of the Tenth Legion, Cornelius, to faith, to name just three (8: 9–13, 18–24; 9: 1–19; 10: 1–48). The 'age of the church' in Luke's programme must really be subdivided into three geographical stages (1: 8; cf. 1: 15–8: 3; 8: 4–11: 18; 11: 19–28: 31) or into 'apostolic' and 'sub-apostolic' periods (the Miletus address by Paul marks a turning-point: 'After my departure, fierce wolves will come in', Paul says, at 20: 29). It was the church fathers, not Acts, who argued that miracles and other endowments were given only for a foundational period; in Acts, tongues and astonishing happenings continue until the end of the book (19: 6; 27: 3–6). Yet here in Acts 20: 29 is the germ of the idea that after the apostles came a 'fall' into heresy (after the apostles and Paul, slippage comes in the next generation). As sketched above, Acts has resulted in all sorts of Christianity.

Childs (*The New Testament as Canon*, 225–40) has argued that in the Lucan picture one sees 'the church of the future'. In particular, Paul is presented in a 'theological composite', based not so much on Paul's letters as on the way 'he was received and heard within the early Christian community' (p. 233). Thus Paul, presented through his address at Miletus in Acts 20 'as the last of the apostles', is both 'representative of the Twelve' and 'dependent on them', a 'model for Christian ministry'. Future leaders are to build upon the apostolic foundation and the pattern modelled by Paul as bearer of the apostolic message. But it is a 'canonical' Paul (better: a Lucan Paul) who is thus presented, a theological composite, bridging not just Jesus and a world-wide church but also the Old Covenant and the Gentile mission (cf. 15: 28–9; 21: 20–5). The location of Acts in the canon before Paul's letters (so that Paul's arrival in Rome in Acts 28 is followed by Paul's Letter to the Romans) has provided a new frame of reference (or distortion) for the historical Paul as seen in his own letters. That is to create a canonical personage at the expense of history (and literature) and warrants further discussion (see Ch. 17).

As for Luke's wealth of motifs, narratives, and emphases, is it too simple to say that this author just loved a good story? Luke told a variety of them about God's activity in Jesus and through Spirit-filled apostles and believers, without fitting all together in a systematic way. For Luke, the experiences, even though he moulded them into a certain unity, were too powerful to be put into a neat uniformity of doctrine. Ever since, readers, preachers, and hearers have been moved by these stories of what can be expected when one trusts in Jesus Christ (Schweizer, *Luke: A Challenge*, 55).

PART IV

The Oneness of the Many in New Testament Faith

The 'epichristian' literature of the apostles and Paul and the after-shocks, volcanic, sometimes lava-hot, creating new peaks and islands in the New Testament archipelago of early Christianity, raise the question of an 'epicentre' for it all and, in Moffatt's words (*The Theology of the Gospels*, 24), how 'to view "the parts/As parts but with a feeling of the whole" '.

Jesus alone, 'since he knew how to serve God', 'standing in the middle between God the unbegotten and those begotten after him ... is called the Father's anointed [Christ]', many 'among the Hebrews being called anointed [christs]' (Eusebius, *The Proof of the Gospel*, 4. 10).

'Christ is *punctus mathematicus sacrae scripturae*', the centre of the circle (Luther, 1532; *Werke*, Weimarer Ausgabe, *Tischreden* (Weimar: Böhlaus), ii (1913) 439, 25).

'The only answer' to the question of how 'the degree of unity that was achieved through all the differences and varieties', writes C. F. D. Moule, 'is that the common factor holding all together is devotion to the person of Jesus Christ—the historical Jesus acknowledged as continuous with the one now acknowledged as the transcendent Lord' (*The Birth of the New Testament*, 17).

Does that hold, in a time when historical variety and reader-oriented interpretations abound?

Will a Centre Hold?

WE began this volume on variety and unity in the New Testament by asking what holds the 27 books of the canonical collection together. Is there a centre for the New Testament and early Christianity? Our examination has shown how modern scholarship has moved again to stress the pluralism of these writings. This exacerbates the unity question. The matter is difficult enough for the gospels, Jesus, and Paul's letters (see Ch. 6 for comparison and 'trajectory' here). It is far more complicated when the other 16 books taken up in Part III above are included as factors in the total equation. It is now time to ask whether there is any centre to New Testament Christianity as a focus for unity, and to what extent it is valid today.

Of course, one should speak, as past ages often did (although usually without total agreement on the answer), about *the* centre of the New Testament, for there should be only one mid-point within the contours of a circle or other configuration. But, not only because so many interpretations have been proposed to point up unity (see Ch 3; Pt. III has laid bare even more), but also because some question whether there is *any* centre, it must first be asked whether any theme designated as central can hold up today.

Many a generation seems to feel that the analysis articulated in W. B. Yeats's poem applies to it: that things are falling apart, and whatever has been considered central can no longer hold up. It is worth recalling that his famous lines written in 1921 were in a poem entitled 'The Second Coming', and are filled with apocalyptic imagery about some anti-Christlike beast figure slouching its way to Bethlehem for birth. The ever-widening spirals or 'gyres', as Yeats called them, using a Greek derivative (cf. 'gyration'), suggest a centrifugal force, such as many have seen at work in biblical studies, ever expanding outward until any core is so distant as to be forgotten. This is the reverse of the centripetal direction stressed by C. H. Dodd in his study of the kerygma in 1936 (*Apostolic Preaching*) and by others in the biblical theology movement (see Ch. 1). We are by no means today in a Yeatsian period of anarchy, where 'the worst' dominate and 'the best' are lacking in conviction. But the very insights of contemporary biblical scholarship, whether deemed good or bad, make one ask the more intensely about any unity.

In spite of all the variety we have laid out, certain observations are possible. A great deal depends on the methods we employ and how we use them. Yet some proposals can be made concerning unity in the New Testament.

Some observations

1. The use of historical–critical methods to examine Scripture enables one to see a greater variety in its contents, possible backgrounds, and therefore meanings than non-critical, literally 'historical' approaches of prior centuries ever did. (These older approaches often took the text, or the critics' reconstruction of it, as 'straight history'.) In some instances, such thoroughgoing modern interrogation of the text leaves us, unfortunately, more uncertain than ever about the original setting and meaning (e.g. the circumstances prompting Hebrews or the authorship and date of James). In other instances, such critical examination can enrich our understanding (as with the reconstruction of the setting for John and 1 John), or removes a book (like Revelation) from absurd misapplications, or is crucial to the very essence of Christian faith (the insistence on Jesus as a historical figure and recovery of something of what he taught and stood for).

2. To employ literary methods of interpretation, while likewise helpful, in no way of itself leads to a greater unity for early Christian literature. The New Testament books, to say nothing of those outside the canon, exhibit a wide variety of

genres. As oral forms, their subsections differ too. The redactional and rhetorical methods of each evangelist and of other writers likewise show great variety. If we focus on narrative, the plot lines and characters even in the Jesus story are not set down in uniform style. Left solely to literary judgements—such as style, whether a document 'grips' one, or to what extent the readers profit with delight—the writings in the New Testament differ all the more when it seems a matter of each modern reader's tastes. To each, his or her own! For 'there's no use disputing over tastes'.

3. The canon as a collection becomes more problematical when one sees how varied are the writings that have been included (and how some of those left out are by no means intrinsically inferior in style or later in date) or how opinions differed over some of these writings in the patristic centuries. The diversity among the writings canonized grows as one becomes more familiar with all of them, and the question of the relative value of each in relation to the others is thereby raised. Can an heir love all 27 ancestors equally, the short and the tall, the angry and polemical along with the calm and pastoral, those that edify and those that devastate? Does each book have the same authoritative hold on us, or is its effect tempered by historical and literary impressions? Some canonical criticism is committed to having no favourites; other critiques of the canon elevate a centre.

4. The many other voices in the New Testament chorus—the 16 books we have referred to as the 'et cetera' after the gospels and Paul's own letters—compound the picture of New Testament diversity. The four gospels, which early caused 'embarrassment over the differences in which opponents took particular delight', can be said to have 'slid into existence almost furtively' as a canonical collection (Stanton, *The Gospels and Jesus*, 133–5). The theology of the Pauline letters 'has a different look and feel' from the synoptic gospels, even if a certain continuity can be sketched; perhaps 'the whole structure' of Paul's thought could not be maintained when Christians no longer felt they were eschatologically 'living on the edge of the times' (Ziesler, *Pauline*

Christianity, rev. edn., 145–9). But whether in eschatology, or in the view of Jesus, or in a host of other topics, the 16 documents discussed in Part III spread the variations yet more widely, far beyond those in the 11 noted in Part II. One can also find literary expression, in those books we discussed in Part III, of all the chief currents which Dunn proposed for diversity amid early Christian unity, namely, Jewish Christianity (cf. James), Hellenistic Christianity (cf. 1 Peter), Apocalyptic Christianity (as in Revelation), and Early Catholicism (Pastorals, 2 Peter).

5. Nevertheless, many of the writings we have especially considered do relate to Paul or the gospels. Those with Pauline links include Colossians, Ephesians, 2 Thessalonians, the pastoral epistles, 1 and 2 Peter, and Hebrews. In the Johannine circle are to be reckoned 1, 2, and 3 John and Revelation. Synoptic connections were noted in James and elsewhere. Hebrews, Revelation, and in many ways 1 Peter emerge as distinct, if not also major, independent theological types of New Testament thought, alongside Pauline, Johannine, and synoptic 'schools'.

6. While many of the books we have treated need be no later than the gospels, few, if any (James? 1 Peter? 2 Thessalonians? Colossians?), are earlier than Paul's acknowledged letters. The 16 generally reflect later developments. These developments include growing persecution, widening contacts with the world of the day, and calls to fuller social responsibility. By now, Christianity was no 'hole-and-corner business' (Acts 26: 26 NEB).

7. These generally later writings therefore reflect development or maturing within Christianity, much of it inevitable, some of it to be applauded, other parts to be lamented, depending on one's viewpoint. Certainly, some of the original vigour and rigour was lost, or at least authors were fighting to sustain it (cf. e.g. Heb. 6: 1–9). Eschatological fervour comes and goes. Christ's meaning must be extended to new realms. Communities are confronted with thoughts that they decide are unacceptable, and so 'heresy' arises. Structures of organization must, as in any social group, become more complex. The ministry of all believers is increasingly related to ministerial leadership worked out along more formal lines.

8. If one has not otherwise thought about it, these (16) writings clearly pose questions, not merely of how Christianity may remain relevant by growth in its thought, adaptation of new ideas, or mutations of old ones, but also of whether its writings (and the views expressed in them) should be prioritized among themselves; further, how the emerging collection is to be viewed in relation to later Christian thinking, creeds, writings, and authority. Thus are raised the problems of a canon within the canon of 27 books and of a 'canon' (in the sense of rule or norm) after the New Testament ecclesiastically.

Our methodologies

The examination above of individual New Testament books for signs of unity has assumed attention to 'the wider issues, both historical and theological, with which the Bible is concerned', as the General Editors' Preface to The Oxford Bible Series puts it, and that especially by use of the historical-critical method (on which, cf. Brown, *The Origins of Christianity*, 7–21; Stanton, *The Gospels and Jesus*, 139–64). In this process, literary aspects of the New Testament writings have often been noted too, and some use made of rhetorical, social, and other approaches. But what one concludes about unity or variety is often influenced by which of the many disciplines or sub-disciplines among the historical, literary, and other criticisms we allow to be dominant.

For most centuries of the Christian era, biblical studies were under the management of systematic theology (or dogmatics or doctrine) or of philosophy. Certainly that was true for the church fathers, with their creeds, Stoicism or Neoplatonism, or the late Middle Ages with its Schoolmen and rediscovery of Aristotle. It continues in some quarters to the present day in Thomism, Existentialism, or Process philosophy. There have accordingly been efforts to view the author of the Epistle to the Hebrews as 'the first Christian philosopher', or to claim that Greek categories underlie New Testament concepts like 'soul' or 'life'. In general, the more 'Semitic' a document, the further away it is from the Greek spirit: but already in the first Christian century Philo was treating all the books of Israel's Torah allegorically, in order to make them speak to the Greek mind.

Since the Renaissance and Reformation, however, there has been a swing away from the dominance of dogma and philosophy over biblical exegesis, and, since the Enlightenment, more and more a move toward history as the chief frame of reference. As Professor Johann Tobias Beck of Tübingen put it in the early nineteenth century, 'History is god nowadays'. Critical methodologies evolved accordingly, in the spirit of the period, to interrogate documents about 'what really happened'. (See Krentz, *Historical-Critical Method* or Morgan and Barton, *Biblical Interpretation*, 44–166, for exemplification.)

More recently, however, it has been claimed that a further shift in paradigm and dominant model has taken place: the new emphasis is on literary approaches. Indeed, this change has been termed a revolution (Macky, 'The Coming Revolution'). There can be reasons for turning one's back on history in favour of literary study of the Bible, among them the failure of historical scholarship to achieve consensus on so many questions (recall the varied theories in Part III about the background, author, date, and audience for document after document); the student's sense of being overwhelmed by the sheer volume of data and opinions on historical matters; and the common-sense reaction (in Henry Ford's dictum), 'History is bunk'.

In The Oxford Bible Series, this change to 'the literary frame of reference', rather than approaching the Bible 'as a historical or theological source', has been vigorously championed in *Biblical Interpretation* by Barton (203–68) and Morgan (1–43, 269–96; quotations above from p. 215). Specifically, the 'breakthrough' is 'characterized as a shift in the focus of interest from past persons, events, traditions, literary forms, and conventions, to the now available texts and their impact upon present-day hearers and readers' (221). The trend is toward 'reader-oriented criticism' (McKnight, *Post-Modern Use of the Bible*).

One needs to ponder this position. It holds that texts are 'inert objects' with 'no rights, no aims, no interests'; the original author's intention is respected only when it is in the modern interpreter's 'interest to do so' (7–8, 269–71). The aim is still to bridge 'the gulf between critical scholarship and religious faith' (25), only now not via historical understanding (167–85) but through a literary paradigm (198–200). To concentrate on the modern reader's perceptions is said to fit well with our 'radically pluralistic society' and to be 'one way of making religious talk of God intelligible in a secular culture' (218–19). The method is deemed particularly helpful in the British university scene, although departments of religion in secular institutions in the USA faced the issues even earlier (138–47) and the description of German university faculties in religion as 'oriented to training clergy to preach on the biblical text' (134, 138) rings a little hollow when the German academic penchant for radical criticism of the Bible is recalled. The underlying assumption, however, is that the theological interpretation of each person or community is the 'middle term' between reason (working now along literary lines) and faith (281, 284).

Under this 'literary frame of reference' can be grouped all sorts of critical methods. Morgan and Barton list structuralism (meagre results, potential importance, 255); deconstructionism ('which denies to any text a fixed and stable meaning', 256–7); rhetorical criticism (215–16); social anthropology (143–51, 218); and reader response (218, 257–9), among others.

A major distinction can be made between approaches that regard the text as a window and those that see it as a mirror. The former assume that one can go back through and behind the window, to earlier sources, oral forms, and, behind these, by judicious use of historical-critical methods, to 'what happened', the event. The latter approaches accept the text as a mirror, behind which it is not desirable or really possible to go, for the meaning lies on this side of it. The readers get caught up in the text, its narrative, plot, characters, and values, and if the story is well told, they find themselves so enmeshed in its symbolic world as to bring back the claims and values of that text to impinge on their own 'real' world of today. The choice is whether to go to the looking-glass (with all its threats of narcissism) or through the window opened by historical criticism (with all the problems of an antique world behind it).

The options can be posed thus. Does the significant 'moment of meaning' occur, for example, in the case of Jesus' death on the Cross, at the very hour Jesus was nailed to the crossbar and expired? Or in the theological reflection found within the earliest oral passion narrative or in the L source? Or in an evangelist's artful retelling? Or in Paul's propositional assertions, such as 'Christ died for our sins'? Or after all the New Testament documents were written, in a canonical combination of them? In a 'biblical theology'? The *Christus Victor* or Anselmic views of the atonement? Or when a preacher proclaims the text so as to get through to hearers today? (Cf. Reumann, 'Methods' and 'Exegetes'.)

The implications of the new literary approaches for unity and variety in New Testament thought are far from clear. In most cases, the thought or theology of each entire New Testament book has not yet been definitively worked out, let alone the totality of the canonical collection. Among structuralists, Daniel Patte's work on Paul (1983) and Matthew (1987) represents a beginning but in terms of the biblical writer's 'faith' (seen as 'a system of convictions' or 'being held by a system of convictions') rather than as 'theology' (a further level, involving 'the logic of the rational mind', Patte holds). Under the heading of rhetoric, fruitful work has been done in the New Testament letters (Stowers, *Letter-Writing in Greco-Roman Antiquity*) for example, in a commentary on Galatians (Betz). Narrative criticism functions best with the gospels and Acts. The social-world approaches, which may be related to historical and/or to literary criticism, work well on the gospels, many of the letters, and apocalyptic writings. Numerous books and articles in the last 20 years or so illuminate these methodologies.

But against all of these examples can be levelled two charges that were also often applied against much historical–critical research: the findings by practitioners do not agree with each other; and advocates do not produce results much beyond what had been achieved by other methods. Patte's commentaries have to promise a further volume that will compare Paul's faith with 'various "theologies of Paul"' and a subsequent monograph systematically presenting Matthew's faith. Yet surely 'faith' had long been perceived as important for each New Testament writer by scholars using non-structuralist methods. As for rhetoric, Luther had, centuries earlier, begun to compare Galatians to Graeco-Roman rhetoricians (Betz, *Galatians*, xv, 14 n. 97). The result of Kee's sociological approach to New Testament interpretation, *Knowing the Truth*, is to elevate 'covenant' as the prime form of social identity for early Christianity; but advocating the covenant theme for either testament (or covenant!) is scarcely new. Our point is not to argue about the truth or usefulness of any of these findings, but simply to point out that the emerging results from new literary and sociological approaches may not be all that different from conclusions reached in previous periods of scholarship.

Obviously, several ways for dealing with the Bible (or other texts) have by now emerged. In addition to the approaches where (1) some system of doctrine or philosophy provides the framework into which passages are to be fitted, there has long existed (2) the historical approach. Here interpreters examine texts by methods that assume, as part of criticism, the principles of analogy and correlation to our understanding of how cause and effect work. There is also now offered (3) a literary frame of reference for understanding the New Testament. But this must be subdivided into (3a) a literary approach that makes some use of historical techniques to grasp the sense intended in the ancient writing, and (3b) a literary approach that is not only ahistorical (with regard to the past) but also clearly determined by the modern reader's interests.

Canonical criticism is more or less of type 3a. It gives the canonical text very high rights and authority, although much depends on whose version of canonical criticism is involved (cf. Morgan and Barton, *Biblical Interpretation*, on Childs and J. A. Sanders). A danger in approaches which exalt the 'canonical world' of the New Testament collection or which emphasize the modern reader's interests (3b) is the creation of a sort of 'Bible land' that never existed—save in the constructs that emerge from combining varying views within the canonical sub-collections (Childs's 'canonical construals'). But even if one accepts such combinations, it is still a question of whether Luke's Paul, or the Paul of Paul's acknowledged letters, or the Paulinists' Paul of the pastorals should dominate. A further problem for Childs seems to be New Testament pseudepigraphy. Some of the same objections apply to the concatenations modern readers make out of texts which they have brought into accord with their own contemporary interests. Certainly, approach (3b) accords well with modern subjectivity, whether in the interests of liberation, feminist, or other theologies. But who will verify (or falsify) the multitudes of results, when each is guided by what is right in his or her own heart? How, indeed, will ecumenical advance be possible if each religious community remains firm in its own reading of the texts, invulnerable to historical critique?

Toward unity in reading the New Testament: Jesus and the experience of faith

Can anything be proposed to bring a sense of oneness amid the varieties of New Testament contents and the pluralism into which our plethora of methodologies has brought us? Plainly, early Christianity, like Israel of old with its cry of 'One God' (Deut. 6: 4), thought so, for it spoke of 'seven unities': one God and Father; one Lord (Jesus Christ), one faith, one baptism; one Spirit, one body, one hope (Eph. 4: 4–6). Early Christianity found its centre in one Jesus—even if depicted in four canonical gospels (Dunn, *Unity and Diversity*, 216: 'One Jesus, Many Christs'). We rightly speak of one gospel (in the sense of message of good news), although we seem to find four Jesuses, each slightly different, in the depictions by Matthew, Mark, Luke, and John, and many facets to 'the gospel'.

Of the ways, initially listed in Chapter 3, that have often been used to point up unity to the New Testament, Jesus and some sort of Christology, it can now be said, appear in every New Testament book. But the christological understandings of Jesus have varied considerably. 'Gospel' has appeared throughout the New Testament books, but the precise definition shifts somewhat because it is responsive to needs and situations addressed. Almost always, the good news had to do with God's work in and through Jesus. (1 Thess. 3: 6, about the good news of the Thessalonians' continuing faith and love, may be the only instance of the term *euangelion* applied to a post-Easter event not directly about Christ.)

The term 'kingdom of God' tended to recede in use outside the synoptics and Paul, but never wholly disappeared. 'Love' is prominent in the Fourth Gospel and 1 John for God's person and actions, but emerged as a demand in the synoptics and elsewhere (Jesus' twofold love command, Mark 12: 29–31 and parallels). The kerygma as apostolic preaching was most prominent in Acts; as Jesus' preaching, in Mark. Credal slogans and hymns that are proclamatory appear in Paul, 1 Peter, and elsewhere. Proclaiming the word is emphasized in Mark, Luke–Acts, and Paul. A plan of salvation is seen with clarity in Luke–Acts, to some extent in Paul, but 'salvation' is a more widespread theme. Eschatology, usually of the 'now' and 'to come' types, can be found in virtually every book. As for 'faith', a striking array of references and nuances have emerged. Details on each item can easily be reviewed for most New Testament books by checking the relevant passages above on that document (see also the General Index).

Repeated references have also been made in Part III to how the Spirit, the church community (ecclesiology), ethics, and the New Testament understanding of what a human being is before God ('anthropology') are part of the thought of these writings. The ministry emerged, especially in later books, as perhaps the least unified topic. Baptism proved more prominent than the Lord's Supper as a subject. Covenant, law, judgement, relations to the world, images of redemption (especially righteousness/ justification), priestly and prophetic aspects of the community— these and other themes were all pointed out.

Can any single unifying emphasis now be charted for this sprawling archipelago of themes? The idea of the New

Testament as a Jesus book, advanced by Moule (*The Birth of the New Testament*, 17, 217, 231, 247), Dunn (*Unity and Diversity in the New Testament*, 59, 371, 382), and others (see above, pp. 28–9), can be said to have found support document by document: Jesus as a Jew who lived and died in Palestine and whom God exalted in life and glory; Jesus now Lord, Christ, Saviour, confessed and adored through a host of other titles.

But it can also be proposed that along with Jesus regularly goes the experience of faith. Jesus is the object of faith (eventually alongside God). On occasion Jesus may even be a paradigm of believing, trusting, and obeying God, as the subject of faith, the one who has faith (cf. Phil. 2: 5–11 in its context; Heb. 5: 7–8). But of perhaps greater prominence is the way that hearers or readers are asked to respond in faith, by believing in God and Jesus Christ, trusting, living with the obedience of faith. One can easily review these rich references under 'faith' for each segment of the New Testament in Parts II and III, where an effort has been made to distinguish objective and subjective genitives, i.e. faith as teaching, assertions to be believed, doctrines to which one commits oneself, and faith as personal, trusting, obedient response.

To couple 'faith' with 'Jesus Christ' as the heart of the New Testament and expression of its unity has several advantages, besides its statistical prominence and a variety of nuances within its basic sense of meaning. The 'experience of faith' can be said to run through the entire biblical story from Abraham's day until the consummation in the Book of Revelation. The New Testament itself (Paul and James!) highlights Gen. 15: 6, 'Abram believed God, and it was reckoned to him as righteousness'. Hab. 2: 4 ('the righteous shall live by faith' or 'the person righteous by faith shall live') is a key thought in Paul (Rom. 1: 17) and Hebrews (10: 38). Faith continues until it turns to sight at the end.

The varied New Testament uses of faith well reflect and do justice to the manifold historical settings of the documents. These include believing when one can no longer see an earthly Jesus (John 20: 29), continuing to trust under pressure of persecution (1 Peter), and faith as orthodox belief (the pastorals), or as practical action in the face of intellectual apathy (James). But this theme also fits the stance called for in the new literary approach emphasized in Morgan and Barton, *Biblical Interpretation*: the New Testament concept not only provides content to confront the reader, but also calls to religious faith. Faith, as content, is thus what reason, working along literary (or historical) lines, finds in numerous passages. It is also a 'middle term', leading one to faith itself, i.e. belief, trust, and obedience. Faith therefore becomes the means for linking Jesus and readers.

The importance of faith in its several aspects has long been appreciated ecumenically. In issuing the call to the Life and Work Conference in Stockholm, 1925, Nathan Soderblom wrote, 'The nearer we come to Christ, the nearer we also come as Christians to one another. For Christ is the centre of faith and of the church. Every drawing near to Christ also draws us near to one another.'

A recently published *Handbook of Faith* (edited by J. M. Lee, 1990) seeks to set forth 'a somewhat comprehensive overview of faith from a wide variety of contrasting but complementary perspectives' so that 'persons of all religious persuasions will better understand the concept of faith'. There are, admittedly, Catholic and Protestant perspectives on the topic as well as concepts of it in philosophy, psychology, and comparative religions. Yet there are 'religionists like James Fowler' who regard faith 'as the central category of human existence' (vii, xii).

The Faith and Order Movement, in its bold project for the year 2000 of a 'common expression of the apostolic faith today', envisions the possibility of a new Christian creed (*fides quae creditur*, content we believe) but also renewal of believers (*fides qua creditur*, the faith with which we believe, expressed in worship, life, and service). It is consonant with our survey of New Testament unity and variety to say,

'Faith' indicates at the same time a decisive act and a continuing attitude of believing (*fides qua creditur*) as well as a set of beliefs and convictions (*fides quae creditur*). . . . This *fides qua* can never be without or separated from the content of faith (*fides quae*). . . . The content of faith is determined by the One toward whom it is directed. The *fides quae* can be expressed in a great plurality of forms, ranging from short biblical affirmations such as 'Jesus is Lord' to massive theological expositions.

The apostolic faith is grounded in the 'testimony of those who preached Jesus in the earliest days', expressed in various ways, 'having its centre in the confession of Jesus as Christ'. But ever since Abraham it has been 'future-directed and opens the future' (Link, *Roots of Our Common Faith*, 20, 38).

Faith, as it has been put in a volume of essays celebrating the 100th anniversary of the publication of *Lux Mundi* in 1889—that important volume which first accepted historical criticism (of the Old Testament) in the Church of England (and the opening essay of which, by Henry Scott Holland, was on 'faith')—faith is 'the setting of a whole life story in the context of God's dealings with humanity through his peculiar people'. As Christian faith, it is 'necessarily and characteristically resurrection faith'. For those who believe, faith is 'the intention and passion which move a believer's self-understanding into the narrative of the people of God and sustain it there' (Sykes, 'Faith', 20–1).

Faith, that is, in Jesus the Christ.

BIBLIOGRAPHY

General books on the New Testament

Anderson, B. W. (ed.), *The Books of the Bible*, ii: *The Apocrypha and the New Testament* (Scribner's, New York 1989). Between a commentary and Bible dictionary; introductory essays, book by book, for the general reader, reflecting shifts beyond the historical approach.

BEM: Baptism, Eucharist and Ministry, Faith and Order Paper No. 111 (World Council of Churches, Geneva 1982).

Brown, S., *The Origins of Christianity*, Oxford Bible Series (Oxford Univ. Press, Oxford and New York 1984).

Bultmann, R., *Theology of the New Testament* (2 vols., Scribner's, New York 1952, 1955). Thorough historical, theological analysis, stressing Paul and John.

Charlot, J., *New Testament Disunity: Its Significance for Christianity Today* (Dutton, New York 1970). Makes a virtue of variety.

Childs, B. S., *The New Testament as Canon: An Introduction* (Fortress Press, Philadelphia 1985). Book by book, within the canonical framework.

Conzelmann, H., *An Outline of the Theology of the New Testament* (SCM Press, London and Harper & Row, New York 1969). Along Bultmannian lines but briefer, more balanced (taking Jesus and the gospels into consideration).

Dunn, J. D. G., *Unity and Diversity in the New Testament* (SCM Press, London and Westminster, Philadelphia 1977; 2nd edn., Trinity Press, Philadelphia 1990). Arranged topically and by types of Christianity (Jewish, Hellenistic, Apocalyptic, and Early Catholic).

Goppelt, L., *Theology of the New Testament*, i: *The Ministry of Jesus in its Theological Significance*; ii: *The Variety and Unity of the Apostolic*

Witness to Christ (Eerdmans, Grand Rapids 1981, 1982). Not purely historical but more historical-positive and salvation-historical, emphasizing Jesus; vol. ii posthumous and less complete but often stimulating.

Hanson, P. D., *The People Called: The Growth of Community in the Bible* (Harper & Row, San Francisco 1986). Jesus and the Church in continuity to themes traced back to the Yahwistic notion of community.

Jeremias, J., *New Testament Theology: The Proclamation of Jesus* (SCM Press, London and Scribner's, New York 1971). The kerygma and call of Jesus as revelation; vol. ii, on the answer of the church, was never completed.

Johnson, L. T., *The Writings of the New Testament: An Interpretation* (Fortress Press, Philadelphia and SCM Press, London 1986). Literary approach, strong on content, abandoning some of the older historical questions.

Kennedy, H. A. A., *The Theology of the Epistles* (Duckworth, London 1919). An old and once standard treatment.

Koester, H., *An Introduction to the New Testament*, ii: *History and Literature of Early Christianity* (Fortress Press, Philadelphia and de Gruyter, Berlin and New York 1980). Vol. i deals with the world of the New Testament, especially Graeco-Roman influences; the canonical writings are rather briefly treated, within the framework of other early Christian writings, by geographical areas of origin.

Kümmel, W. G., *Introduction to the New Testament* (rev. edn., SCM Press, London and Abingdon, Nashville 1975). Standard, detailed overview, book by book; plus canon and text.

— *The Theology of the New Testament According to Its Major Witnesses: Jesus—Paul—John* (Abingdon, Nashville 1973). Readable, helpful on these three chief voices.

Ladd, G. E., *A Theology of the New Testament* (Eerdmans, Grand Rapids 1974). Conservative, detailed.

McCurley, F. R., and Reumann, J., *Witness of the Word: A Biblical Theology of the Gospel* (Fortress Press, Philadelphia 1986). 'Good news' as hermeneutic in a historical-literary approach for laity and students.

Morgan, R., and Barton, J., *Biblical Interpretation*, Oxford Bible Series (Oxford Univ. Press, Oxford and New York 1988). See above, Ch. 17.

Morris, L., *New Testament Theology* (Zondervan, Grand Rapids 1986). Conservative, uniformly structured treatment of chief theological themes in New Testament blocks of literature.

Moule, C. F. D., *The Birth of the New Testament*, Black's/Harper's New Testament Commentaries (3rd edn., rev., Black, London and Harper & Row, San Francisco 1981). A unique overview, falling between an introduction and a New Testament theology.

NTMI: The New Testament and its Modern Interpreters, ed. E. J. Epp and G. W. MacRae (Fortress Press, Philadelphia and Scholars Press, Atlanta 1989). Surveys of international scholarly literature since 1950.

Reumann, J., with responses by J. A. Fitzmyer and J. D. Quinn, *'Righteousness' in the New Testament: 'Justification' in the United States Lutheran–Roman Catholic Dialogue* (Fortress Press, Philadelphia and Paulist, New York 1982).

Richardson, A., *Introduction to the Theology of the New Testament* (SCM Press, London and Harper & Row, New York 1959). Topically organized, often emphasizing patristic links.

Robinson, J. A. T., *Redating the New Testament* (SCM Press, London and Westminster, Philadelphia 1976). A *tour de force*, arguing that all New Testament books can be dated before AD 70, an unlikely conclusion, but compelling critical scholarship to re-examine its positions on late datings.

Schüssler Fiorenza, E., *In Memory of Her: A Feminist Reconstruction of Christian Origins* (Crossroad, New York 1984). A pioneering hermeneutic, historical reconstruction, exegesis, and advocacy for 'the ekklesia of women'.

Stanton, G. N., *The Gospels and Jesus*, Oxford Bible Series (Oxford Univ. Press, Oxford and New York 1989).

Stauffer, E., *New Testament Theology* (SCM Press, London and Macmillan, New York 1955). Succinct, systematically theological in structure, with attention to apocalyptic aspects.

Ziesler, J., *Pauline Christianity*, Oxford Bible Series (Oxford Univ. Press, Oxford and New York 1983; rev. edn. 1990).

Reference works cited

Charlesworth, J. H. (ed.), *The Old Testament Pseudepigrapha* (2 vols., Doubleday, Garden City, NY 1983).

IDB Sup.: The Interpreter's Dictionary of the Bible, Supplementary Volume, ed. K. Crim (Abingdon Press, Nashville 1976).

Link, H. G. (ed.), *The Roots of Our Common Faith: Faith in the Scriptures and in the Early Church*, Faith and Order Paper No. 119 (World Council of Churches, Geneva 1984).

Robinson, J. (ed.), *The Nag Hammadi Library in English* (Harper & Row, San Francisco 1977; rev. edn. 1989).

Commentaries

Some series cited below are detailed and technical, often using Greek; examples include the Anchor Bible (Doubleday, Garden City, NY); Cambridge Greek Testament Commentary; Hermeneia (Fortress Press, Philadelphia); and Word Biblical Commentary (Word Books, Waco, Tex.).

Other series are less technical, briefer, but scholarly; e.g. Augsburg Commentary on the New Testament (Augsburg, Minneapolis); Black's/Harper's New Testament Commentaries (Black, London; Harper's, New York, later Harper & Row, San Francisco); New Century Bible (Oliphants, London; Eerdmans, Grand Rapids); New Clarendon Bible (Oxford Univ. Press, Oxford and New York); or Westminster Pelican Commentaries (Westminster, Philadelphia; Penguin, Harmondsworth).

Among one-volume commentaries of importance are *Peake's Commentary on the Bible*, ed. M. Black and H. H. Rowley (Nelson, London 1962); *The Jerome Biblical Commentary* (*JBC* 1962) and *The New Jerome Biblical Commentary* (*NJBC*, 1990), both ed. R. E. Brown, J. A. Fitzmyer, and R. E. Murphy (Prentice-Hall, Englewood Cliffs, NJ).

Proclamation Commentaries are introductions to biblical books, especially for preachers, a sort of *vade mecum* for those using Scripture, which update one's knowledge on each book of the Bible (not section-by-section commentaries), and Guides to Biblical Scholarship seek to acquaint readers with methods of scholarly study (both series published by Fortress Press, Philadelphia; since 1989 Minneapolis).

For the general reader, Torch Bible Commentaries (SCM Press, London; Macmillan, New York) and the series A Good News Commentary (Harper & Row, San Francisco) are typical of the many available.

PART I: UNITY AND PLURALISM IN NEW TESTAMENT STUDIES TODAY

Chapter 1: Is There a Centre to the New Testament?

Cullman, O., *Christ and Time: The Primitive Christian Conception of Time and History* (SCM Press, London and Westminster, Philadelphia 1950; rev. edn. 1964).
— *Salvation as History* (SCM Press, London and Harper & Row, New York 1967).
Divino Afflante Spiritu, in *Rome and the Study of Scripture* (7th edn., Grail Publications, St Mcinrad, Ind. 1962).
Dodd, C. H., *The Apostolic Preaching and its Developments* (Hodder & Stoughton, London 1936).
Eichrodt, W., *Theology of the Old Testament* (2 vols., Westminster, Philadelphia 1961, 1967).
Filson, F. V., *Jesus Christ the Risen Lord* (Abingdon, New York and Nashville 1955).
Rad, G. von, *Old Testament Theology* (2 vols., Harper & Row, New York 1962, 1965).
Schweitzer, A., *The Mysticism of Paul the Apostle* (Black, London and Holt, New York 1931; Seabury, New York 1968).
— *The Quest of the Historical Jesus: A Critical Study of its Progress from Reimarus to Wrede* (Black, London 1910).

Chapter 2: The New Testament Canon and the Techniques of Modern Scholarship

Aland, K., *The Problem of the New Testament Canon* (Mowbray, London 1962).
Freedman, D. N., 'Canon of the OT', *IDB Sup.* 130–6.
Gamble, H. Y., 'The Canon of the New Testament', *NTMI* 201–43.
— *The New Testament Canon: Its Making and Meaning*, Guides to Biblical Scholarship (Fortress Press, Philadelphia 1985).
Harrington, D. J., *Interpreting the New Testament: A Practical Guide*, New Testament Message, 1 (Glazier, Wilmington, Del. 1979).
Kümmel, W. G., *Introduction to the New Testament*, 475–510.
Sanders, J. A., *Canon and Community: A Guide to Canonical Criticism*, Guides to Biblical Scholarship (Fortress Press, Philadelphia 1984).
— *Torah and Canon* (Fortress Press, Philadelphia 1972).

Sundberg, A. C., Jr., 'Canon of the NT', *IDB Sup.* 136–40.

Tuckett, C., *Reading the New Testament: Methods of Interpretation* (Fortress Press, Philadelphia 1987).

Chapter 3: Ways Proposed toward New Testament Unity

Barrett, C. K., *From First Adam to Last: A Study in Pauline Theology* (Scribner's, New York 1962).

Braun, H. 'The Meaning of New Testament Christology', in *God and Christ: Existence and Province, Journal for Theology and the Church* 5 (Mohr-Siebeck, Tübingen and Harper & Row, New York 1968), 89–127.

Ebeling, G., 'The Meaning of "Biblical Theology"' and 'Jesus and Faith', in *Word and Faith* (SCM Press, London and Fortress Press, Philadelphia 1963), 79–97, 201–46.

Fuller, R. H., 'New Testament Theology', *NTMI* 565–84.

Perrin, N., *Jesus and the Language of the Kingdom: Symbol and Metaphor in New Testament Interpretation* (Fortress Press, Philadelphia 1976).

PART II: JESUS, THE GOSPELS, AND PAUL

Chapter 4: Jesus of Nazareth as Starting-Point

Blenkinsopp, J., *Wisdom and Law in the Old Testament: The Ordering of Life in Israel and Early Judaism*, Oxford Bible Series (Oxford Univ. Press, Oxford and New York 1983).

Conzelmann, H., *Jesus: The Classic Article from RGG³ Expanded and Updated* (Fortress Press, Philadelphia 1973). The 1959 article in *Die Religion in Geschichte und Gegenwart*, 3rd edn., is supplemented with later bibliography.

Freyne, S., *Galilee, Jesus and the Gospels: Literary Approaches and Historical Investigation* (Fortress Press, Philadelphia 1988).

Hoskyns, E., and Davey, N., *The Riddle of the New Testament* (Faber & Faber, London 1931).

Reumann, J., 'Jesus and Christology', *NTMI* 501–64.

— *Jesus in the Church's Gospels: Modern Scholarship and the Earliest Sources* (Fortress Press, Philadelphia 1968; SPCK, London 1970).

Schillebeeckx, E. C. F., *Jesus: An Experiment in Christology* (Seabury, New York 1979).
Stanton, G. N., *The Gospels and Jesus*, 137–274, 281–5.

Chapter 5: The Witness of the Four Gospels

Johnson, S., *The Theology of the Gospels* (Duckworth, London 1966).
Kee, H. C., 'Synoptic Studies', *NTMI* 245–69.
Moffatt, J., *The Theology of the Gospels* (Duckworth, London 1912).
Smith, D. M., 'Johannine Studies', *NTMI* 271–96.
Stanton, G., *The Gospels and Jesus*, 34–135, 276–81.
Talbert, C. H., 'Luke–Acts', *NTMI* 297–320.

Mark
Achtemeier, P. J., *Mark*, Proclamation Commentaries (2nd edn., Fortress Press, Philadelphia 1986).
Best, E., *Mark: The Gospel as Story* (Clark, Edinburgh 1983).
Guelich, R. A., *Mark 1–8: 26*, Word Biblical Commentary 34A (Word Books, Waco, Tex. 1989).
Kee, H. C., *Community of the New Age: Studies in Mark's Gospel* (SCM Press, London and Westminster, Philadelphia 1977).
Schweizer, E., *The Good News According to Mark* (Knox, Atlanta and SPCK, London 1971).

Matthew
Guclich, R. A., *The Sermon on the Mount: A Foundation for Understanding* (Word Books, Waco, Tex. 1982).
Kingsbury, J. D., *Matthew*, Proclamation Commentaries (2nd edn., Fortress Press, Philadelphia 1986).
— *Matthew as Story* (2nd edn., Fortress Press, Philadelphia 1988).
Luz, U., *Matthew 1–7: A Commentary* (Augsburg, Minneapolis 1989). Vols. ii and iii to come.
Patte, D., *The Gospel According to Matthew: A Structural Commentary on Matthew's Faith* (Fortress Press, Philadelphia 1987).
Schweizer, E., *The Good News According to Matthew* (Knox, Atlanta and SPCK, London 1976).
Smith, R. H., *Matthew*, Augsburg Commentary on the New Testament (Augsburg, Minneapolis 1989).

Luke

Danker, F. W., *Luke*, Proclamation Commentaries (2nd edn., Fortress Press, Philadelphia 1987).

Fitzmyer, J. A., *The Gospel According to Luke*, Anchor Bible 28, 28A (2 vols., Doubleday, Garden City, NY 1981, 1985).

— *Luke the Theologian: Aspects of His Teaching* (Paulist, New York 1989).

Schweizer, E., *The Good News According to Luke* (Knox, Atlanta and SPCK, London 1984).

— *Luke: A Challenge to Present Theology* (Knox, Atlanta and SPCK, London 1982).

Tannehill, R. C., *The Narrative Unity of Luke–Acts: A Literary Interpretation*, i (Fortress Press, Philadelphia 1986).

Tiede, D. L., *Luke*, Augsburg Commentary on the New Testament (Augsburg, Minneapolis 1989).

John

Brown, R. E., *The Gospel According to John*, Anchor Bible 29, 29A (2 vols., Doubleday, Garden City, NY 1966, 1970).

Bultmann, R., *The Gospel of John* (Blackwell, Oxford and Westminster, Philadelphia 1979).

Culpepper, R. A., *Anatomy of the Fourth Gospel: A Study in Literary Design* (Fortress Press, Philadelphia 1983).

Kysar, R., *John*, Augsburg Commentary on the New Testament (Augsburg, Minneapolis 1986).

— *John's Story of Jesus* (Fortress Press, Philadelphia 1984).

Smith, D. M., *John*, Proclamation Commentaries (2nd edn., Fortress Press, Philadelphia 1986).

Chapter 6: Pauline Theology

Beker, J. C., *Paul the Apostle: The Triumph of God in Life and Thought* (Fortress Press, Philadelphia 1980).

— *Paul's Apocalyptic Gospel: The Coming Triumph of God* (Fortress Press, Philadelphia 1982).

Deissmann, A., *Paul: A Study in Social and Religious History* (Hodder & Stoughton, London 1912; 2nd edn. 1927; repr. Harper, New York 1957; Peter Smith, Gloucester, Mass. 1972).

Fitzmyer, J. A., *Pauline Theology: A Brief Sketch* (Prentice-Hall, Englewood Cliffs, NJ 1967); *JBC* 79. 2nd edn. *Paul and His*

Theology: A Brief Sketch (Prentice-Hall, Englewood Cliffs, NJ 1989; *NJBC* 79, 82.

Furnish, V. P., 'Pauline Studies', *NTMI* 321–50.

Keck, L. E., *Paul and His Letters*, Proclamation Commentaries (Fortress Press, Philadelphia 1979; 2nd edn., 1988).

Meeks, W., *The First Urban Christians: The Social World of the Apostle Paul* (Yale Univ. Press, New Haven 1983).

Sanders, E. P., *Paul and Palestinian Judaism: A Comparison of Patterns of Religion* (Fortress Press, Philadelphia and SCM Press, London 1977).

Ziesler, J., *Pauline Christianity*, 145–8, rev. edn., 150–4 (bibliography).

PART III: THE MANY OTHER VOICES OF FAITH WITHIN THE CHORUS OF THE NEW TESTAMENT CANON

Chapter 7: Introducing the Other New Testament Books

Collins, R. F., *Letters That Paul Did Not Write: The Epistle to the Hebrews and the Pauline Pseudepigrapha*, Good News Studies 28 (Glazier, Wilmington, Del. 1988).

Fuller, R. H., Sloyan, G., Krodel, G., Danker, F., and Schüssler Fiorenza, E., *Hebrews, James, 1 and 2 Peter, Jude, Revelation*, Proclamation Commentaries (Fortress Press, Philadelphia 1977).

Reumann, J., 'A History of Lectionaries: From the Synagogue at Nazareth to Post-Vatican II', *Interpretation* 31 (1977), 116–30.

Sampley, J. P., Burgess, J., Krodel, G., and Fuller, R. H., *Ephesians, Colossians, 2 Thessalonians, the Pastoral Epistles*, Proclamation Commentaries (Fortress Press, Philadelphia 1978).

Chapter 8: The Pauline School: Colossians, Ephesians, and 2 Thessalonians

Caird, G. B., *Paul's Letters from Prison (Ephesians, Philippians, Colossians, Philemon)*, New Clarendon Bible (Oxford Univ. Press, London 1976).

Houlden, J. L., *Paul's Letters from Prison: Philippians, Colossians, Philemon, and Ephesians*, Westminster Pelican Commentaries (Westminster, Philadelphia and Penguin, Harmondsworth 1977).

Colossians

Lohse, E., *Colossians and Philemon*, Hermeneia (Fortress Press, Philadelphia 1971).

Moule, C. F. D., *The Epistles of Paul the Apostle to the Colossians and to Philemon*, Cambridge Greek Testament Commentary (Cambridge Univ. Press, New York and Cambridge 1957).

Reumann, J., *Colossians*, Augsburg Commentary on the New Testament (Augsburg, Minneapolis 1985).

Schweizer, E., *The Letter to the Colossians* (Augsburg, Minneapolis 1982).

Ephesians

Barth, M., *Ephesians: Introduction, Translation and Commentary*, Anchor Bible 34, 34A (Doubleday, Garden City 1974).

Mitton, C. L., *Ephesians*, New Century Bible (Eerdmans, Grand Rapids 1976).

Taylor, W. F., Jr., *Ephesians*, Augsburg Commentary on the New Testament (Augsburg, Minneapolis 1985).

2 Thessalonians

Best, E., *The First and Second Epistles to the Thessalonians*, Black's/Harper's New Testament Commentaries (Black, London and Harper & Row, San Francisco 1972).

Bruce, F. F., *1 & 2 Thessalonians*, Word Biblical Commentary (Word Books, Waco, Tex. 1982).

Chapter 9: The Pauline School: Three 'Pastoral' Epistles to Timothy and Titus

Dibelius, M., and Conzelmann, H., *The Pastoral Epistles*, Hermeneia (Fortress Press, Philadelphia 1971).

Fee, G. D., *1 and 2 Timothy, Titus*, Good News Commentary (Harper & Row, San Francisco 1984).

Kelly, J. N. D., *The Pastoral Epistles: I Timothy, II Timothy, Titus*, Black's/Harper's New Testament Commentaries (Black, London and Harper & Row, San Francisco 1963).

Macdonald, R. D., *The Legend and the Apostle: The Battle for Paul in Story and Canon* (Westminster, Philadelphia 1983).

Wilson, S. G., *Luke and the Pastoral Epistles* (SPCK, London 1979).

For discussion of the problem of *pseudepigraphy*, see the titles in Childs, *The New Testament as Canon* 376–8 (chiefly in German) and in R. F. Collins, *Letters*, 242–63. For 'The Acts of Paul', see *Edgar Hennecke, New Testament Apocrypha*, ed. H. Schneemelcher (Lutterworth, London and Westminster, Philadelphia 1963–4), ii: 322–79, esp. 364.

Chapter 10: 1 Peter

Balch, D. L., *Let Wives Be Submissive: The Domestic Code in I Peter*, Society of Biblical Literature Monograph Series 26 (Scholars Press, Chico, Calif. 1981).
Beare, F. W., *The First Epistle of Peter* (Blackwell, Oxford 1947).
Elliott, J. H., *A Home for the Homeless: A Sociological Exegesis of 1 Peter, Its Situation and Strategy* (Fortress Press, Philadelphia 1981).
— *I–II Peter/Jude*, Augsburg Commentary on the New Testament (Augsburg, Minneapolis 1982).
Michaels, J. R., *1 Peter*, Word Biblical Themes (Word, Waco, Tex. 1989).
Pearson, B. A., 'James, 1–2 Peter, Jude', *NTMI* 376–82.
Reicke, B., *The Epistles of James, Peter, and Jude*, Anchor Bible 37 (Doubleday, Garden City, NY 1964). Reviewed by P. Minear in *Journal of Biblical Literature* 84 (1966), 181–4.
Selwyn, E. G., *The First Epistle of Saint Peter* (Macmillan, London 1958).

Chapter 11: Enigmatic Hebrews

Attridge, H. W., *The Epistle to the Hebrews: A Commentary on the Epistle to the Hebrews*, Hermeneia (Fortress Press, Philadelphia 1989).
Buchanan, G. W., *To the Hebrews*, Anchor Bible 36 (Doubleday, Garden City, NY 1972).
Hughes, P. E., 'The Epistle to the Hebrews', *NTMI* 351–70.
Käsemann, E., *The Wandering People of God: An Investigation of the Letter to the Hebrews* (Augsburg, Minneapolis 1984).
Moffatt, J., *A Critical and Exegetical Commentary on the Epistle to the Hebrews*, International Critical Commentary Series (Clark, Edinburgh and Scribner's, New York 1924).
Montefiore, H., *A Commentary on the Epistle to the Hebrews*,

Black's/Harper's New Testament Commentaries (Black, London and Harper & Row, New York 1964).

Vanhoye, A., *Our Priest Is Christ: The Doctrine of the Epistle to the Hebrews* (Biblical Institute Press, Rome 1977).

Chapter 12: The Wisdom of James

Davids, P. H., *The Epistle of James: A Commentary on the Greek Text*, New International Greek Testament Commentary (Eerdmans, Grand Rapids 1982).

Dibelius, M., and Greeven, H., *James: A Commentary on the Epistle of James*, Hermeneia (Fortress Press, Philadelphia 1976).

Laws, S., *The Epistle of James*, Black's/Harper's New Testament Commentaries (Black, London and Harper & Row, San Francisco 1980).

Martin, R. A., *James* (with J. H. Elliott, I–II Peter, Jude), Augsburg Commentary on the New Testament (Augsburg, Minneapolis 1982).

Pearson, B. A., 'James, 1–2 Peter, Jude', *NTMI* 371–6.

Reicke, B., *The Epistles of James, Peter, and Jude*, Anchor Bible 37 (Doubleday, Garden City, NY 1964). Reviewed by R. W. Funk, *Interpretation* 19 (1965), 468–72.

Via, D. O., Jr., 'The Right Strawy Epistle Reconsidered: A Study in Biblical Ethics and Hermeneutic', *Journal of Religion* 49 (1969), 253–67.

Chapter 13: The Johannine Line of Development: Three Letters

Brown, R. E., *The Community of the Beloved Disciple* (Paulist, Paramus, NJ 1979).

— *The Epistles of John*, Anchor Bible 30 (Doubleday, Garden City, NY 1982).

Bruce, F. F., 'Johannine Studies Since Westcott's Day', in B. F. Westcott, *The Epistles of St. John* (1892; repr. Eerdmanns, Grand Rapids 1966), pp. lix–lxxvi.

Houlden, J. L., *A Commentary on the Johannine Epistles*, Black's/Harper's New Testament Commentaries (Black, London and Harper & Row, San Francisco 1973).

Chapter 14: The Johannine Line of Development: Revelation

Beckwith, I. T., *The Apocalypse of John: Studies in Introduction with a Critical and Exegetical Commentary* (Macmillan, New York 1919; repr. Baker, Grand Rapids 1967).

Caird, G. B., *A Commentary on the Revelation of St. John the Divine*, Black's/Harper's New Testament Commentaries (Black, London and Harper & Row, San Francisco 1966).

Collins, A. Y. (ed.), *Early Christian Apocalypticism: Genre and Social Setting*, Semeia 36 (1986).

Elliott, E. B., *Horae Apocalypticae* (4 vols., 4th edn., Seeley, London 1851).

Ford, J., M., *Revelation*, Anchor Bible 38 (Doubleday, Garden City, NY 1975).

Krodel, G. A., *Revelation*, Augsburg Commentary on the New Testament (Augsburg, Minneapolis 1989).

Minear, P., *I Saw a New Earth: An Introduction to the Visions of the Apocalypse* (Corpus, Washington, DC 1968).

Preston, R. H., and Hanson, A. T., *The Revelation of Saint John the Divine: Introduction and Commentary*, Torch Bible Commentary (SCM, London 1949).

Schüssler Fiorenza, E., *The Book of Revelation: Justice and Judgment* (Fortress Press, Philadelphia 1985).

— 'Revelation', *NTMI* 407–27.

Sweet, J. P. M., *Revelation*, Westminster Pelican Commentaries (Westminster, Philadelphia and Penguin, Harmondsworth 1979).

Chapter 15: Jude and 2 Peter

Bauckham, R. J., *Jude, 2 Peter*, Word Biblical Commentary (Word Books, Waco, Tex. 1983).

Elliott, J. H., *I–II Peter, Jude, James* (with R. A. Martin), Augsburg Commentary on the New Testament (Augsburg, Minneapolis 1982).

Käsemann, E., 'An Apologia for Primitive Christian Eschatology', in his *Essays on New Testament Themes* (SCM Press, London and Fortress Press, Philadelphia 1964), 169–95.

Kelly, J. N. D., *The Epistles of Peter and Jude*, Black's/Harper's New Testament Commentaries (Black, London and Harper & Row, New York 1969).

Pearson, B. A., 'James, 1–2 Peter, Jude', *NTMI* 382–7.
Reicke, B., *The Epistles of James, Peter, and Jude*, Anchor Bible 37 (Doubleday, Garden City, NY 1964).

Chapter 16: Another Look at Luke's 'Acts of the Apostles'

Conzelmann, H., *Acts of the Apostles: A Commentary on the Acts of the Apostles*, Hermeneia (Fortress Press, Philadelphia 1987).
Haenchen, E., *The Acts of the Apostles: A Commentary* (Blackwell, Oxford and Westminster, Philadelphia 1971).
Krodel, G. A., *Acts*, Augsburg Commentary on the New Testament (Augsburg, Minneapolis 1986).
Pervo, R. I., *Profit with Delight: The Literary Genre of the Acts of the Apostles* (Fortress Press, Philadelphia 1987).
Tannehill, R. C., *The Narrative Unity of Luke–Acts: A Literary Interpretation*, ii (Fortress Press, Philadelphia 1990).

PART IV: THE ONENESS OF THE MANY IN NEW TESTAMENT FAITH

Chapter 17: Will a Centre Hold?

Aune, D. E., *The New Testament in Its Literary Environment*, Library of Early Christianity (Westminster, Philadelphia 1987).
Betz, H. D., *Galatians: A Commentary on Paul's Letter to the Churches in Galatia*, Hermeneia (Fortress Press, Philadelphia 1979).
Kee, H. C., *Knowing the Truth: A Sociological Approach to New Testament Interpretation* (Fortress Press, Philadelphia 1989).
Krentz, E., *The Historical-Critical Method*, Guides to Biblical Scholarship (Fortress Press, Philadelphia 1975).
Lee, J. M. (ed.), *Handbook of Faith* (Religious Education Press, Birmingham, Ala. 1990).
Link, H.-G. (ed.), *The Roots of Our Common Faith: Faith in the Scriptures and in the Early Church*, Faith and Order Paper No. 119 (World Council of Churches, Geneva 1984).
Mack, B., *Rhetoric and the New Testament*, Guides to Biblical Scholarship (Fortress Press, Minneapolis 1990).
Macky, P., 'The Coming Revolution: The New Literary Approach to the New Testament', *Theological Educator* 9 (1972), 32–46, repr. in

A Guide to Contemporary Hermeneutics: Major Trends in Biblical Interpretation, ed. D. K. McKim (Eerdmans, Grand Rapids 1986), 263–79.

McKnight, E. V., *Post-Modern Use of the Bible: The Emergence of Reader-Oriented Criticism* (Abingdon, Nashville 1988).

Patte, D., *Paul's Faith and the Power of the Gospel: A Structural Introduction to the Pauline Letters* (Fortress Press, Philadelphia 1983). See also above, Ch. 5, Matthew.

— *Structural Exegesis for New Testament Critics*, Guides to Biblical Scholarship (Fortress Press, Minneapolis 1990).

Reumann, J., 'Exegetes, Honesty and the Faith: Biblical Scholarship in Church School Theology', *Currents in Theology and Mission* 5 (1978), 16–32.

— 'Methods in Studying the Biblical Text Today', *Concordia Theological Monthly* 40 (1969), 655–81.

Stowers, S. K., *Letter-Writing in Greco-Roman Antiquity*, Library of Early Christianity (Westminster, Philadelphia 1986).

Sykes, S., 'Faith', in *Keeping the Faith: Essays to Mark the Centenary of Lux Mundi*, ed. G. Wainwright (Fortress Press, Philadelphia and Pickwick Publications, Pittsburgh 1988), 1–24.

INDEX OF PASSAGES CITED

Apocrypha, Pseudepigrapha, and other Ancient Writings

INDEX OF CHIEF THEMES IN
NEW TESTAMENT THOUGHT

Pentateuch - Pete Diamond

72 - use as intro in Paul
82 - expiation - paper

why blood - life of body in blood

85 - Paul's letters & evangelism

89 - Paul's themes

200ff Luther contro - James works -
6ar - Abra faith - work use - NEW
167 - Hebrews does not allow 2nd chance
Luther pastor periphery of NT 179

11 - read Origins of Xianity

34 - outline of book
254 - early Cath' formation